Riding Jane Crow

D0870196

WOMEN, GENDER, AND SEXUALITY IN AMERICAN HISTORY

Editorial Advisors:
Susan K. Cahn
Wanda A. Hendricks
Deborah Gray White
Anne Firor Scott, Founding Editor Emerita

A list of books in the series appears at the end of this book.

Riding Jane Crow

African American Women on the American Railroad

MIRIAM THAGGERT

UNIVERSITY OF ILLINOIS PRESS
Urbana, Chicago, and Springfield

Furthermore:
a program of the J. M. Kaplan Fund

This publication is made possible with support from
Furthermore: a program of the J. M. Kaplan Fund.

Library of Congress Cataloging-in-Publication Data
Names: Thaggert, Miriam, author.
Title: Riding Jane Crow : African American women on the
    American railroad / Miriam Thaggert.
Other titles: African American women on the American
    railroad | Women, gender, and sexuality in American
    history.
Description: Urbana : University of Illinois Press, 2022.
    | Series: Women, gender, and sexuality in American
    history | Includes bibliographical references and index.
Identifiers: LCCN 2021059030 (print) | LCCN 2021059031
    (ebook) | ISBN 9780252044526 (cloth ; alk. paper) | ISBN
    9780252086595 (paperback) | ISBN 9780252053528 (ebook)
Subjects: LCSH: African American women—United States—
    History. | Railroad travel—United States—History. |
    African Americans—Legal status, laws, etc. | United
    States—Race relations.
Classification: LCC E185.86 .T385 2022 (print) | LCC E185.86
    (ebook) | DDC 305.896/073—dc23/eng/20211215
LC record available at https://lccn.loc.gov/2021059030
LC ebook record available at https://lccn.loc.gov/2021059031

For Mom, Always

Contents

Acknowledgments

Everyone has a train story. I am blessed that I am able to add this book to my own collection of railroad tales. I'd like to recognize a large community of supportive colleagues, friends, and family who helped me on this journey.

There were several readers of the manuscript or sections of the manuscript at the University of Iowa, including Bluford Adams, Jill Davis, Kathleen Diffley, Mary Lou Emery, Claire Fox, Ellen Lewin, Judith Pascoe, Laura Rigal, Phillip Round, Leslie Schwalm, Claire Sponsler, Susan Stanfield, Doris Witt, and Catherine A. Stewart of Cornell College. I'd also like to thank Florence Boos, Lori Branch, Matthew Brown, Jennifer Buckley, Corey Creekmur, John D'Gata, Cherie Hansen-Rieskamp, Kevin Kopelson, Marie Kruger, Teresa Magnum, Christopher McMillan, Dee Morris, Peter Nazareth, Horace Porter, Robyn Schiff, Jennifer Sessions, Anne Stapleton, Garrett Stewart, Rachel Williams, and Fred Woodward. Librarians at the University of Iowa, Amy Chen and Janalyn Moss, were always ready to answer my questions. A Developmental Studies Hybridoma Bank (DSHB) Fellowship at University of Iowa was helpful as I completed portions of the book. A very special thank-you to my friend and colleague Janette Taylor.

At SUNY-Buffalo, readers of the manuscript included Carrie Bramen, director of the Gender Institute; Stacy Hubbard; Cristanne Miller; and Victoria Wolcott. For their support, I thank Rachel Ablow, David Alff, Barbara Bono, Susan Eilenberg, Cecil Foster, Judith Goldman, Walter Hakala, Jim Holstun, Damien Keene, Chad Levin, Ruth Mack, Carine Mardorossian, Patricia Matthew, Elizabeth Mazzolini, Theresa McCarthy, Kristen Moore, Eric Pritchard, William Solomon, Lillian Williams, and Despina Stratigakos with the Office of Inclusive Excellence. A very special thank-you goes to my writing partner and colleague Nicole Morris-Johnson.

A fellowship at the Newberry Library was fundamental to the initial ideas in the book; the time and people I met there will always be special to me. I'd like to especially thank D. Bradford Hunt, JoEllen Dickie, Diane Dillon, Kristen Emery, Keelin Burke, and the amazing fellows I met during my fellowship year. Alex Schneider introduced me to the world of railroad model and history enthusiasts and helped me identify the time period of trains and compartments.

A fellowship at the Virginia Humanities and the University of Virginia enabled me to delve more deeply and significantly into the lives and experiences of the waiter carriers of Virginia. It also very importantly gave me time to experiment with how to tell their stories. I'd like to thank Susan Bratton, John Deal, Don DeBats, Matthew Gibson, Russell Halley, Deborah Lee, Dianne Martin, Rich Martin, Deborah McDowell, Ann B. Miller, Brenda Marie Osbrey, Justin Read, Aron Shetterly, Jeanne Siler, Jane Smith, Edwina St. Rose, and Earl Swift. I am very much indebted to Gloria Johnson Gilmore and Doretha Taylor Dickerson for sharing their knowledge of the waiter carriers, Gordonsville, and Black Virginia with me and for giving me a memorable personal tour of Gordonsville (and nearby areas). Psyche A. Williams-Forson graciously offered feedback on a section of the waiter carriers chapter presented at a conference.

I had the opportunity to participate in Georgetown University's Second Book Institute, directed by Robert Patterson and supported by the dean of Georgetown College, Christopher S. Celenza.

Several people drew my attention to the images that appear in the book or granted permission to use the images. I'd like to thank Larry Z. Daily, Earnestine Jenkins, Lisa Renee Johnson, Gloria Johnson Gilmore, Jane Smith, and the following institutions: the David Rumsey Historical Map Center of Stanford University, the Newberry Library, the California State Railroad Museum, the Library and Archives of Canada, the Minnesota Historical Society, the Estate of Pauli Murray, and the Virginia Museum of History and Culture. There were several archives that I consulted but did not quote or reference within the text. These include the A. Phillip Randolph Papers at the Library of Congress and the Mississippi Department of Archives and History in Jackson, Mississippi.

Scholars and colleagues offered expert guidance and feedback along this trip, including Maria Cotera, Madhu Dubey, Daylanne English, Sheri Englund, Rachel Farebrother, Nathan Grant, Thabiti Lewis, Barbara McCaskill, Koritha Mitchell, Joycelyn Moody, William Pretzer, Amy Richter,

Phillip Round, Shawn Michelle Smith, Valerie Smith, Ann Twinam, and Ben Vinson. Noaquia Callahan shared some of her archival work on Mary Church Terrell.

Portions of this research were presented at talks given at Rutgers University–New Brunswick and the University of Georgia. I thank Carter Mathes, Evie Shockley, and Cheryl Wall (Rutgers); and Nell Andrew and Susan Rosenbaum (Georgia).

Dawn Durante expressed interest in the book when it was still a hazy idea, read early chapters, and discussed the book with me several times over the years. I am deeply appreciative of her engagement and support. The manuscript then came into the expert hands of Dominique J. Moore, Alison K. Syring, and Ellie Hinton of the University of Illinois Press.

Finally, for keeping me "on track," literally and figuratively, and for listening to me talk about "the railroad book," I thank my friends and family, including my parents; M. M. Smith; Sheila; Florence; Rachel; Thuc Tran and James, Jessica, Jonathan, Jackson, Jillian, and Sister Therese; and Henry, Tammy, Kat, Sunny, and Lucy.

Riding Jane Crow

Introduction

Off the Tracks: Race, Gender, and the American Railroad

Train's at the station, I heard the whistle blow
The train's at the station, I heard the whistle blow
I done bought my ticket and I don't know where I'll go.
—Gertrude "Ma" Rainey, "Traveling Blues"

The Napa Valley Wine Train succeeded only too well in re-creating an earlier era of American railroad travel. According to the company's website, "great effort was exerted to ensure that the interior of the railcars evoked the spirit of opulent rail travel at the beginning of the twentieth century."[1] The wine train replicated not just any type of train car but the first-class compartment familiar during the golden age of railroad travel. Passengers sampled wine, cheese, and the luxuries of yesteryear as the train traveled throughout the Napa Valley, through thirty-six miles of "some of the most expensive and famous farm real estate in the country."[2]

In 2015, a group of African American women sued the wine train, precisely because wine employees replicated another detail of the golden age of railroad travel: Jim Crow segregation. A Black women's book club boarded the train and were seated "in the back of the last train car." Before the train left the station, a train employee admonished the women, claiming that their "noise level was offensive to other passengers." When the women asked which passengers were offended, the employee replied that she "[could] see it on the face[s] of other passengers when you laugh out loud."[3] While train employees claimed that the women were unusually loud and boisterous, the members of Sistahs on the Reading Edge, the Black women's book club, noted that, as a group of eleven women, ranging in ages between thirty-four and eighty-five, they were no louder than any other groups on the train. Wine employees posted an online statement, later admitted to be false, claiming that the Black women were verbally and physically abusive to other passengers and staff. Before the three-hour excursion could conclude, train employees escorted the club members off, "parad[ing]" the women through the cars to the police who were waiting on a station platform.[4] The women reported feeling "like criminals" when they were forced to leave the train in full view of other, mostly white, passengers. The train company, then, succeeded in duplicating the late nineteenth-century, first-class American train car experience. Indeed, the president of the book club felt she was "transported back in time and these were tales my grandmother and great-grandmother should have been telling me about." The book club members sued the train company, settling for an undisclosed amount.[5]

Figure 0.1: Members of Sistahs on the Reading Edge, sitting in the train compartment of the Napa Valley Wine Train, August 2015. Photograph courtesy of Lisa Renee Johnson.

I begin this book with this incident because it demonstrates how, however obsolete the railroad may appear now, the racial, class, and gender dynamics of railroad travel in the nineteenth and twentieth centuries linger potently into the twenty-first. The event offers an unsettling commentary on Black femininity, mobility, and spatiality—the ways in which the upscale train compartment and related travel spaces define and shape gender, race, and class identities and understandings of U.S. citizenship. *Riding Jane Crow* details the experiences of nineteenth- and early twentieth-century African American women on or near American trains and discloses the displaced social history of African American women and U.S. train travel. Despite the storied position the railroad occupies in American cultural memory and numerous books on American railroad history, the experiences of African American women are notably absent. Previous scholarship on Black male

Figure 0.2: Members of Sistahs on the Reading Edge, after being removed from the Napa Valley Wine Train, August 2015. Photograph courtesy of Lisa Renee Johnson.

"Pullman porter blues" and white middle-class women who made a "home on the rails" have obscured accounts of Black female train workers and riders.[6] *Riding Jane Crow* foregrounds the experiences of Black female passengers and workers, reading the train compartment as a contested space of leisure or as a problematic work site. Just as the United States was entering a more industrial, technologically advanced moment in the late nineteenth century, Jim Crow laws—regulations that restricted the mobility of African Americans in public space—were becoming more prevalent. This new "unregulab[le] freedom" was enabled in part by technology such as the railroad.[7] I am interested in this twin occurrence, arguing that the nation's mechanical trajectory "forward" is entwined with the attempted retrenchment of African American social progress. Further, the experience of Black women in relation to the railroad questions the forward linear movement normally associated with "progress." Indeed, American technological progress has often meant the ejection or displacement of Black women.

The question of African American women on railroads reflects the larger ambiguity of the law after the Civil War and the citizenship status of African Americans, even after the passage of three constitutional amendments. The U.S. railroad was the first mass form of technology actively policed in an effort to assert and maintain white political, social, and economic dominance. Thus, I focus on the period from 1860 to 1925, the era between depictions of train travel as a mode of escape in slave narratives and the formation of the Brotherhood of Sleeping Car Porters and Maids (BSCP), the labor union representing mostly African American male porters. These years witnessed the emancipation of enslaved persons and the Great Migration, the mass movement of African Americans from the South to the North and West, a movement facilitated in part by one specific railroad, the Illinois Central.[8] This sixty-five-year period brought radical changes to African American identity and citizenship, as well as momentous social and technological transformations in the country. Because mobility is a significant sign of U.S. privilege and citizenship, Black mobility on the nation's railroads became a key issue to assess new, constitutionally granted rights. Railroads, and specifically first-class train compartments, became one of the most contested spaces of experimentation for white supremacy and Black assertiveness. While other scholars have examined Black men's relationship with the railroad as a symbol representing a blues-inflected freedom or Jim Crow segregation, I argue that a focus on Black women more fully depicts the paradoxical progress and retrenchment, mobility and stasis of Black travel during this period, as Black women determined if and how feminine respectability could travel with them on the train. Looking at the railroad—the period's most triumphant technological achievement—through the eyes of a group that routinely had its citizenship and femininity questioned reveals the train car as a political space, where racial and gender identities were performed and contested. If, as the familiar celebratory narrative goes, railroads united the country after the Civil War and were signs of national progress and American ingenuity, then Black mobility—and particularly Black female independence—was a significant threat to the nation's fragile unity, meriting repressive policing from train employees and fellow passengers, with only occasional reprieve through the courts. I argue that it is the African American woman who most fully measures the success of American freedom and privilege, or "progress," through her travel experiences.

While recognizing the significance of the train in Black culture, *Riding Jane Crow* travels down new tracks by examining Black women's different relationship to the railroad compared to Black men. Houston A. Baker Jr., in a discussion of African American blues culture, perhaps unintentionally captures the phallic possibilities of the railroad, describing "the locomotive's drive and thrust, its promise of unrestrained mobility and unlimited free-dom." But as Hazel Carby and Angela Y. Davis note, reflecting on the lyrics of Black female blues singers, the railroad was often a melancholy object in the blues, transporting men and family members away from home. And yet Davis and Carby caution us that Black women did not necessarily have an antagonistic relationship to the train. As Carby notes, although some sounds associated with the train were "mournful signal[s] of imminent desertion and future loneliness," Black female blues singers "reclaimed" these sounds "as a sign that women too were on the move."[9] Black women's blues songs are, in fact, one of the few places where Black female travel pleasure may be found.[10] For some Black women, the railroad was a mode of travel away from difficult circumstances or offered brief pleasurable trips away from local com-munities. In addition, the railroad was a relatively well-paying worksite that provided alternatives to women with limited occupational choices, despite having advanced degrees. Fully examining the multiple ways Black women interacted with this form of transportation complicates the celebrated notion of progress associated with the railroad as well as the emancipatory potential of trains so often evoked in Black song.

Throughout the book, I investigate the large cultural archive of the railroad in the United States and that archive's notable absence of women of color, studying how the space of the archive replicates some forms of the American train car. The book questions how we position Black women in transportation history by noting how Black women have been *dis*-remembered in railroad history.

The book began, as I describe in a later chapter, during a research trip at the Newberry Library in Chicago, which holds the massive Pullman Company business and personnel records. Searching for first-person narratives of Pullman porters and their work on the railroads, I came across a folder containing the application of an African American woman seeking employment as a Pullman maid. The Pullman porter has long been a celebrated figure in African American history and culture, but surprisingly, the experiences of women such as Frances Albrier, one of the hundreds of women who worked as "handmaidens for travelers" for the Pullman Company, has not garnered similar attention. The Newberry's Pullman Company records are both deep and lacking—just enough of an archival history to tantalize the researcher but missing important information about the women who worked as maids. This presence-absence within the archive functions for many of the women I examine in this book. Drawing on the work of scholars who interrogate archives and the archival absences of African-descended peoples, the book troubles the space of the train car and the space of the archive, two repositories that imperfectly hold the African American woman.[11]

Earlier Train Rides

To write this book I have had to go off the tracks, so to speak. I have had to reread standard sources of railroad history and texts about travel and transport, always on the lookout for where Black women may be found. Two important earlier works on the social and literary history of the railroad offer useful points of departure and a guide: Leo Marx's *The Machine in the Garden* (1964) and Wolfgang Schivelbusch's *The Railway Journey* (1986). Marx studies the presence of the train on the external American landscape, while Schivelbusch focuses on the subjective, perceptual effect of the railroad on the passenger. Both books delineate the subtle impact of the railroad on national consciousness and individual subjectivity beginning in the 1830s, in England and the United States, into the late nineteenth century, when the economic, political, and social power of the train became undeniable in the two countries.[12] Both disclose the mood of a period and the subtle power of the railroad in U.S. and European culture. It is precisely in these analyses of amorphous, intangible feelings fostered by the train that we could expect, at least in in the U.S. context, to find some discussion of the impact of a racial caste system based on skin color.[13] But in their attention to the influence of the railroad on individual or national consciousness, these works overlook how the railroad shaped that most socially constructed category, "race," during a period of U.S. history when the category held indomitable weight. Nor do the books, which have influenced a generation of scholarship on railroad and technology studies, fully consider gender or the perspective of the everyday railroad laborer. Rereading these books with the history of African Americans and train workers in mind, along with the special dilemmas of Black female travelers, guides us to a new recognition of the power of the railroad in shaping Americans' ideas of race and gender and the politics of class.

Leo Marx's *The Machine in the Garden* reveals how the "machine" came to occupy American consciousness, from a hazy idea when early nineteenth-century Americans sought to bring European industrialization to the United States to a potent national symbol. Marx highlights the moment when "the startling shriek of the train whistle" interrupted American authors' idyllic outings in nature, most famously Henry David Thoreau as he sat in Walden. This "little event" occurred repeatedly in mid-nineteenth-century U.S. literature as the railroad became more prevalent in American towns. The motif helped U.S. writers reconcile "the political and the psychic dissonance associated with the onset of industrialism," a reconciliation that reflects "the subtle influence of industrialization upon mass consciousness."[14] As a sign of just how influential the book has been, Oxford University Press published a new edition of *The Machine in the Garden* in 2000 to mark the book's thirty-fifth anniversary, and a 2015 collection of essays by contemporary scholars evaluates the enduring significance of Marx's work.[15]

In the many reviews and analyses of *The Machine in the Garden*, none have considered the brevity, and offhandedness, of its discussion of slavery, for the train whistle was not a "startling shriek" to all ears and may have imparted different meanings to other Americans. Consider, for example, how the train may have sounded to Jourden Banks, who was fleeing slavery, and for whom the sound of a locomotive was a harbinger of possible escape. Banks, according to historian William G. Thomas, had "a long experience on the railroad, first as a slave being transported into the market, then as a slave hired to work on the line, and finally as a fugitive on the railroad."[16] The railroad was Banks's technological "North Star;" he used his deep familiarity with the tracks, and, most likely, the sound, as a guide to the North.

What if we included other American authors of the 1840s and 1850s in Marx's study, authors whose lives intersected with the railroad at significant moments? Frederick Douglass, a "serious writer," referenced the train in his autobiography—not as a startling interruption but as the means by which he effected his escape to freedom.[17] He passed as a sailor and boarded a train to Philadelphia. While fleeing on the train, he successfully evaded the railroad conductor's questions and the stares of a fellow white passenger who recognized him but did not alert anyone to Douglass's identity. Similarly, the railroad appears in the writings of another important early African American author, Martin Delany, "the principal progenitor of Black nationalism in

America," and perhaps the quintessential figure of African American mobility in the early nineteenth century.[18] The railroad runs through Delany's works in a quite "American" fashion. He developed a train-related invention that would allow "locomotives to cross mountains under their own steam," but unfortunately for him and other free Black inventors before 1865, U.S. patents were given to African Americans only if they were enslaved and applied through their owners. As a free person of color, Delany was not a citizen and could not file a patent.[19] I focus on Douglass and Delany in order to suggest how the inclusion of African American writers or texts that dealt specifically with slavery in the United States could further strengthen Leo Marx's work and to suggest alternative readings of the machine in America's garden.

Wolfgang Schivelbusch, like Leo Marx, does not discuss railroad workers. Instead, *The Railway Journey*, "perhaps the single most innovative contribution to scholarship on the cultural history of railways," analyzes the subtle perceptual shifts engendered by the train in both England and the United States.[20] *The Railway Journey* is important because Schivelbusch delineates the less concrete, more subjective effects of the railroad and the dramatic effect this technology had on conceptions of self, time, space, and nation. Railroad travel "alter[ed] the consciousness of the passengers: they developed a new set of perceptions," that were then registered in various forms such as literature and visual art. But Schivelbusch's perceptive history and analysis of the railroad in the United States overlooks how much the complex history of skin color in the United States contributed to what he calls "an American transportation consciousness." This is evident particularly when he discusses two topics: the shortage of labor during the mid-nineteenth century and what he calls a "classless American railroad system." When Schivelbusch notes "the shortage of capital and labor in the United States," he fails to distinguish between the U.S. North and South.[21] The enslaved population played a pivotal role in the early construction of the railroad in the South. Railroad companies such as the Mississippi Central Railroad purchased enslaved people in order to build track lines, contributing to "the rise in slave prices throughout the region in the two decades before the Civil War."[22] While transportation companies in the Northeast hired immigrant wage labor, southern railroads relied on the boundless possibilities that slavery offered them, and by the start of the Civil War there was an ironic interdependence between slavery and southern trains.[23]

We can also complicate *The Railway Journey*'s interpretations by comparing Schivelbusch's analyses of the traveling public to the real, physical conditions of Black travel on the early U.S. railroad, especially for those African Americans who were enslaved. Schivelbusch notes, for example, that early passengers were disturbed that they felt like the baggage: "Bourgeois first-class travelers complained that they no longer felt like travelers but like parcels."[24] These tender feelings contrast strongly with the lived experience of enslaved people such as Henry "Box" Brown, who escaped to freedom by literally having himself mailed on a train via the Express Delivery Service of Adams and Company of Richmond, Virginia; or William Craft, who passed as the enslaved property of his disguised light-skinned wife and, at one point, rode in a train's baggage car.[25]

Schivelbusch also concludes that the class-based system of trains in the United States developed comparatively later than it did in Europe, noting that Pullman cars were developed in 1859 and "with them, a 'first class' was introduced into the until then classless American railroad system."[26] But many earlier incidents make it clear that from their earliest days, the divisions within U.S. trains were not just economic but epidermic. Louis Ruchames's research on antebellum railroads in Massachusetts identifies a series of incidents that took place in 1841, demonstrating the segregation of African American passengers, including Frederick Douglass, from first-class cars.[27] These events helped to mobilize northern abolitionists and brought the issue of racially segregated cars to wider public attention. We also know from the narratives of enslaved people, such as Harriet Jacobs's *Incidents in the Life of a Slave Girl* (1861), that the U.S. railroad was, if not class-based, at the very least, attuned to dividing passengers based on servitude or color.[28] Other slave narratives recount the various laws that restricted the movements of free people of color. William Craft and Ellen Craft's 1860 narrative, *Running a Thousand Miles for Freedom*, details a long-standing law in Tennessee that prohibited free African Americans from traveling on the railroad without a white person to "vouch for the character of said free Negro in a penal bond of one thousand dollars"—an extraordinary and prohibitive sum.[29] These narratives indicate that color and elements of social class played a persistent and early role in the history of the American railroad and were common forms of segregating passengers.

Other points raised by Schivelbusch gain further meaning when the nineteenth-century African American woman's traveling experience is considered. The distinctions between U.S. and European railcars illustrate this point. Schivelbusch notes that, crucially, U.S. cars were more "democratic" than the British railways. He observes that "travel in the [European] compartment was characterized by immobility." European train cars were comparatively small, private, and confined, becoming the location of both real and imagined crimes.[30] In contrast, passengers in U.S. cars could move about the train more freely; the larger cars, with seats positioned down either side of a

Figure 0.3: The Crafts would have encountered warnings such as this one as they traveled by train from the South to the North. The notice informed colored passengers that they are "required to bring with them . . . some responsible white person." "Notice to Colored People." Schomburg Center for Research in Black Culture, Photographs and Prints Division, New York Public Library Digital Collections, https://digitalcollections.nypl.org/items/510d47dd-f22b-a3d9-e040-e00a18064a99.

walkable aisle, enabled better opportunities for movement and communication. The relative freedom of movement and the "democratic" qualities of the U.S. train car may have contributed to the need, in the minds of white Americans, for segregation from racial others. Whites and emancipated southern Blacks mingled more frequently in public spaces during Reconstruction, when the growth of Black economic and political success threatened white supremacy.[31] Ida B. Wells explicitly linked Black upward mobility in the South and the increase of lynchings of Black men and women between the 1870s and 1890s when the visual sight of Black middle-class propriety challenged concepts of Black racial inferiority. Visiting England in 1893, Wells commented on the design difference between the wider U.S. cars and the cramped English compartments, noting how she disliked English "narrow railway compartments, with seats facing each other, knees rubbing against those of entire strangers, and being forced to stare into each other's faces for hours." But Wells also importantly noted one benefit of the English trains never raised by Marx or Schivelbusch: "I as a Negro can ride in them free from insult or discrimination on account of color, and that's what I cannot do in many states of my own free (?) America."[32]

As foundational works in transportation history, *The Machine in the Garden* and *The Railway Journey* shaped a generation of cultural studies of the railroad. But, remarkably, neither race nor gender nor the common railroad laborer registers in these works, particularly when the scholars theorize the train in the United States from the 1830s to the late nineteenth century, a period that witnessed not only dramatic American technological transformation but also the growing regimentation of race as a sign of servitude in the United States and the increasingly public role of American middle-class women. The daily humiliations and frequent clashes that occurred on trains and the numerous debates surrounding who could enter designated cars make the railroad a fruitful site for thinking through the practices of abstract concepts such as race and citizenship during and after the Civil War. Studying how Black women in particular fared on the railroad reveals how gender and class intersected with race in the crucible of cramped public spaces.

In *Riding Jane Crow*, I argue that the American train compartment was so deeply contested precisely because it served as a mobile repository of a larger culture's racial, gender, and class practices and tensions. If technology impacts such abstract concepts of space and time, if the effect of technology can be felt and registered through painting and novels, as Schivelbusch argues, what sort of impact does technology have on such important concepts as "race" and gender in the United States? If the train is the site of "an extraordinary bundle of relations," or as Ralph Ellison notes describing the Chehaw train station near his college in Tuskegee, train stations are "meeting places for motley mixtures of people . . . gathering places as juncture points for random assemblies of sensibilities," how does a mode of transportation that brings diverse strangers together impact conceptions of nationality and identity?[33] What, in short, is the effect of a technology like the railroad on racial and gender constructions?[34] And how have these effects been archived and remembered in American culture?

Race-ing the Railroad in Time and Space

Fully understanding the significance of Black female railroad travel requires an understanding of the social and psychological underpinnings of travel and the significance of travel in shaping subjectivity, identity, and citizenship. As Elizabeth Pryor and Paul Gilroy perceptively note, the history of the African American's identity has been closely tied to the *in*ability to freely move from one location to another.[35] The early African's experience in the Americas has been one of contested movement. From the hold of a slave ship of the Middle Passage, moving across the Atlantic, to restricted movement in the Americas, the African American's relation to movement has been one of "successive displacements, migrations, and journeys (forced and otherwise) which have come to constitute . . . Black cultures' special conditions of existence."[36] Thomas Jefferson, in the infamous section 14 of his *Notes on the State of Virginia*, written during the 1780s, noted that laws proposed in the newly formed republic wanted "to make slaves distributable among the next of kin, as other *moveables*."[37] The U.S. Supreme Court's 1857 Dred Scott decision rendered insignificant Scott and his family's movement from the slave state of Missouri to the free areas of the Midwest to a return to Missouri, ensuring their status as property rather than as citizens. During the Civil War, the amorphous political and social conditions of fugitive enslaved people were marked with a special word, "contraband," a term that continued their status as property even though they escaped the plantation or their masters' space.[38] When African Americans who were enslaved learned of Emancipation, testing their ability to move was one way they assured themselves of freedom. As Booker T. Washington noted, newly freed people felt they had to "leave the old plantation for at least a few days or weeks in order that they might really feel sure that they were free."[39] And yet, *Plessy v. Ferguson* (1896) would, in time, affect the train and later bus travel of African Americans for well over half a century.[40] In all of these historical peak points, from the Middle Passage to Emancipation to the post-Reconstruction era, mobility functioned for Black Americans as a sign of citizenship and self-ownership.

Travel was and is a particular conundrum for African American women. One of the more common forms of "gender deference" granted to middle-class traveling women were "ladies' cars," train compartments so-called because they were primarily for white women traveling alone or with a male relative or companion. But could Black women occupy such compartments when a larger culture routinely denied the term "lady" to them? Black women learned that access to comfortable and safe travel spaces often necessitated the successful performance of a classed femininity or the willingness to contest their removal, physically or financially, through the courts.

In addition to exploring the material forms and conditions of Black female travel, I am also interested in the subjective impact of Black female travel, elusively captured in fiction, short stories, diaries, and letters, and recorded as injury in lawsuits initiated by African American women. Black female geography—a conscious attention to the depiction and movement of Black female bodies in public and private spaces—helps articulate the subtle pains—and pleasures—of travel and the significance of travel spaces that are consciously and unconsciously gendered.

Scenes of Reading, Scenes of Riding

"If you wish to ride with me, you must come into the Jim Crow car"—so begins the reader's metaphorical journey with W. E. B. Du Bois into Georgia and the Black Belt, one stop as he lifts the veil for white readers in *The Souls of Black Folk* (1903).[41] Like his other metaphors, this journey in a Jim Crow car, occurring in chapter 7 of *Souls*, explains the internal dilemmas of the educated African American subject. Segregated cars appear frequently in *Souls*, so much so that one could use the Jim Crow car to rephrase that other well-known line in the collection of essays: the problem of the twentieth century is the problem of the (rail) line.

In order to understand why the train appears frequently in *Souls* and other Black literature, and to measure the symbolic power of the train in Black culture, one can start with the feeling one has within the train car, in the period between departure and destination. I have long been fascinated with that period of time and space that resides within the train compartment. A paradoxical feeling of stability and movement mark the experience. It is a peculiar sensation: the impression of being stable within the compartment while the vehicle itself is in rapid forward movement. This apparently contradictory physical sensation of mobile but stalled progress is one that the Jim Crow car renders into fact. As Robert Stepto notes, discussing the image of the train in *Souls*, the segregated Jim Crow car is a "despised and imposed conveyance, employed rather ingeniously to inflict the stasis of social structure upon Blacks in motion."[42] In other words, the train car reflects the dual condition the African American holds in American culture, a condition of both aspirational mobility (up from slavery, to use Booker T. Washington's words) and forced stasis. The Jim Crow car, as with other forms of racial segregation, keeps Black people "fixed," even as Black subjects attempt forward, or upward, movement. The tension between stasis and mobility, that troubled feeling of suspended time and motion, of feeling in abeyance, is a central one that undergirds most depictions of the train, particularly the Jim Crow car, in African American fiction. Because scenes of what Du Bois called "double consciousness" are so frequent on trains, one can think of the repeated trauma of fixed mobility while train riding as a spatial and temporal form of double consciousness. The "scene of reading" so pivotal to African American slave narratives of the mid-nineteenth century became a "scene of riding" by the end of the century, as the difficulties of rail travel figured prominently in Black letters and as African Americans worked to transform segregated practices in this and other public spaces.[43] As I discuss in the first chapter, the train compartment has even more resonances for African American women, for the space becomes the material embodiment of the interiorized Black female experience of upward, yet stalled, movement. Or as Stephanie Camp, termed it, in regards to enslaved women, "mobility in the face of constraint."[44]

It is a mistake to assume that only a Jim Crow car provoked anxiety in the Black passenger. The first-class car was also the site of racial antagonisms. Indeed, it was the location where Black passengers faced the most extreme form of violence in others' efforts to displace them, since a Black passenger's treatment within the car depended on who else was present. In the first-class car, we see what I call situational riding—a condition of riding in which the probability of being treated fairly is always contingent on who else is in the car. Derived from Ariela Gross and Ann Twinam and their discussions of "situational differences," and R. Douglas Cope and his theorization of "situational classification," the idea of situational riding takes into account how the traveler of color presents him- or herself as the car moves through space and as various people enter and depart the train car.[45] As with scenes of racial passing, situational riding comes into play in the presence of another race.[46] This, then, is one reason for the popularity of the Pullman car with African American travelers. The respite offered by the Pullman compartment was not just solitude but safety. The Pullman car enabled travelers to travel long distances with comfortable accommodations but also with as little interaction with others as possible: the self-segregation available there enabled the Black rider to maintain a sense of self. Pullman offered a reprieve to travelers of color, so much so that some prominent African American intellectuals included the cost of a Pullman car in their expenses when traveling to speak to organizations.[47] As I discuss briefly in chapter 4, the protection offered in a Pullman compartment was just one of the many ways in which the Pullman Company affected nineteenth- and twentieth-century Black culture.

One historical figure can help us to continue to explicate what I call situational riding and its role in shaping a spatialized and gendered double consciousness. A ride in disguise with Ellen Craft can help map the changing and challenging transitions of Black female subjectivity on, or nearby, the rails.

A Ride with Ellen Craft

Perhaps the best example of gendered double consciousness and situational riding occurs in William Craft and Ellen Craft's slave narrative, *Running a Thousand Miles for Freedom*.[48] For the Crafts, as it will be later for many African Americans of the Great Migration, freedom occurs in the act of boarding the train. Their 1861 account narrativizes the drama in the train compartment. Although the Crafts used various modes of transportation to effect their escape—in addition to the railroad, they also traveled by steamboat, carriage, and ferryboat—the train compartment is the most significant. Mid-nineteenth-century racial and gender travel conventions dictate the Crafts' escape plans, which necessitates that Ellen don masculine clothing and pass as a white male planter. The cross-dressing element of the escape captured readers' attention, then and now. What has gone unnoticed is how the design of mid-nineteenth-century American railroad cars impacted their travel and continually exposed them to capture. I am interested in the spatial design of the first-class train compartment and the effect of this design on the Crafts' interaction with others. The compartments' designs facilitate conversation among passengers, the very act that can threaten the Crafts' escape.

The Crafts dramatize the paradoxical concept of progress in relation to African Americans and the train: they are stilled even while moving forward, wrestling with mobility and stasis as they run "a thousand miles to freedom." The rhythm of the railroad informs the structure of the first section in which the Crafts escape by steamboat and train. Geoffrey Sanborn, in his reading of *Running a Thousand Miles*, notes that there is a "start-and-stop feel" to this narrative, a sense in which the author "suspend[s] the forward movement of the text, over and over." According to Sanborn, these stops and starts create a theatrical effect.[49] I would also argue that these repeated starts and stops in the Crafts' narrative mirror the jolts and disjunction of the railroad. But, more dangerously, every time the Crafts set foot on a different train or steamship or in a hotel, they are, in essence, beginning the travel experience again, experiencing the anxiety of "situational riding" with new fellow passengers who may be able to determine their disguised identities.[50]

Part of the drama of *Running* also derives from the interior design of the first-class car, which contributes to a continual threat of exposure. Traveling in her disguise as a wealthy white man enables Ellen to occupy first-class compartments, or what William calls "the best carriages."[51] At several moments in the narrative, William informs the reader about the construction of these exemplary spaces, mapping the compartment's layout in narrative form. The design of the vestibule lends itself to what I call the precarity of proximity, that is, the design of the first-class train compartment contributes to the exposure and possible capture that renders the escape so suspenseful. The Crafts are in danger of discovery even before they leave their home of Macon, primarily because of the arrangement of the first-class car. As William explains to the reader, after they have separately traveled to the train station and Ellen settles into her seat: "The doors of the American railway carriage are at the ends. The passengers walk up the aisle, and take seats on either side; and as my master [Ellen in disguise] was engaged in looking out of the window, he did not see who came in."[52] The person who came in—a resident of the town they are fleeing and a friend of Ellen's master—sits next to Ellen. Because the "democratic" American design encourages passengers to talk to each other, Ellen escapes conversation only by pretending to be deaf. Unlike the other forms of transport the Crafts use, the train forces Ellen to remain relatively immobile. In the hotel or in the steamboat, Ellen walks away from talkative Southerners; she can walk further along the deck, retire to a cabin or her room. In the train compartment, she is, to use Michel de Certeau's words, "pigeon-holed" in the train car.[53] The immobility ensures that Ellen will have to speak to others or find credible ways to avoid conversation.

The design of the first-class compartments continues to play a subtle role as the Crafts escape further North. During one episode, when Ellen meets two young ladies who become enamored with her, William again remarks on the layout of the train compartment: "I have stated that the American railway carriages (or cars, as they are called), are constructed differently to those in England. At one end of some of them, in the South, there is a little apartment with a couch on both sides for the convenience of families and invalids; and as they thought my master was very poorly, he was allowed to enter one of these apartments at Petersburg, Virginia, where an old gentleman and two handsome young ladies, his daughters, also got in, and took seats in the same carriage."[54] While the father questions William Craft about his master, the two young ladies engage in conversation with Ellen, who, to avoid further dialogue, pretends to sleep on the compartment's couch and overhears the affection the women have developed for her.[55] The encounter and the conversation reveal the public nature of the enclosed space. But fortunately, Ellen can take advantage of the resting couch—available only in the first-class car.

A second episode occurs when an elderly woman enters the train compartment in Richmond. This scene does not highlight the structure of the compartment as much as it demonstrates the unsettledness of suspended mobility, the uncanny feeling one can have while riding the train. Unlike the protected white femininity of the two young female railroad travelers, the

Richmond woman presents a type of femininity that caricatures the grossest elements of the white men the Crafts meet on the steamer and in the hotel. The Richmond woman first loudly mistakes William for her own runaway property, then she informs the two passengers in her compartment, Ellen and a young southern white man, how she sold off the "ungrateful" July, even though her dead husband's will emancipated her. The woman's volubility in discussing the ingratitude of her human property increases the sense of insularity or imprisonment of the space.

Other scholars of the Crafts' narrative have remarked on the oddity of this scene—its "ridiculous aspects," its "internal contradictions."[56] With the three participants in the confined car—a white man, a white woman, and the race-gender-class-passing Ellen—this strange scene ruptures conventional expectations of slavery and gender: the white male passenger, whose mother was a slaveholder, is the figure who seems most sympathetic to July's plight. A series of uncanny doublings begin when the woman mistakes William Craft for the runaway Ned. The doublings continue in that Ellen could stand in for "July," the woman whom the Richmond woman sold and who, unfortunately, experiences what Ellen herself is trying to avoid, the breakup of her family. That all of this occurs in the presence of the "Black" Ellen heightens the sense of gender and racial inversion being performed before the Richmond woman's unknowing eyes.[57] Ellen's and William's doubling in this scene contributes to its destabilizing effect. As Freud notes, an uncanny feeling results not only when experiencing something weirdly familiar; it also derives from the oddity of finding likenesses of yourself in spaces of transience such as "hotel rooms [and] compartments in railways."[58] Here, the strangeness of this scene springs from the ways in which the main participants can stand in for other people.

Running a Thousand Miles for Freedom, as an antebellum railroad narrative, exemplifies several qualities of train travel, particularly Black female train travel, revealed in my book's later chapters. The Crafts are suspended between capture and freedom in the first half of their narrative. They embody the lived, traumatic elements experienced during the suspension of time and space that occurs between arrival and destination—that is, traveling "in abeyance." The train compartment is a paradox of mobility and stasis: it moves from one locale to another while the passenger is stable within.[59] The various ways in which the Black female subjects—whether fictional characters, activist "club" women, legal plaintiffs, or entrepreneurs—negotiate mobility and stasis helps to disrupt fixed ideas of Black femininity. The Crafts are hypervisible even though they are in disguise—both free and enslaved passengers throughout their trip are frequently attracted by the appearance of the ill white gentleman and his devoted enslaved man. *Running a Thousand Miles for Freedom* registers the performative component riding on a train often required of African Americans, especially African American women. Finally, the Crafts reveal the deep uncertainty and unpredictability of railroad travel, especially for Black travelers both during and after slavery and the studied plotting necessary in order to travel safely.[60] These fraught conditions mark Black and female travel in abeyance, inside the train car in which time and space seem stilled or dormant, in quiescence.[61]

Following the Tracks

This book engages with the previous scholarship of Mia Bay, Melinda Chateauvert, Blair L. M. Kelley, Amy Richter, and Barbara Welke, feminist historians whose work developed my interest in railroad history and marginalized groups.[62] I engage with and extend from these works by examining the railroad and, specifically, the first-class train compartment, as a site of work, travel, or pleasure for Black women and by noting how "gender deference" traditionally granted to traveling white women was continually denied to traveling Black women; by studying how the railroad shaped ideas about belonging—to a community as well as a larger nation; and by detailing the history of Pullman maids before the BSCP was recognized by the American Federation of Labor (AFL) in the 1930s—which was also the moment when the number of maids in the Pullman Company decreased and BSCP removed the term "Maids" from its name. This period and later is archivally rich: it is after this period that we have comparatively more information about the Black women who worked for a railroad or were involved with porters' auxiliaries or women's groups. The early period of Black female railroad labor history is the more challenging, and the more fascinating, story to tell because of the paucity of sources on these women.

Riding Jane Crow is not a comprehensive history of the railroad in Black culture, nor is this a book about the history of specific railroads or a study of the economic impact and influence of trains. Instead the book traces an overlooked dimension of U.S. travel: the material and psychic costs of gender and racial discrimination on the rails and the difficulties—and liberties—segregated travel created for Black women. I look at Black women, as passengers and as workers, on and outside the train car. I examine four specific forms or instances of railroad travel—early Black female intellectuals who described Black female travel as passengers, Black middle-class women who sued to ride in first-class passenger cars, Black women railroad food vendors, and Black maids on Pullman trains—to see the nineteenth and early twentieth centuries' most important form of public transportation through the eyes of African American women. By studying the multiple ways Black women experienced the enclosed space of the train car and how Black women's mobility fluctuated throughout the train compartment and related spaces, the book reveals the cultural impact of the railroad on Americans' shifting perceptions of race, gender, class, and nationality. For women of color, the train car was a transforming and transformative space, revealing a gendered and spatialized form of double consciousness. Reading literature and legal, labor, and travel history; maps, census records, and town directories; newspapers and town council records; lithographs, photographs, and film stills; and diaries and letters, I bring to life the different geographic strategies African American women employed to navigate the train car and related spaces.

I begin with an examination of the spatial and temporal dynamics of the train compartment by reading the writings of Anna Julia Cooper, Mary Church Terrell, and, briefly, Ida B. Wells. These three highly mobile and intellectual women recorded the difficulty of Black female railroad travel. Each author's difficulty on or near a railroad articulated the unique dilemmas of the Black female middle-class traveler. Cooper's discourse on Black female spatial politics comes most pointedly, in fact, when she critiques the spaces of travel and writes of her experiences within them. The women's common narrative strategy of paralepsis—emphasizing a point by claiming not to discuss it—revealed their embarrassment of not receiving the respectability they expected as accomplished women. Terrell, for example, frequently discussed the difficulty of train traveling as a Black woman and "like a lady," particularly in her autobiography, *A Colored Woman in a White World* (1940) and in an unpublished short story, "Betsy's Borrowed Baby." Betsy, a southern Black college student, fears returning to college in the North, for she would have to make the trip on a Jim Crow car. Her solution—passing as a Black nanny—plays on accepted notions of Black femininity of the time and enables Betsy to "borrow" the security and comfort usually granted to traveling white women. Terrell's work elucidates the drama in the usually uneventful period between departure and destination within the compartment space. For Terrell's fictional character, the "lull" during railroad travel is not one of subjective pleasure but one of acute fear of sexual or racial violence. Curiously, the frequent references to the difficulty of Black female railroad travel includes an inability to be fully forthcoming about the unique predicament railroad travel places on Black women. Reading Terrell with Cooper, I detail the performative aspect of being in temporal and spatial abeyance in the first-class train car and the material and psychological dynamics of riding first and second-class as a Black woman. All three women illustrate how the country's racial and social progress can only be measured by the travel experiences of Black women who test what Cooper calls "national courtesy."

I continue a study of the interior of the train compartment by examining the history of racial segregation on the railroad by analyzing lawsuits filed against railroad companies by African American women. The second chapter studies Black women who destabilized racial, gender, and class conventions both in first-class travel spaces and in the U.S. courtroom in the 1880s: Jane Brown of Corinth, Mississippi, and Sallie Robinson, also of Mississippi. I analyze legal documents, trial transcripts, newspapers, and county and census records to understand how these lawsuits differed from Homer Plessy's landmark case: their suits were based not only on their race but also on their gender. The women sued to ride in "ladies' cars," designed for first-class, white, female passengers who traveled alone or were accompanied by a male relative. By suing to ride in those cars, the women exploited conventional conceptions of femininity. They affirmed *gender* segregation to subvert *racial* discrimination. The very attempt to create a "ladies' space" depended on what one judge called "a strained construction of the term 'ladies'" and what legal scholar Joan R. Tarpley calls "jezebel jurisprudence," that is, the supposed sexual proclivities of Black women.[63] The railroad defended itself in both suits by identifying the women as prostitutes. I argue that it was not just their race that contributed to these assumptions. It was their race, gender, and their *mobility* that led weight to the perception. The women and their lawsuits illustrate one of the more troubling aspects of Black female train travel: the sexualization of Black female mobility.

Sallie Robinson's lawsuit was one of five that came to be known as the *Civil Rights Cases of 1883*. This set of cases was important for two reasons: first, the majority U.S. Supreme Court opinion negated the 1875 Civil Rights Act that prohibited discrimination in public accommodations. Passed after the death of Massachusetts senator Charles Sumner, the 1875 law was repeatedly invoked by African Americans fighting segregation in the late 1870s and early 1880s. The U.S. Supreme Court's decision in the *Civil Rights Cases* nullified that law. Second, the Supreme Court's 1883 decision would prefigure another legal case the court would decide thirteen years later, *Plessy v. Ferguson*.[64] Although Jane Brown and Sallie Robinson sued the same railroad company, the success of one and the failure of the other demonstrated the regression of Black social and legal rights during the Post-Reconstruction period, particularly for African American women who resisted riding Jane Crow.

As Anna Julia Cooper and Mary Church Terrell reveal, we should expand discussion of the railroad space to include not only the compartment but also the station platform, the ticket counter, and the waiting room—in short, all of the areas people must encounter in order to travel. Chapter 3 looks closely at the interstitial space between the train car and the train depot: the railroad platform. Here I examine waiter carriers, a group of African American women who worked as food vendors to train passengers before and after the Civil War and well into the twentieth century. These women had a thriving business in two railroad towns of the South: Corinth, Mississippi, and Gordonsville, Virginia. Psyche Williams-Forson's *Building Houses out of Chicken Legs* (2006) first drew wider attention to these women and discussed them in terms of food studies and their significance in developing a Black female economic independence.[65] I shift the discussion of these women by looking at the spatial politics of the towns in which the women lived and by studying how the train and community politics impacted their occupation. Remembered primarily in old postcards and newspapers and by word of mouth, as well as in a short story, waiter carriers are different from the women of the earlier chapters. I re-create the experiences of waiter carriers in Virginia to analyze the despatialization of Black women in relation to the railroad: As railroad technologies improved and as their platform business became more profitable, the women were forced to move from the platform to sell from an even more marginal location—on the very railroad tracks. Waiter carriers were displaced as white community members struggled to assert other aspects of the community's local history and promote a tourist economy. Ironically, Gordonsville's "Fried Chicken Festival," celebrating the most popular food sold by the waiter carriers, is now the primary fame of the Virginian town.

A study of the waiter carriers highlights how precariously Black women survive in the archival record and how infrequently they are remembered in railroad history. I found information about these women from a dispersed and disparate archive. The eclectic nature of Black women's railroad history is further revealed when researching another group of women not normally discussed with train travel, the women who worked for the once powerful Pullman Palace Car Company as Pullman maids. The fourth chapter examines the development of the Pullman railroad car and the practices that regulated "transportable" Blackness in this space. The Black male Pullman porter symbolized the elegance of the Pullman car but complicated ideas of racial segregation because of his necessary presence in all areas of the train. I focus, however, on the comparatively unknown story of the Black *women* who worked for Pullman—the Pullman maid and female attendant. Analyzing the employee files of Pullman maids helped me to understand the dynamic of a mixture of races and classes in the confined space of a train car and the economic and sexual exploitation that occurred on the trains. The Pullman instruction manual for maids, employee cards, and an anonymous grievance letter together help to reconstruct the experiences of the Pullman maids and illustrate how their service enabled the Pullman Company to demonstrate its remarkable progress in transportation but at the expense of Black women's labor. The experiences of these women as well as other overlooked women of color, such as the Asian American women who worked as Pullman maids on the western train lines, reveal that the Pullman car was perhaps one of the most problematic spaces for traveling women of color.

As the book progresses, I detail the challenges of finding Black women in the archive. The second half of the book attempts to install African American women more concretely in the archive of U.S. railroad history: How *do* we measure progress when the advancement of the race or the improvement in technologies leads to the erasure of Black women? How do we record and remember the impact of the railroad on Black female lives? *Riding Jane Crow* explores the links between two spaces: the archive as a space of knowledge production, the train car as a space of identity construction. It expands the valences of the term "archive" to include the material space holding the limited documentation of these women's lived experiences, and considers the train car as an archival imaginary, the collective space of railroad history attuned to the varied ways African American women interacted with the railroad and their experiences that were not fully, if ever, recorded.

When I thought of the title "Riding Jane Crow," I assumed that readers would know and understand the reference. To "ride Jim Crow" for most of the nineteenth century and for at least the first half of the twentieth meant to travel in a segregated space. Louis Ruchames, the researcher who studied segregated railroads in Massachusetts, also noted that the term Jim Crow first appeared in 1841 when the Black abolitionist David Ruggles was forced to ride in a "dirt car" instead of a first-class railroad compartment, even though he had a first-class ticket.[66] Because T. D. Rice's minstrel performance of the song "Jump Jim Crow," was so popular, it may have taken little imagination, or as Ruchames notes, it was "a natural development," for the public to come up with a phrase that would signify the less desirable travel spaces that would be set aside for African Americans.[67] "Jane Crow" is not simply the femininized version of "Jim Crow." It is rather a sustained analysis of how the legal arguments to combat racial discrimination in the United States could be used in the late twentieth century to fight entrenched forms of gender and sexual discrimination. The term was developed by Pauli Murray, the writer, lawyer, scholar, poet, and priest who had a public feminine gender expression, identified privately as male, and, significantly, wrote about multiple train travel experiences.[68] The book concludes with a seeming paradox: one of the places where I found pleasurable Black "female" train riding was in the private papers, scrapbook, and photographs of Murray. Murray's identification as male is revealed more openly in his private archival records of the 1930s, and obliquely in a short narrative "Three Thousand Miles on a Dime in Ten Days" (1934), than in a 1987 autobiography, *A Song in a Weary Throat*. By comparing the public and private accounts of Murray's travel episodes, several of which took place on freight cars when Murray presented to others as male, we catch a rare, queer glimpse of Black (fe)male railroad pleasure. Like the young woman who graces this book's cover with a peculiar smile of quiet self-confidence as she hangs off a boxcar, the private Murray enjoyed the pleasures and freedoms of travel only outside of the confinement of the first-class and second-class passenger cars discussed throughout the book.[69] The term "Jane Crow," then alters as the book travels to a conclusion. The middle-class women of chapters 1 and 2 who actively sought travel in first-class spaces experienced Black female train travel as one of heightened awareness of their Black and female bodies. The Black female workers of chapters 3 and 4 had to navigate travel spaces on which they were financially dependent, an occupationally inflected Jane Crow. And Murray's travel experiences suggest a subversive redefinition of the term. One Murray biographer notes that an initial title for the autobiography *Song in a Weary Throat* was, in fact, "Jane Crow," a title that would have signaled how Murray reinvested the legal concept with a more personal meaning.[70] In these different iterations of "Jane Crow," the meaning is very much dependent on how the Black subject experiences space, travel, and gender.

"Progress" and Black Female Subjectivity

In the U.S. context, the train is usually read in light of progress and ingenuity, of uniting the nation after the Civil War, or, as I noted earlier, a "machine in an [American] garden." But the railroad in America served many masters and many purposes. Notably, it was the first technology that white America used after the Civil War to assert white supremacy. It became a battleground between new scenarios made possible by the end of slavery and old, institutionalized habits that emancipation did not remove. As such, it is an evocative symbol of the contradictory progress and disappointments of the post-Reconstruction era for African Americans. Du Bois mused "on the meaning of [this contradictory] progress" in the fourth chapter of *The Souls of Black Folk*. The chapter is noteworthy not only because of its ambivalent view of progress but also because it depicts such ambivalence through the dual concepts of the railroad and Black female immobility.

Chapter 4 recounts Du Bois's time as a teacher near Alexandria, Tennessee, roughly fifty miles east of Nashville, a trip he makes by foot and on horseback ("I feel the deep weariness of heart and limb as ten, eight, six miles stretch relentlessly ahead").[71] The chapter fully registers the frustrations with prohibitive or stalled movement, also subtly signified by the spiritual that opens the chapter, "My Way's Cloudy."[72] Hope and promise fill the chapter, even as Du Bois wonders how he will provide seats for his students in the old log hut that serves as the schoolhouse. He is inspired by his students, especially one, Josie: "She had about her a certain fineness, the shadow of an unconscious moral heroism that would willingly give all of life to make life broader, deeper, and fuller for her and hers."[73] Du Bois returns to the area ten years later and finds some improvements. The schoolhouse log cabin, for example, is gone: "In its place stood Progress; and Progress, I understand, is necessarily ugly." He also learns that Josie died after working hard to provide for her family. Musing about the various improvements in the small town, DuBois states, in an anticlimactic conclusion:

> My journey was done, and behind me lay hill and dale, and Life and Death. How shall man measure Progress there where the dark-faced Josie lies? How many heartfuls of sorrow shall balance a bushel of wheat? . . . is it the twilight of nightfall or the flush of some faint-dawning day?
> Thus sadly musing, I rode to Nashville in the Jim Crow car.[74]

This moment in *Souls* reveals the deep ambivalence of "progress" through the images of Black femininity and the railroad. Hazel Carby's spatial and geographic reading of *Souls of Black Folk* details the troubling place Josie Dowell has in the chapter, for her "life and death become a measure for the historical progress of the folk as a whole."[75] Josie's demise is in marked contrast to the technological progress of the town, signified by the improved forms of transportation. Du Bois's literal and figurative advancement is limited by discrimination but is at least better than whatever progress lies where the dark-faced Josie is: immobile, inert, dead in the ground. His progress is tempered by the fact that he has to ride a Jim Crow car, but he does ride away, where he previously walked tirelessly over hills, and he leaves behind the small, constrictive town still confronted with economic and social injustices.

In this jumble of racial and gender strictures, we see a common trope of gender and the railroad: men traveling away and women remaining. What happens when America's Josies are the ones who ride away on that whistling train?

1 Ladies' Space

An Archive of Black Women's Railroad Narratives

There can be no true test of national courtesy without travel.
—Anna Julia Cooper, "Woman vs. The Indian,"
  A Voice From the South (1892)

In her slave narrative *Incidents in the Life of a Slave Girl* (1861), Harriet Jacobs deliberates on the injustice of her confinement in a cramped space. The uncomfortable interior she describes is not the "loophole of retreat" of her grandmother's attic, where she hid for seven years to evade her owner's father, but the crowded environment of a Jim Crow train compartment. Indeed, her reflections occur *after* she is nominally "free"—that is, after she has escaped from the South and is preparing to board a train in Philadelphia to New York. The passage records her shock on experiencing discrimination in the northern states because "they don't allow colored people to go in the first-class cars": "This was my first chill to my enthusiasm about the Free States. Colored people were allowed to ride in a filthy box, behind white people, at the south, but they were not required to pay for the privilege. It made me sad to find how the north aped the customs of slavery." Jacobs is well-versed in the dynamics of confined areas and skilled in withstanding difficulties in restrictive environments, but her new status as a fugitive slave dawns on her here, in a train compartment. The spatial specificity of this new experience with Jim Crow segregation—"*in* a filthy box, *behind* white people, *at* the south"—mark just how startled she is that the coordinates of northern segregation simulate the spatial and racial hierarchies of the South.[1] Jacobs continues with a description of the materiality of the filthy box, conveying the full sensory and physical experience to the reader:

> We were stowed away in a large, rough car, with windows on each side, too high for us to look out without standing up. It was crowded with people, apparently of all nations. There were plenty of beds and cradles, containing screaming and kicking babies. Every other man has a cigar or pipe in his mouth, and jugs of whiskey were handed round freely. The fumes of the whiskey and the dense tobacco smoke were sickening to my senses, and my mind was equally nauseated by the coarse jokes and ribald songs around me. It was a very disagreeable ride.[2]

The brief time Jacobs spends riding in a dirty train car is a relatively small discomfort compared to years of confinement in the "loophole of retreat," but the abominable conditions in the train compartment disrupt her expectations of freedom she anticipated while hiding in the garret space. It is fitting that Jacobs's inaugural lesson on Black life in the North takes place on the railroad, for if Jacobs's garret was a space of alternative freedom, a place from which she became skilled in "geographic possibilities" and learned "spatial strategies" to survive slavery, then the Jim Crow car teaches her the failure of the North's concept of freedom, and, indeed, the North's complicity in segregatory practices.[3] The North's mimicry of the South calls into question the freedom of the "Free States," and Jacobs's exclusion from the first-class car can be read as a larger exclusion from the definitions of U.S. citizenship. As I argue throughout this book, the enclosed area of the train car was a microcosm of the United States, and, as such, became one of the most contested public spaces in the late nineteenth and early twentieth centuries. Neither citizenship nor respectability necessarily traveled with the African American woman in the antebellum Jim Crow car.

Jacobs's is one of the earliest, but certainly not the only, examples in black letters of the Black female railroad travel experience. Jacobs's 1860 recording of her train ride is repeated in various ways by several African American women throughout the mid to late nineteenth and early twentieth centuries. As I detail at the end of this chapter, a range of African American women—from Sojourner Truth and Harriet Tubman to Francis Ellen Watkins Harper and Susie King Taylor to the female members of the Fisk Jubilee Singers—discussed or wrote about their difficult experiences traveling by rail or streetcar in various locations of the United States throughout the nineteenth century, helping to construct a literary archive of railroad narratives. Train travel was of particular concern to African American intellectual "race" women, such as Anna Julia Cooper, Mary Church Terrell, and Ida B. Wells (see chapter 2), whose activist work necessitated lecturing throughout the country and abroad. In addition to commenting on the major race and gender issues of the time, the women used their public and private writings to expose the physical hardships and ideological dilemmas train travel posed to Black female subjectivity. The apprehensions each writer detailed—the racism and sexism within the railroad's built environment, the sexual assumptions made of mobile Black women riding a train, and the inability to travel safely in a train compartment within the United States, particularly below the Mason-Dixon Line—all reveal the ensemble of power relations embedded in the U.S. train car and the train car's ability to define and reflect social and racial hierarchies.

I am interested in the deeply *spatial* way the women disclose their travel difficulties—by using the built or travel environment to metaphorize the internal dynamics and interior dilemmas that take place within the Black female traveling subject. Cooper and Terrell reveal what Jacobs's first train ride also conveyed: that gendered and racial discrimination are, quite literally, built into the nineteenth-century railroad environment. By doing so, the authors present the train compartment as the material embodiment of Black women's social mobility: they go forward yet are stilled by others, a paradoxical movement and stasis identified with the inner time and space within the train car. Moreover, their writings, when taken together, tell an alternative story of the railroad and America's "progress" narrative. Indeed, they challenge the mythos of the train as the nation's symbol of civilization and advancement. The assemblage of their writings together constructs a counter-archive of the American railroad, or what I have earlier termed a railroad imaginary.

The African American woman's travel experience, whether by train or by steamboat, the other common form of nineteenth-century public transportation, differed significantly from the romanticized conceptions of travel frequently invoked by white male writers. Jacobs's account of her first railroad trip is revelatory for its contrast to descriptions that present an idealized experience of riding the rails, one of leisured introspection. In Wolfgang Schivelbusch's reading, for example, the railroad passenger "savor[ed]" what Schivelbusch calls that "in-between or travel space," the period of time between departure and destination. The velocity of the train contributed to an imagined movement into a private world and the creation of an aesthetically gratifying perspective.[4] By reading a book or gazing out of the train window, the passenger pleasantly "forgot" the external world, an amnesia that led to productive artistic musings. The in-between space within the train car and the in-between time linking departure and destination facilitated a traveler's expanded sense of identity and enabled him to "lose himself" while contemplating the passing landscape. Speed, the motive force of the railroad, furthered "freedom," "the dissolution of the outer world by means of velocity."[5] The train ride, apparently, was conducive to introspection and intellectual passions.

Yet, like Jacobs's description of her disagreeable ride, the writings of Cooper and Terrell challenge this description of leisured introspection. I argue that when African American women ride the railroad, the "hiatus" during the travel journey—that specific temporal and spatial period within the train compartment itself—is one of keen hypervigilance and possible anxiety. In order to fully explicate this disparity between leisured introspection and heightened awareness while within the train car, this chapter studies the concept of what Anna Julia Cooper calls "national courtesy," a form of deference and consideration usually granted to traveling white women, but a consideration on which Black women could not reliably count, particularly in the South and particularly when they traveled away from home. Travel courtesy was routinely denied to Black women, despite their sometimes conscious efforts to behave and dress as "ladies." In addition, Cooper and Terrell employ a writing strategy also present in Jacobs: they center their discussions of the problems of train travel by invoking the materiality of the train ride experience. While Anna Julia Cooper's writings reveal how gendered discrimination was reflected in the built environment of the train station, Mary Church Terrell depicts the material conditions usually found in Jim Crow cars and their difference from the first-class cars set aside for white ladies. As I show, presenting this concrete experience of train travel is important in their efforts to theorize the injustices they encountered as they traveled. Their insights are rendered not through intellectual abstraction but through concrete information about the material conditions of travel. They both detail the assumptions made of Black women traveling alone and the performative qualities Black women adopted to borrow or appropriate the courtesy usually granted to traveling white women. In fact, their writings reveal that the time within the space of the train car can be one of heightened anxiety made more acute because of possible assault on their persons, primarily because of their race and sex. For women of color traveling on trains, the inability to "lose *herself*" is one of the more momentous forms of riding Jane Crow, of gender and racial discrimination on the rails.

The Steamboat: The Other Form of Nineteenth-Century Travel

Some background on other forms of travel available in the mid to late nineteenth century can help explain the significance of train travel and its difficulties for African American women. The railroad was not the only form of long-distance, public travel that was commonly available to nineteenth-century travelers. Steamboats on major American rivers remained popular for passenger travel until several years after the Civil War, but several factors contributed to the railroad as, arguably, the more contested racialized space of public transport. There were two main areas usually available for passengers on steamboats: the cabin and the deck. The deck, the unenclosed area of the steamboat, cost less than cabin space. Before Emancipation, slaves were allowed in cabins only as servants of white passengers and even then were forced to sleep on the saloon floor at night.[6] After the Civil War, African American passengers who could afford a cabin ticket were relegated to what was pejoratively called "the freedmen's bureau," "a segregated compartment above the main cabin and to the rear of the pilothouse and officers' quarters," in a space frequently subject to winds.[7] Throughout the latter half of the nineteenth century, the steamboat declined as the preferred mode of passenger travel and distribution of goods. Steamboat navigation was subject to favorable weather and river water levels. At its swiftest, a mid-century steamboat traveled five to six miles per hour upstream, compared to the approximately twenty-five to thirty miles per hour of mid-century railroads. Steamboats lost passengers to the faster railroad, and by the end of Reconstruction and with the increase in the miles of tracks throughout the United States, railroads were the more common form of passenger travel.[8]

Unlike steamboats, which were "the most consistently segregated [form of transport] in the postwar South," according to Barbara Welke, railroads had somewhat arbitrary segregation policies, at least before the 1890s.[9] A single line or run of a railroad company usually consisted of three types of compartments: the first-class car, the second-class car, and the luggage car.[10] These cars were roughly fifty feet in length and nine to ten feet wide, with two seats forming a row down a narrow aisle.[11] Unlike contemporary understandings of "first-class" travel spaces, the first-class railroad car was often the *last* car of the train. This car was located away from the engine at the front of the train, thus, passengers in first-class were protected from smoke, soot, and the other dirt associated with train travel. First-class cars were further distinguished from the others by the comfort provided, namely upholstered, padded seats. Second-class cars, closer to the front of the train, were for those who could not afford first-class and for men who wanted to smoke. Segregation policies on American railroad lines varied but African Americans were often relegated to second-class cars, even when they paid for first-class tickets.

The railroad cars reflected the divisions that pervaded America throughout the late nineteenth century. Analyzing the changing dynamic of the post–Civil War South as African Americans gradually received rights previously denied to them, Edward Ayers notes the charged atmosphere of the train compartment and the distinctions between first and second class:

> In the first-class car rode women and men who did not use tobacco, while in the second-class car rode men who chewed or smoked, men unaccompanied by women, and people who could not afford a first-class ticket. To travel in the second-class car was to travel with people, overwhelmingly men, who behaved very differently from those in the car ahead. The floors were thick with spit and tobacco juice, the air thick with smoke and vulgarities. The second-class car had hard seats, low ceilings, and no water; frequently, it was merely a part of the baggage car set off by a partition. . . . And was often invaded by smoke and soot. The cars saw more crowding of strangers than in any other place in the New South.[12]

Ayers's description indicates how the differences of the cars reflected the class distinctions of passengers. And these divisions of train cars into first and second class inevitably sharpened into racial divisions. An 1890 editorial in a New Orleans newspaper asserted the need to keep African Americans out of first-class cars, otherwise the races would be "crowded together, squeezed close to each other in the same seats, using the same conveniences, and to all intents and purposes in social intercourse."[13] Notably, there was no concern about the intimacy possible in second-class cars, or the smokers.

Although Tennessee was the first state after the Civil War to enact a segregated railcar law in 1881, separate but equal statutes did not appear in any extensive fashion until the 1890s; nine southern states enacted such laws between 1887 and 1901.[14] Prior to those laws, African Americans who could afford the legal cost used the courts to challenge unfair treatment on the railroads and tested the power of postwar constitutional amendments and the Civil Rights Act of 1875, which, among other items, prohibited discrimination in public accommodations.[15] Since it was uncertain "what institutions or laws or customs would be necessary to maintain white control now that slavery was gone," as C. Vann Woodward notes, railroads, and specifically first-class compartments, became one of the most disputed spaces of experimentation for white supremacy and Black assertiveness.[16] The Black traveler's ability to pay for a first-class railroad ticket signified not his or her desire to separate from other African Americans or to be in the presence of first-class white passengers but rather to have some comfort, if not respect, during the travel experience.

Black women's travel experiences question the assumed "naturalness" of travel spaces and reveal how a history of undervaluing Blackness and female-ness contributed to practices that have cohered into racial and spatial hier-archies. In her analysis of Black female geographies, Katherine McKittrick identifies such sites as the slave auction block and the plantation as settings that materialize "the spatialization of the racial-sexual black subject."[17] A first- or second-class train compartment, in contrast, may appear to be not as racially loaded as these other spaces but we should theorize this place pre-cisely because nineteenth-century railroad passengers generally accepted the class and gender divisions of train cars as "natural." Moreover, attending to the specifics of the travel experience, the materiality of the built environment, can help us trouble assumptions of public travel as a neutral activity that simply occurs. As Mark Simpson suggests, we should "understand mobility not as a naturally occurring phenomenon but more rigorously as a mode of social contest decisive in the manufacture of subjectivity and the determination of belonging."[18] As I argue, Cooper and Terrell disclose and critique the role of race and gender in the production of travel space. Their writings reveal what it may have meant for Black middle-class women to travel on Jim Crow trains in the late nineteenth-century and early twentieth-century United States, a period of intense racial activity when Black political and economic advancements precipitated widespread violence against Blacks throughout the country. This experience I call "riding Jane Crow" to indicate the highly gendered and heightened experience of Black women on these trains during and following post-Reconstruction segregation.[19]

Cooper's and Terrell's writings metaphorize Black women's "inner lives" as the time and space within the compartment, as the train car becomes the physical embodiment of the forward yet stilled/stifled movement as described by Robert Stepto.[20] Cooper and Terrell indicate how the travel interval, the in-between period within the time and space of the train compartment, can be a burdensome weight for women, instead of an experience of newness and adventure or leisured introspection. These railroad experiences do not make the women "journey-proud," Thomas Mann's term for a satisfying, almost narcissistic understanding of train travel in which "a pleasing relax-ation takes place, the mind turns to fresh concerns, the unknown unfolds itself beyond the expanse of the window-pane, and [one is] consumed with joyful anticipations."[21] Their experience instead can be found in the words that concern one of Terrell's fictional characters as she plans her trip home: "getting there's the thing." These four simple words emphasize the anxiety of the actual, physical process of moving through the segregated United States on public transportation as a woman of color. The phrase reflects not just metaphorical or class mobility popular during contemporaneous discussions of the "New Woman," but the specific, literal activity of movement that Black women must consider, particularly as the rise of Black women's clubs in the late nineteenth century necessitated travel throughout the country.

Demonstrating how the first-class train car is a metonymic space of U.S. race and gender relations, Cooper's and Terrell's writings provide a larger context to Black women and American public travel. Their archive of Black female travel writing reveals that, in public travel spaces, the Black female body is hypervisible, simultaneously sexualized and policed—even as the train architecture erases the individual Black woman's identity. Ultimately, their writings provide insight into the dynamics of the train car environment, the liminal position of Black women who travel in public space, and the conditions necessary to survive the time and space within the train car. In order to combat the gender inequities of racialized travel spaces, particularly in the compact area of the American train car, Black women relied on complex planning to enact a raced and gendered resistance.

National Courtesy and the Infrastructure of Jane Crow Travel

Booker T. Washington experienced an unusual form of discomfort while traveling south in a Pullman sleeper. He met "two ladies from Boston" who knew him and who, unfortunately for Washington, were "perfectly ignorant of the customs of the South." The women insisted that he sit with them, all while the compartment was "full of Southern white men, all of whom had their eye on our party." Washington was embarrassed but did not want to be rude and so continued to sit with the ladies, even after he learned they had ordered dinner to be served. After the meal, the trauma was not yet quite over: "To add further to the embarrassment of the situation, . . . one of the ladies remembered that she had in her satchel a special kind of tea which she wished served, and as she said she felt quite sure the porter did not know how to brew it properly, she insisted on getting up and preparing and serving it herself." Mortified, Washington finally left the women to join the male passengers in the smoking car and to determine the consequences for breaking so many travel protocols, or "to see how the land lay." Knowledge of his identity fortunately reached the white men while he was eating. Instead of being angry, the men "thanked me earnestly for the work that I was trying to do for the whole South." An episode rife with travel embarrassment, and with the potential for violence if it had involved any other Black man, ended with expressions of gratitude.[22]

We may look askance at Washington's account of his train travels because his form of embarrassment is so very different from the humiliation experienced by the women who appear in this chapter. Although much could be said about the Boston ladies' appropriation of the porter's work, as well as the gender and racial expectations parodied, I am more interested in Washington's description of his discomfort brought on by the women's solicitude. If politeness was a weapon, Washington would have been wounded. Washington recounts the episode, it appears, to be humorous. But for many African American women of the same period, traveling in a Pullman, or indeed, any first-class or second-class train car, did not leave them feeling amused. In fact, it is precisely the *absence* of such politeness, what Anna Julia Cooper calls "national courtesy," that marks and delimits the Black female travel experience as recorded, preserved—archived—in the writings of two African American intellectual women of the late nineteenth and early twentieth centuries, Cooper and Mary Church Terrell.

Anna Julia Cooper's writings are important not only for her early insight into the "intersectionality" of race and gender, the ways in which race and gender overlap in the construction of the Black female subject, but also for her ability to cast her eye over the entire architecture associated with the travel experience. It is not just the train compartment that presents difficulties but also the other spaces associated with public travel, such as the waiting room and the platform.[23] If Cooper reveals "the artifice of segregation," as scholar Vivian May notes, Cooper also exposes how that artifice is built through the material structure and design of train stations and the rules and protocols of the train cars.[24] While Ida B. Wells employs legal remedies to combat discriminatory travel, and Mary Church Terrell exposes the concrete hazards within the particular area of the train compartment in fiction and autobiography, Cooper uses her writings to survey the train car and train depot building, rendering her philosophical ideas of overlapped identities into the built environment of the train station.

Geography and mobility shape Cooper's argument throughout her 1892 collection of essays, *A Voice From the South*, but she discusses her train travels specifically in "Woman vs. The Indian," a wide-ranging essay, moving from the racial bias of nineteenth-century white women's organizations to the North's complicity with southern slavery to the reasons for the eventual failure of Reconstruction. Cooper compares the United States, particularly the southern United States, to other nations—and the United States fails in that comparison. Drawing on the work of Percival Lowell in *The Soul of the Far East* (1888), who claimed that nations are more "polite" as one travels east, Cooper argues that the United States is the least polite country.[25] Traveling in Great Britain, Cooper compares the courtesy she receives there to her familiar treatment in the United States. England comes out better under the assessment, although not because of any overt demonstration of solicitude.[26] In fact, the politeness Cooper received was a "uniform, matter-of-fact courtesy," but it was in marked contrast to what she normally receives in her home country and in contrast to other women.

Three issues most concerned female travelers of color: efficiency, safety, and courtesy. "Woman vs. The Indian" details how, for the Black female traveler, the lack of the last item compromises the first two. Cooper drapes her critique of railroad travel with her not-so-subtle sarcasm, noting that a group of young white women attempted to study the U.S. woman's travel experience and celebrate the nation's railroad proficiency: "Some American girls, in search of novelty and adventure, were taking an extended trip through our country unattended by gentleman friends; their wish was to write up for a periodical or lecture the ease and facility, the comfort and safety of American travel, under our well-nigh perfect railroad systems and our gentlemanly and efficient corps of officials and public servants. I have some material I could furnish these young ladies, though possibly it might not be just on the side they wish to have illuminated" (89). Just as W. E. B. Du Bois will do years later in *Souls of Black Folk*, Anna Julia Cooper invites us to travel with her on a train trip through the South. This time, the trip is less sanguine. Where discomfort "lies chiefly in [Du Bois's] heart," distress and more wounds Cooper. Where the young girls think of their trip as a "novel" adventure, it is a necessity for Cooper. "The Black Woman of the South has to do considerable travelling in this country, often unattended. She thinks she is quiet and unobtrusive in her manner, simple and inconspicuous in her dress, and can see no reason why in any chance assemblage of *ladies*, . . . she should be signaled out for any marked consideration" (89–90). Cooper's emphasis on "ladies" is significant, cognizant as she is of how the term was routinely denied to African American women. The word "lady" is charged with social and racial meanings.[27] The lack of courtesy given to traveling Black women was a form of de-gendering, despite, or one could argue because of, her physical dress as a "lady." In contrast to the experience of the "American girls," a ladylike appearance and behavior made the African American traveling woman more susceptible to violence rather than less. As I discuss in more detail with Terrell later in this chapter, a middle-class appearance drew attention to Black women. Cooper's statement about "some American girls" is significant also because of the way she derisively sutures the naïveté of the young women to their nationality. These American girls, like Washington's Boston ladies, have unquestioned faith in the efficiency and safety of the railroad, even when "unattended by gentlemen friends."

For Anna Julia Cooper, national courtesy was the consideration given to women especially as they journeyed far from home or familiar surroundings. It occurred not in one's hometown with friends or neighbors but with unfamiliar people in unfamiliar, distant places—now made easier to travel to because of the reach of America's railroad system. The railroad brought together people who did not know each other, a potentially volatile mixture when it occurred between Blacks and whites. Mark M. Smith observes that, "in less mobile times, whites just recognized an individual's race because they knew the individual's genealogy and history."[28] The mobility fostered by the railroads made determining the race and class of individuals less certain. For African American intellectual women, their bearing would confirm first-class treatment with the expectation that courtesy could travel with them.

National courtesy depended not only on the etiquette of others but also others' recognition of a ladylike manner. One way to ensure courtesy was the display of proper female travel etiquette. As an experienced traveler, Cooper would have been familiar with the various etiquette instructions imparted to women who rode the rails. Travel was so central to late nineteenth-century Black female respectability and racial uplift that educator Charlotte Hawkins Brown included a section on travel in her etiquette manual for African American girls and young women, *The Correct Thing to Do and Say*. Published in 1941 but derived from the instruction given to girls beginning when Brown's school, Palmer Memorial Institute, was founded in 1902, *The Correct Thing* encouraged travel by African American women because "it offers a source of learning and appreciating, of improving the mind and satisfying the soul." Among the suggestions Brown made for the traveling woman was to not carry packages wrapped in paper or newspaper and to "not use the train or public conveyance for grooming which should be done in private quarters. The inconspicuous use of a powder puff or the smoothing of ruffled hair is all right."[29] Ideally, Brown's instructions would help strangers to identify the traveling African American woman as a "lady" so that she could be treated accordingly; it assumed, of course, that a mobile and recognizable Black femininity would be acknowledged by others. Annie E. Hall, deaconess of the Woman's Home Missionary Society, also offered suggestions to Black women while traveling, but she had harsh criticisms of "the railroad deportment of our young people." Hall was particularly critical of Black women who wore loud colors, talked loudly on the train, and who seemed flattered by the attentions of male passengers, conductors, and porters: "What traveler has not noticed the wink of the eye, the glances full of meaning, the contemptible smile received by our young women on cars, won by their carelessness?"[30]

A scene in Toni Morrison's *Sula* (1973) captures the significance of etiquette for traveling Black women even as it reveals the ineffectiveness of good fashion and behavior as a form of defense on a train. Helene, Nel's mother, worries about a trip south on a train "but decided that she had the best protection: her manner and her bearing, to which she would add a beautiful dress" (19). Morrison depicts in one brief sentence the over-planning necessary to travel safely as well as the significance of a proper etiquette which is intended to shield the traveling Black woman from assault or other indignities. Unfortunately for Helene, her carefully constructed railroad armor offers little safety. She is demeaned before she can even find the "right" train car. Mistakenly entering the white, first-class compartment, Helene prepares to leave but is stopped by a white conductor: "What you think you doin' gal?" (20). The deep de-personalization of the conductor's question as well as Helene's need to be recognized as not just a woman but as a *lady* explains the "foolish" coquetry she exhibits to the white conductor (22). Unfortunately, there will be no courtesy, nor bathrooms, for Helene as she and Nel travel in the South.[31]

Despite practicing correct etiquette, Cooper, like Helene, experienced rudeness during her train journey. Cooper first draws our attention to the lack of courtesy from a variety of train officials. The travel examples in "Woman vs. The Indian" all reveal the railroad official's inability to respond to her demeanor primarily because of color, and Cooper describes the incivility and the lack of courtesies that result. Acts of kindness shown to traveling Black women signify whether or not a man is a true gentleman, because the gentleman, not knowing the woman, does not know if she has "position or influence."[32] Cooper offers, as an example, the methods southern railroad conductors employ in order to get an African American woman to move from a first-class car to a Jim Crow car, noting the distinctions between a conductor who, being a "gentleman," discretely informs Cooper that "I had made a mistake and offer[s] to show me the proper car for black ladies" versus "a great burly six feet of masculinity with sloping shoulders and unkempt beard [who] swaggers in [and] . . . growls out at me over the paper I am reading, 'Here gurl,' (I am past thirty) 'you better git out 'n dis kyar 'f yer don't, I'll put yer out" (94, 95), in a near foreshadowing of Helene's experience in *Sula*. The form of deference shown by the first kind of conductor makes the request to move from one space to another, though unjust, more palatable.

Second, Cooper studies the actual construction of the environments she encounters while traveling—the physical layout of the train depot. While analyzing the train depot building, Cooper makes one of her most famous formulations about the intersectional nature of African American femininity. Having departed from the train car and "with a trying leap" jumped to the train platform, because the conductor refuses to assist her as she departs,

Cooper enters the station, glances at her surroundings, and faces what was a common dilemma for nineteenth and early twentieth-century Black female travelers.[33] Surveying the train station, Cooper's eyes stop at two signs that, though they reference parts of her identity, effectively function to erase her: "Looking a little more closely, I see two dingy little rooms with 'FOR LADIES' swinging over one and 'FOR COLORED PEOPLE' over the other; . . . wondering under which head I come" (96).[34] Cooper's gaze at the dual signs has been recognized as a powerful metaphor to explain the interlocking concerns that women of color face. As Elizabeth Alexander notes, the division "renders [Cooper] a literally impossible body in her time and space," an impossibility that neglects the experiences of African American women.[35] Cooper experiences yet another form of what we can call de-gendering; the waiting rooms "de-race" her as well.

Blueprints of southern train stations of the 1890s visualize Cooper's conundrum. Station plans of two passenger depots on the Louisville and Nashville Railroad (L&N) line, which covered the southeastern part of the United States from St. Louis to New Orleans, render concrete the abstract concepts underlying gender and racial segregation and their inconvenience for African American women.[36] The design of the first blueprint makes Cooper's dilemma tangible: The dimensions of each room are given: the ladies' waiting room is 18 by 16 feet, the gentlemen's waiting room is 16 by 16 feet, and the colored waiting room is 15 by 15 feet (fig. 1.1). In addition to being the largest room in the depot, the ladies' room also offers a convenience lacking in the others:

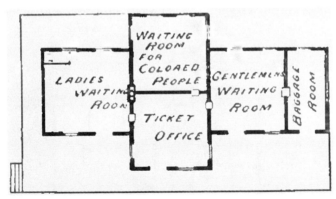

Figure 1.1: Black female railroad travelers like Anna Julia Cooper encountered train station waiting rooms for white "ladies," white men, and African American women and men. Blueprint, Local Passenger Depot, Louisville & Nashville Railroad. From Walter G. Berg, *Buildings and Structures of American Railroads* (1893), 291.

a bathroom. If we recall Toni Morrison's *Sula* (in which Helene traveling into the South on a train for the first time gradually learns how to "squat" in the woods in order to relieve herself because the stations lack restrooms for African American women), we understand the value, and, indeed, luxury, of a bathroom in a specified women's location. Cooper's impossible choice has real-world implications for her safety and comfort, while the (white) female passenger does not need to exit the room to address personal or biological needs.[37]

Studying the blueprints reveal even more slights to the African American traveler. The blueprint in figure 1.2 is of another depot on the L&N line, this one located in Columbia, Kentucky.[38] Again a woman's restroom is located inside the women's waiting room (in the back and to the right). Inequities exist not just in the signs "Ladies" and "Colored" but also in the physical layout. The "colored room" in the first blueprint is located at the back of the building, farthest from the train platform, a location that complicates viewing of the arrival or departure of the trains. The "colored" room of the second blueprint is the farthest from the restaurant—if Blacks were even allowed to eat there. Cooper's powerful metaphor of the impossible positions railroad travel places African American women in is made more prescient by the fact that, just a few months after *A Voice From the South* was published, Cooper herself was forcibly ejected from a woman's waiting room at a train station in North Carolina, even though she had a first-class ticket.[39]

Cooper's use of spatial references to describe African American female experiences continues with another well-known statement about the

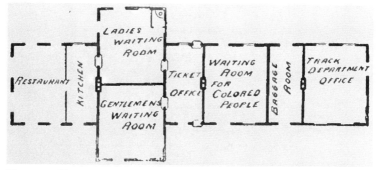

Figure 1.2: Blueprint, passenger depot at Columbia, Kentucky, Louisville & Nashville Railroad. From Walter G. Berg, *Buildings and Structures of American Railroads* (1893), 291.

universality of the Black woman's experience in time and space, as a marker of the race's progress: "When and Where I enter, in the quiet undisputed dignity of my womanhood, there the whole race enters with me" (31). If the space the black woman enters is a train car, then Cooper's experience indicates that racial progress is still very much in the future. In fact, twenty-seven years after Emancipation, Cooper can look outside of her train compartment window while passing through a section of "our enlightened and progressive country" and observe African Americans still in chains, victims of the convict lease system. Their feet are "chained together and heavy blocks attached—not in 1850, but in 1890, '91, and '92" (95–96).

Cooper's writings are important, then, because she broadens our understanding of the difficulties of Black female travel and highlights that it is not just the train compartment but multiple areas associated with travel that can impede the mobility of the Black woman. These obstacles reveal the lack of racial and gender progress of the nation. In a forceful refutation of the concept of leisured introspection, Cooper offers a studied deliberation of travel space. It is not just the train compartment but related spaces such as the railroad station, platform, and the waiting room that can cause particular predicaments for African American women. How Black women navigate these different areas says as much about national and regional perspectives on femininity and race as it comments on the racial progress of the nation. Or, as Cooper states much more succinctly, "There can be no true test of national courtesy without travel."

While Cooper draws our attention to the train station and briefly recounts the indignities in the train car, Mary Church Terrell offers a sustained discussion of the difficulties of Black female travel within the train compartment space. Although both writers convey the specificities of the inequities in the Jim Crow and first-class train car, Terrell particularizes the various ways in which the Jim Crow car, and sometimes the first-class car, disempowers African American female travelers.

Borrowed Time

"Betsy's Borrowed Baby," an unpublished, undated short story by Mary Church Terrell, illustrates the hazards experienced by Black women traveling by railroad during the late nineteenth or early twentieth century. A Black student at Ralston College, a fictional version of Terrell's alma mater Oberlin College, Betsy dreads going home—not because she does not want to see her family, but because she will have to travel from her school in Ohio to her home in the South on a Jim Crow, or second-class, train car. While her friends plan their summer vacations "taking ocean dips near Portland, Maine," Betsy worries about the trip to Magnolia, Kentucky, because "the conditions under which the white girls travel are totally different from those which confront" her. The story details Betsy's travel for two nights in a segregated train car and the difficulties she faces, including a sexually threatening encounter with male passengers and starving because the vendor runs out of food after selling to white passengers first. Determined not to repeat the experience when she returns to college in the fall, Betsy comes up with an idea: she agrees to travel with a white neighbor's young relative on a train to bring the child to her grandmother in Ohio. Betsy "passes" as a nanny to the white child in order to ride in a first-class car and avoid the hazards she experienced earlier. The grandmother offers to pay Betsy for escorting the child, but Betsy refuses. No amount of money can compensate her for traveling with the little girl, for as she tells herself at the end of the story, "I actually borrowed that baby to return to college in comfort, safety and peace."[40]

"Betsy's Borrowed Baby" was likely written after 1900 but drew on Terrell's personal travel experiences in the nineteenth century. Born in Memphis, Tennessee, in 1863, Mary "Mollie" Church grew up in an upper-class Black family, her father's wealth derived from real estate ventures. She attended Oberlin and graduated in 1884 in the same class as Anna Julia Cooper.[41] After teaching at the famed M Street School in Washington, D.C., and touring Europe, she married Robert Terrell, an African American judge, in 1891. Terrell was best known for her "club work." She was the founder and president of the National Association of Colored Women (NACW), formed in 1896. She wrote for prominent Black journals and magazines, including the *Washington Evening Star*, the *Chicago Defender*, and the *New York Age*. Terrell frequently traveled for the NACW, most notably speaking in fluent German to a predominantly white audience in Germany in 1904. Like Cooper and Ida B. Wells, Terrell documents her difficulties with traveling as a Black woman but does so in a much more expanded archive consisting of fiction, autobiography, and personal diaries. Collectively, these writings of her travel experiences reveal the perils of traveling Black and "like a lady." Money is not an issue, but, as it is for Betsy, "getting there's the thing" (2).

In her 1940 autobiography, *A Colored Woman in a White World*, for example, Terrell devotes an entire chapter to describe not one but several traumatic railroad experiences, beginning when she was five years old.[42] Each episode demonstrated how the rules, protocols, and assumptions of nineteenth- and early-twentieth-century American culture seep into the confined space of the train car. In the first incident, her father left her in the first-class car to smoke in the smoking car. When the white conductor spied her by herself, he asked of the other passengers, "Whose nigger is this?" For Terrell, this instance was the first time that "the Race Problem [was] brought directly home to me," a troubling incident that reflected not just racial but also gender inequities.[43] The courtesies most women or girls assumed in the late nineteenth century were not available to Terrell, even as a small child. Importantly, Terrell tried to understand the confrontation in terms of appropriate gender behavior and proper female appearance. She's puzzled because she looks presentable: "my hands were clean and so was my face. I hadn't mussed my hair; it was brushed back and was perfectly smooth." When she recounted the incident to her mother, she noted, "I assured my mother I was 'behaving like a little lady,' as she told me to do . . . but she explained the incident by telling me that sometimes conductors on railroad trains were unkind and treated good little girls very badly."[44] The episode was one filled with instruction. Terrell learned that her race trumps her class, family, and deportment—that is, she learned what kind of treatment she will receive in public spaces when she travels independently and "like a little lady."[45]

The respectability Terrell gains from her comportment or from her family will not necessarily travel with her. Other railroad incidents occurred when, as teenager, a conductor tried to seat Terrell in the Jim Crow section. When she protested, the conductor "assured me with a significant look that he himself would keep me company and remain in there with me."[46] The sexual suggestion of the remark stays with her, particularly during yet another incident, an event that shaped the story of "Betsy's Borrowed Baby." Terrell cryptically describes the experience of being alone in a train car when a white man propositioned and grabbed her:

> As the passengers reached their destination and left, one by one, I realized to my horror and dismay that I was left alone. A white man from the smoker came into the car and began to talk to me. I told him I was sleepy and to leave me alone. He refused to do so and made some ugly remarks. I was terror stricken and started to the door when the train slowed to stop. He seized me and threw me into a seat and then left the car. No pen can describe and no tongue portray the indignities, insults and assaults to which colored women and girls have been subjected in Jim Crow cars.[47]

Although all of these episodes reveal the danger posed to Terrell as she travels alone or is perceived to be alone by others, this last episode is particularly important. It depicts the paradoxical manner in which Terrell discusses her many domestic and international trips. Terrell's recounting dances between confession and muteness—"no pen or tongue" capable of revealing the true cost of being Black, female and alone on public transport. As I argue at the end of this chapter, train travel for Terrell is a repeated, though strangely stifled, concern in her autobiography. There is a disclosure of some harm, even as she expresses an inability to be fully forthcoming.

Compared to Anna Julia Cooper's essay, the detailed depiction of the multiple ways in which second-class travel dispossesses the Black female traveling subject is expanded on in Terrell's short story. Fifteen typewritten pages long, "Betsy's Borrowed Baby" is unusual because significant portions of the story take place within the confines of the train compartment. Terrell details two lengthy episodes of riding on a train as a Black woman. In the first trip, in a second-class segregated car traveling south, Betsy experiences a near-rape and the trip is filled with tense dread. During the second train trip, on a North-bound first-class car, passengers and railroad officials assume she is a nanny, and she is the only person of color in a predominantly white space. Besides the obvious contrast of her surroundings, the two trips— a kind of a reversed migration narrative—highlight the power, race, and gender relations enabled by and fostered within the confined space of the train compartment.[48] The details allow for a comparison between the two journeys and highlight the injustice of segregation and the threat of sexual violence. By providing this sustained experience of traveling with Betsy, the story troubles our understanding of the "romance of the rails" common to discussions of the U.S. railroad; and the reader obtains not a brief description of injustice but an elongated description of fear and terror.

A Close Reading of a Close Encounter

In contrast to the leisure suggested by earlier examples of railroad passenger travel, Terrell's fiction about Black female travel is a quite different presentation of the interval of time and space within the compartment, of traveling in abeyance. Betsy must actively and strategically consider her movements within the train car, regardless of whether she is in first or second class, or traveling in the North or South. Her strategy to subvert riding Jane Crow consists of strategic omission.

When Betsy leaves Ralston College and boards a train in Ohio, she transitions from accomplished college student to uncertain traveling female. Before this trip, one college friend, implied to be African American, has informed Betsy of some unspoken horror, "an ordeal" that occurred when the friend "spent the major portion of the night alone in a Jim Crow Car" (4). Conscious of possible physical or verbal assault, Betsy reveals the studied over-determination needed to circumvent the danger of railroad travel; she has internal debates with herself about the safety of the train car. Traveling in the North in a first-class car presents comparatively few problems for her. "From Ralston to Cincinnati the journey was delightful," Terrell writes, "but when Betsy reached Cincinnati, it was necessary for her to change cars" (3).[49] Although Betsy considers getting into the first-class train compartment in Cincinnati, a major railroad junction, and hoping that the conductor does not remove her, she eventually decides against it. It is less embarrassing for Betsy to place herself voluntarily in the Jim Crow car, otherwise she would have to be escorted out of first class and forced to walk forward, in full view of other passengers, into the second-class car, becoming "the cynosure of all eyes and, perhaps, the butt of ridicule and jests" (3).

Certain elements of Betsy's train ride exhibit the familiar disadvantages of riding Jim Crow and reveal the "spatial inequalities" of segregated trains.[50] There is a division of an already small space in the second-class car, a further constriction of an already enclosed area. As with Cooper's account of the train station's built environment, Terrell provides a near granular description of a Jim Crow car to make palpable the material inequality of the car: "The Jim Crow car is made by dividing an ordinary day coach into two parts by means of a wooden partition. A section consisting of three or four seats on each side of the aisle is set apart for colored passengers and the remaining portion of the coach behind the partition is generally used as a smoker for white men" (3). Terrell reveals the inequitable access to certain spaces on the train. The least attractive space is further divided, and a space set aside for African Americans is shared with white men who smoke. If we recall Ayers's description of men who "behaved very differently" in second class, the lack of propriety and free-wheeling atmosphere make this an uncomfortable space for any respectable woman, but especially for the Black female college student. Riding second class is not only unjust, it is also unhygienic. Terrell emphasizes the dirtiness of the southern Jim Crow compartment. Betsy has to "close her eyes to scratched and marred woodwork, to the faded and worn covering on the seats and to all the other dilapidated, unsightly and inadequate appointments in the coach" (4). In addition to these discomforts, there is a specific type of fear that expands the danger and threat of riding Jim Crow as a Black woman.

Terrell's extended description of Betsy's experience on the Jim Crow car renders the terror of the unknown. During the trip south in the second-class space, two white men approach and sexually harass Betsy. One man "tr[ies] to catch her eye," but she avoids his gaze. When the man alerts his friend that "there's some good-looker in the Jim," the friend comes over to Betsy to "give her the once over myself" (5). The exchange discloses the men's assumptions of Black female sexual accessibility or promiscuity, particularly within a train car. Betsy eventually falls asleep and wakes up in the arms of one of the men. After she resists him again, he "catches her by the arm, twists it brutally, [and] throws her into her seat." There is a lack of concern from the white conductor, as well as, it is implied, from the Black porter who does nothing to help, and who, by winking at the white men, appears to be complicit in the encounter. The incident reveals that there is white male access to all parts of the train, including those sections established for second-class, mostly African American, passengers. Because white male access within the compartment is uncontested, there is no personal space left for Betsy.

What makes this scene different from the other travel scenes in the African American literary canon is the specific depiction of sexual terror for women of color, a feminized, sexualized Jim Crow, a scene frequently hinted at but routinely elided in Black women's archive of travel experiences. If Jim Crow is a term describing a system of laws that regulated the mobility of African Americans in public space in order "to freeze the place of the Negro in society and guarantee his basic immobility," socially, politically, and economically, then the term Jane Crow acknowledges such racial stasis but also recognizes the additional stagnancy caused by the sexual threats accompanying public travel.[51] Amy Richter has described the "gender deference" granted to white women so that they could create a "home on the rails" on late nineteenth- and early twentieth-century U.S. railroad lines.[52] Black women, however, were routinely denied this deference and were ejected out of such first-class spaces as "women-only" train cars. The transitional space between arrival and departure, what Schivelbusch calls an "in-between or travel space, which . . . was possible to 'savor,'" was not, in fact, possible for African American female riders to enjoy.[53] As Terrell shows in the second part of her story, Black women had to "borrow" these courtesies; they were not automatically granted the privileges assumed of white femininity. Betsy finally "gets there"—she reaches her home in Magnolia, Kentucky. Throughout the summer the thought of "the whole dreadful, vexatious problem of returning to college" in the fall scares her until she comes up with a solution—accompanying a white child on a train trip (10).[54]

The unwanted sexual attention Betsy previously attracted as a single, Black college student is replaced with a different kind of attention when she travels with a cute child. Helen, "a little pink-cheeked, blue-eyed, golden haired three-year old," draws admiration from other passengers, especially white women on the train (11). In contrast to Betsy's treatment on her ride to the South, during which the white conductor laughs at her attempt to fight off men as if she were a "Mrs. Jack Johnson," in the first-class car with a young child Betsy receives courtesy—at least secondhand (8).[55] "Everybody was willing to the nth degree both to serve and entertain" little Helen. Moreover, as Terrell observes, Black caregivers in a public space are often objects of solicitous surveillance. The white passengers on the train do not automatically assume a Black person will be an efficient caretaker. "If the nurse happens to be colored, every white man and woman on the train appoints himself or herself a committee of one to see that the child is not neglected and receives the proper care" (12). This vicarious, secondhand concern from white passengers ensures that Betsy is able to get food when Helen is hungry, even in the traditionally segregated dining car. Only if she is a nurse "could a colored girl's presence in a diner be tolerated, no matter what her attainments or her culture might be" (13).

Setting a significant portion of the story on a train enables Terrell to depict the dynamic of Betsy's social interactions in enclosed spaces; these interactions reveal how the first-class train compartment is raced and gendered white, female, and middle or upper class. In the first half of the short story, when Betsy sits in a second-class car, she encounters a motley group of people of different classes and races. She meets, for example, an elderly Black woman named Aunt Parody who questions Betsy about her background, proud to "se[e] a young woman of her race so well-educated and refined" (4). Here, Terrell's description of lower-class Black travelers escapes the judgmental critique of Charles Chesnutt, who presents a similar scene in *The Marrow of Tradition* (1901). Traveling north in first class, however, Betsy interacts primarily with middle-class white women and does not speak to or interact with any white men. The first-class car remains white and female except for the presence of Betsy. In both first and second class, she is approached by white people, but her sexual availability is limited when she appears to be a nanny. The presence of little Helen Dowling is as important as Betsy's neat appearance, for Helen's cute presence helps to contain Betsy's Black body, making it "knowable" and safe in first class. It is important to note, however, that as a Black woman, she cannot escape surveillance and questions from others. Unlike the white men who threatened her while she rode Jim Crow, the white women in first-class appreciate Betsy's remarkable elocution and poise. Her liberal arts education is a hindrance in one car but to her advantage in another: "The correctness of Betsy's English and her evident refinement of manner" draws approval from white women passengers and offers of employment as a nurse (13). The story concludes by Betsy refusing payment from the toddler's grandmother; and in that act, she refuses to solidify the position as nanny and maintains, discreetly, the much higher class status of Black Ralston College student.

"Betsy's Borrowed Baby" illustrates the circumscription of space because one is afraid to travel—not because of lack of freedom or lack of ownership of one's body but because traveling requires a presence in a second-class car where a person is subject to sexual assaults and lewd approaches by others. Black women, in particular, face "wounded feelings and crushed pride solely on account of [their] color" (3). The fact that such post-Reconstruction strategizing is necessary several decades after slavery suggests the limitations created by Jim Crow segregation and its insidiously gendered versions.

Paralepsis

There is one further distinction about Terrell's story that sets it apart from other Black literary episodes of riding Jim Crow. Other such accounts are justifiably strident in calls for racial protest and anger about the injustice of riding second class. In contrast, Betsy takes a *quiet* means of enabling secure passage. The success of her "loan" is transitory and temporary: it is not a permanent change to a railroad's policies and she will be forced to ride second class when she can no longer find a young white child needing to be accompanied on the train. Similarly, the story does not reference larger historical issues of the time. Terrell does not actively engage with the contemporaneous legal cases that challenged Jim Crow segregation, such as *Plessy v. Ferguson* (1896). As a comparison, Charles Chesnutt fictionalized the Supreme Court decision in his novel. When activist Ida B. Wells was violently removed from the Chesapeake, Ohio, and Southwestern Railroad in 1883, she successfully sued the railroad in the Tennessee Circuit Court, but the verdict was overturned in the state supreme court. While Wells is forceful in her attempts at social justice, the fictional Betsy's quiet confidence of putting one over on the railroad officials is a more discreet reproof against segregation. Terrell's short story offers a very "ladylike" challenge to the system of segregation.

This point about the reservedness in "Betsy's Borrowed Baby" raises an unsettling though shared quality that appears in Anna Julia Cooper's and Terrell's travel writings: they both make use of paralepsis, the rhetorical practice of stating a point by claiming not to speak of it, in order to reveal the slights to Black womanhood on the train. I wrote earlier about Terrell's fragile balance between confession and silence when referencing a near-sexual assault when she was a teenager. Cooper makes a similar rhetorical move when, in "Woman vs. The Indian," after discussing the difficulties of Black female travel, she asserts, "I purposely forbear to mention instances of personal violence to colored women travelling in less civilized sections of our country, where women have been forcibly ejected from cars, thrown out of seats, their garments rudely torn, their person wantonly and cruelly injured" (91)—but, of course, she tells us this concisely in her act of forbearance. Terrell makes a comparable claim in an unusual cover letter for "Betsy's Borrowed Baby";

she posed a tense, truculent question to the editor of *Harper's*: "If [the short story] were a master piece of literature and told the story of a colored girl's *plight* on a Jim Crow car, I fear it would not be accepted by Harper's Magazine. It would be against your policy would it not?" (cover letter).[56] This faux confession or reticence does not happen just once but multiple times.

In contrast, Terrell's private writings divulge a more assertive response to discrimination. Her unpublished diary entry for Monday, July 27, 1908, for example, records an encounter on the streetcar when a white man refused to make room for her. The episode ended in violence—from Terrell's own hand:

> I asked him to make room for me, but when he did not do so, I simply sat down. He said something to me and I said, "When I tell you to move, you move." "I won't be sassed by a nigger," he growled. Before I knew it, I hit him in the face, not very hard, to be sure, for I tried to restrain my hand and I had partially succeeded, but I had slapped him just the same. A tall, lank[y] poor white fellow whose clothes almost hung off him rose and said, "Jim [?], you are not going to let a nigger hit you are you?" "You had better try to protect him," I replied.[57]

Unlike Betsy's, Terrell's anger here is much more forthcoming and acknowledged. The episode is remarkable because the very refined Terrell physically defends herself and because Black female anger is not muted but enacted, "not very hard, to be sure," but more forcefully than what is recounted in Cooper's and Terrell's published writings. These rhetorical, paraleptic moves allow the women to reveal the travel violence experienced by Black women while still maintaining the poise required for Black female respectability. What's remarkable is the fact that the women found such verbal efforts necessary.[58]

Other African American women also experienced hardships on the railroad or street car throughout the mid to late nineteenth century and demonstrate the African American woman's long search for national courtesy. Abolitionists Harriet Tubman and Sojourner Truth both encountered difficulties with train and streetcar travel; Tubman had difficulties even while conducting business on behalf of the U.S. government during the Civil War. While she was traveling as a hospital nurse, a conductor and three men "nearly wrenched her arm off" as they tried to eject her from a railroad car. Her arm remained injured throughout the following winter.[59] When Sojourner Truth was finally able to get on a street car, after being skipped several times by street car conductors, Truth continued riding past her stop, one of the rare pleasurable moments of Black female travel in an expansive archive: "Sojourner rode farther than she needed to go; for a ride was so rare a privilege that she determined to make the most of it."[60] The free-born Frances

Ellen Watkins Harper made observations about the railroads in Philadelphia that resembled the comments noted earlier by the formerly enslaved Harriet Jacobs. Harper, while traveling in Pennsylvania, felt "the shadow of slavery" in the north, particularly while traveling by train: "I have been insulted in several railroad cars. . . . Two men came after me in one day."[61] Notably, both Jacobs and Harper fault Pennsylvania as the site of their train car dilemmas, reflecting the history of segregation of travel spaces in the North.[62] In 1898, Susie King Taylor, a nurse during the Civil War, was rudely questioned by police constables while traveling by train to see her ill son in Louisiana.[63] Even the Fisk Jubilee Singers, those early mobile ambassadors of respectable Blackness, were harassed when they attempted to enter the white waiting room of the notorious L&N Railroad line.[64]

The experience of Amanda America Dickson proved that national courtesy was denied to African American women despite their wealth or married status. Dickson, one of the wealthiest African American women of the late nineteenth century, and her husband Nathan Toomer purchased first-class tickets for a Pullman car traveling from Baltimore to Augusta, Georgia, in June, 1893. The railroad had announced that no Pullman cars would go past Columbia, South Carolina, but unfortunately the Toomers were not informed of this before they purchased their tickets. Their Pullman car was unlinked from the rest of the train line, which preceded south without them. Despite their first-class tickets and Nathan's pleas, they were forced to wait in the Pullman for hours, during which time Dickson became ill from the heat and shock. She died two days after their Pullman car finally arrived in Augusta. Nathan Toomer sued the Pullman Company but lost his case.[65] Charles Chesnutt likely had Dickson's demise in mind in early drafts of *The Marrow of Tradition*. His "plot notes" for a "Jim Crow car story" briefly record that "this story will take a man with a sick wife who for some reason is compelled to take a long journey. Put her thro various experiences, until she dies of the exposure."[66] Neither Chesnutt's fictional character nor Nathan Toomer could participate in a "democratic ideal" defined by train travel.[67]

Both Anna Julia Cooper and Mary Church Terrell traveled widely within and outside the country in the late nineteenth and early twentieth centuries, and their treatment on America's railroads reflected the lack of racial and gender advancement in the American nation. In a Black woman's railroad archive, the train compartment is a repository of travel experiences that challenge America's valued progress narrative, a story so often symbolized by the railroad. The nation's mechanical trajectory "forward" has, embedded within it, the retrenchment of African American social progress.

2 A Kiss in the Dark

Sexualizing Black Female Mobility

The conductor had been a conductor for a long time and his
experience as conductor was that when young white men travelled
in company with young colored women it was for illicit purposes
and that white men so travelling with colored women generally
conducted themselves in an improper manner and in a manner
objectionable to other passengers[.]

—*Robinson v. Memphis and Charleston Railroad* (1883)

A newspaper report published in July 1865 illustrated some of the
social changes brought on by the conclusion of the Civil War. On a train
heading toward Louisville, Kentucky, passengers pleasantly passed the time
talking to each other, since "there was no longer any apprehension of guer-
rillas or marauders on the road." Two women sat opposite each other in the
train compartment, as described by the reporter: "On one of the seats in the
ladies' car was a married lady with a little daughter; opposite facing them was
a colored 'lady'—we believe they are all 'ladies' now—with the baby." When
a Yankee soldier sitting near the white woman got familiar with her—he
told her he would kiss her when the train entered the tunnel—the white
woman used her seating arrangement to her advantage. The train entered
the tunnel; and, when it emerged, "white lady looked amazed, colored lady
bashful and blushing, gay Lieutenant befogged." Somehow, the women had
switched places, resulting in the lieutenant hugging and kissing the Black
woman instead of the white woman, provoking laughter among the other
train passengers. The Yankee, one of "Uncle Sam's pets with shoulder-straps,"
was clearly the butt of the joke. Less humorous was the reporter's derisive

observation of the altered circumstances brought on by the end of the rebellion. Now that the war was over, certain signifiers of class were also gone, for even Black women were "all 'ladies' now."[1] The report illustrated the possibility of unpredictable encounters facilitated by railroad travel, along with the well-known "sexual connotation of trains . . . particularly trains entering tunnels."[2]

Repetitions of this scene occurred frequently in U.S. popular culture in the late nineteenth and early twentieth century. An 1881 Currier and Ives lithograph duplicated the scene just described, for example, but with one important difference (fig. 2.1). Whereas the "colored lady" in the news report was assumed to be a domestic but mockingly called a "lady," the Black woman in the lithograph is clearly marked as a servant and her uniformed presence in a first-class train car seemingly undisputed. Here the episode again plays on the concept of mistaken identities and chance encounters prevalent in railroad lore. The print's left panel depicts passengers on a train and a "mischievous conductor" who informs the passengers that the train will enter a "dark tunnel, through in half an hour." In fact, the train is in the tunnel briefly, and the right panel reveals what happens when the passengers assume their actions will not be witnessed by others: a man previously reading a book now drinks from a flask; and another man, earlier smiling at a white female passenger, attempts "a kiss in the dark"—not with the white woman

Mischievous Conductor. "Dark Tunnel, through in half an hour"!   Scene.- When the Train struck the light in just 3 minutes.
A KISS IN THE DARK.

Figure 2.1: Currier & Ives, "A Kiss in the Dark" (1881). Library of Congress, www.loc.gov/item/2002707713/.

but with an African American nanny. Again, the two women have switched places. The lithograph is clearly a humorous scene—figures in the print are shown smiling and cheering. This culturally familiar gag suggests how a Black woman on a train, even in a first-class compartment, becomes fair game for a sexual affront.[3]

A 1903 silent film further reproduces the scene for dramatic effect in a more improved form of visual technology.[4] In Edwin S. Porter's "What Happened in the Tunnel," released by Thomas Edison's film company, the static images of the lithograph are brought to life. The sixty-second film repeats the Currier and Ives lithograph, depicting a white man, a white woman, a Black woman, and, briefly, a black screen to suggest the darkness in the tunnel. When the passengers emerge, the white man is caught kissing the Black maid. Again, the scene is undeniably comic. While the man is embarrassed, the two women roar with laughter at the practical joke (figs. 2.2a, b).

Figure 2.2a: Before "What Happened in the Tunnel" (Porter).

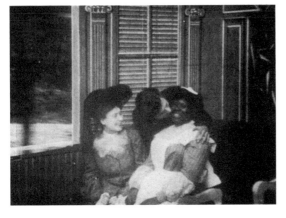

Figure 2.2b: And after "What Happened in the Tunnel" (Porter).

Similar readings of Black femininity are depicted in the news report, litho-graph, and film. Although the man in each scene is laughed at, the "joke" ultimately relies on the presence of the African American woman in the unique space of the railroad compartment. The Black woman in uniform in each example is not considered attractive enough to kiss, even as she is made sexually available in each scene. The Black woman is, as one scholar notes of the film, "invested with the sexuality denied by the white woman."[5] The visual scenes depict with clarity the assumptions of accessible Black female sexuality. The viewer may laugh at the white man, but the joke is always at the expense of the Black woman, who, it is assumed, cannot be as publicly degraded by a kiss in the dark as a white "lady" can. The comedy "works," in other words, because the Black woman cannot be considered a lady—in all senses of the word—despite her presence in the first-class travel space some would call the "ladies' car."

These cross-race, race-switching visual comedies illustrate the conflu-ence of intimate public space, Black femininity, and first-class railroad travel. The episodes, and their various repetitions in U.S. culture throughout the late nineteenth and early twentieth-century, dramatize an issue that would trouble Americans during that period: the presence of African Americans, especially middle-class African American women, on first-class modes of public transportation, and their presence in a specific *type* of train compart-ment suffused with class and racial considerations. The first-class railroad car was distinguished from the other cars by location (at the end of the train, away from the noxious, dirty engine) and the comfort of upholstered seating. During the mid to late nineteenth century, as more women began to travel long distances by rail, middle- and upper-class white women were granted the privilege of riding in first-class "ladies' cars"—clean, nicely upholstered train compartments designed specifically for the comfort of female passen-gers who traveled the rails alone or were accompanied by a male relative or male companion. Smoking—customary only among men, especially in pub-lic—was not allowed in these compartments. "Ladies' spaces" were framed as signs of deference to women, to protect them from the harsher elements of train travel and from the attentions of men, but when African American or mixed-race women attempted to enter these spaces, their presence was forcibly contested. Legal historian Barbara Welke notes that, between 1855 and 1914, a majority of the lawsuits challenging racial segregation on public transportation were initiated by nonwhite women: thirty-one of forty-seven cases "involved injury to a woman of color."[6] The lawsuits took place through-out the country, in the Deep South, such as Mississippi, as well as places such as Washington, D.C., New York, and Ohio. These legal proceedings raise a number of historical and legal questions: What accounts for the larger number of anti-segregation lawsuits among women of color? How do we understand the success of such lawsuits, some of which were litigated decades before Homer Plessy's landmark railroad case, the 1896 U.S. Supreme Court decision that enshrined "separate but equal" travel spaces? What do these lawsuits reveal about Black female travel and the larger cultural assumptions of Black mobile femininity? And what can these lawsuits, and contemporaneous news reports about them, tell us about the perils of traveling Black and "like a lady" in mid- to late nineteenth-century America?

All three cross-race "comedies" capture the American anxiety regarding the presence of Black women in first-class spaces of public travel. By public travel, I mean the public spaces of transportation shared by a wide group of strangers—the transportation available on carriages, steamboats, and trains as transportation technologies in the nineteenth century improved and spread. In the context of mid- to late nineteenth-century America, public travel refers to those forms of transportation known as "common carriers," such as the train, that reveal the paradox of mass transportation: such public spaces enabled intimate private encounters. Because "ladies' spaces" were prevalent and widely accepted, middle-class Black women could exploit this form of segregation to their advantage prior to the Supreme Court's codification of racial segregation in 1896. Before *Plessy v. Ferguson*, Black women sometimes succeeded in subverting *racial* discrimination by using the legitimacy of *gender* segregation. By reading two legal proceedings that debate the presence of Black women in first-class railroad cars, we can begin to understand the period's "constrained construction of the definition 'ladies,'" as noted by one judge, as well as the *effect* of the nineteenth-century railroad on perceptions of gender, class, race, and citizenship during post-Reconstruction America.[7]

Just as the report, lithograph, and film sexualize the Black women within the train compartment space, the sexualization of Black women occurred in two lawsuits against railroad companies in the early 1880s.[8] Two Black female plaintiffs, Jane Brown and Sallie Robinson, sued railroad companies after they were forced to leave first-class train cars—when they were ejected from "ladies' spaces." Taking place after the political and social experiment of Reconstruction, the two lawsuits inform us about the experiences of nineteenth-century African American female travel, the gendered and racialized space of the first-class train car, and the stakes of keeping that space free of Black middle-class women. The cases highlight the contradictory assumptions of mobility for Black women and white men and, in the case of Jane Brown, the reputations of African American women who traveled on the railroad or frequented the train depot. They also illustrate one of the more troubling aspects of Black female train travel: the sexualization of Black female mobility and the suggestion of illicit interracial intimacy hinted at in the episodes with which this chapter begins. In both lawsuits, train conductors contested the women's presence in first-class cars because the women were assumed to be prostitutes. It was not just their race that contributed to these assumptions, I argue, but their race, gender, and *mobility* that lent weight to the perception.

The women's forced ejections, the newspaper reports about them, and the legal documents derived from the trials reveal what I argue throughout this book: that the railroad and related spaces were crucial sites where the performance of race, gender, class, and citizenship were disputed and enacted. Although Jane Brown won her lawsuit, Brown's success could not be duplicated by Sallie Robinson, even though the two women sued the same railroad company, the Memphis and Charleston Railroad. Indeed, Robinson's lawsuit, one of the five cases that made up what came to be known as the *Civil Rights Cases of 1883*, prefigured African Americans' reduced ability to rely on the court for redress from discrimination, later sedimented with *Plessy v. Ferguson*. Read together, Brown's and Robinson's cases reveal how Black female legal success was followed by legal retrenchment, not only for African American women but for larger African American communities as well. Mobility, the very act facilitated by the train, was sexualized, and, in some cases, criminalized, when practiced or performed by African American women.

"A Strained Construction"

The three examples above do not depict, precisely, "ladies' cars." In each incident, a white man travels alone. If the cars were "ladies' spaces," the single men would not have been able to enter and the Black women would have been safe from "kisses in the dark." The terms "ladies' car" and "first-class car" became synonymous in railroad lexicon and, unlike the common assumptions about Black and white femininity, interchangeable in the nineteenth century. In the lawsuits I examine, the first-class compartments—the place from which the Black women were ejected—are often referred to in the legal documents as ladies' cars, even when white men are present. This fact reveals just how slippery and loose the term "ladies' space" was, referring to any public area that was considered first-class, did not allow smoking, and restricted the access of single men traveling alone. There was a certain ambiguity, a frequent indeterminacy, in defining a compartment as first-class or a ladies' car. While all ladies' cars were first-class, not all first-class cars were women-only cars.

The amorous attentions of the white men in the images demonstrate why ladies' cars were necessary: to protect the traveling female public from the unwanted attention of male passengers and from the usually harsh conditions found in second-class cars. Ladies' cars appeared as early in the United States as the late 1830s. Railroad historian August Mencken notes that the Philadelphia, Wilmington, and Baltimore Railroad first advertised special cars for women and children in August 1838, only eight years after the Baltimore and Ohio Railroad first transported passengers.[9] By the 1860s, ladies' cars were common on the railroads, to the point that male passengers traveling by themselves bemoaned the amenities unavailable to them. Writing about the western route on the New York and Erie Railroad, one male correspondent for *Scientific American* in 1860 pointed out that "unmarried men have lungs as well as those blessed with 'better halves'" and encouraged railroad managers to offer "dust-excluding and ventilating arrangements" to a male public willing to pay for those comforts.[10] White men also sued to ride in ladies' cars but were usually unsuccessful when not accompanied by women. The *New York Times*, for example, humorously reported on a Mr. Pike, who throughout the 1870s sued unsuccessfully when he was forced to leave the ladies' car on the Hudson River Railroad.[11] Writing after the success of the Pullman Palace Car Company's sleeping cars, which enabled train passengers to sleep comfortably on the railroad, a female train passenger in 1876 advocated for "separate sleeping cars for women travelers," having just completed a trip on one to awake finding a group of men "gazing smilingly upon [her] sleeping beauty." The female passenger claimed such a car was a way to further improve the American nation. To offer train travelers female-only sleeping cars would "be a great advancement in wayfaring civilization."[12]

Ladies' cars were just one of the many forms of consideration railroad companies granted to middle-class women as they traveled the rails, and companies transformed previously uncomfortable train compartments to accommodate white women travelers. According to historian Amy Richter, women's expectations for "gender deference" encouraged the railroads to include more luxury items, such as better-equipped bathrooms and better amenities in the car.[13] These changes sparked by the female presence enabled railroads to create what Richter calls a "home on the rails," or a public domesticity, "a social ideal that was neither as private as a home, nor as socially unruly as a public street."[14] Such benefits helped to make women feel that they were not as "out of place," less incongruous, in the world of the railroad, traditionally perceived as a highly masculine space. Like the American girls described by Anna Julia Cooper in "Woman vs. The Indian," middle- and upper-class white women found these upgrades convenient and efficient.[15]

Despite these forms of deference, women and trains were still the subject of some jokes in popular culture. Tracking the gradual acceptance of white women on the rails by noting the prevalence of jokes about women and trains, Richter notes that mid-century witticisms, such as "visual puns playing on the trains of ladies' dresses and trains of railway cars," emphasized the incongruity of pairing delicate femininity with masculine machine: "Women, such jokes implied, were out of place among the powerful machines that propelled so much of America's industrial and commercial life."[16] But if we recall the gags of "A Kiss in the Dark" and "What Happened in the Tunnel," although white middle-class women were "out of place" in the public sphere of a train car at mid-century, by the 1880s they belonged in the designated first-class space more than other women, particularly those with dark skin. Indeed, as I argue, the attempt to create an "etiquette" of public travel for white women contributed to the many rationalizations railroad officials presented to explain the removal of Black women from first-class spaces. The very deference railroads wanted to give to white, middle-class women so that these women could create a "home on the rails" was dependent on maintaining a segregated environment that tolerated Black women and working-class women of all races—but only as servants. Black women were not only considered out of place but actively *displaced* unless they were in the first-class car to perform a service role.

Trains were objects of special concern when Americans desired segregation, both in the North and the South. The phrase "home on the rails" highlights why the train received special consideration: having Blacks so close to "home," in a confined space that was both public and private, offered great potential for intimate contact. Additionally, as Evelyn Brooks Higginbotham notes, "Ladies were not merely women, they represented a class, a differentiated status within the generic category of 'women.'"[17] If Black women could, literally and metaphorically, occupy a (white) lady's space, they would then disrupt well-entrenched assumptions of racial hierarchies. If ladies' cars were for those women who had the means to travel first class, and Black women as well as white had those means, what distinguished white ladies from Black, particularly if Black women were not in uniform? To put the question more bluntly, could a Black woman occupy the space—and claim the title—of a "lady"?

Black women who sued to ride in ladies' cars offered a unique challenge to gendered and racialized ideas of travel. Barbara Welke observes that Black women "who could afford first-class fare would seek the privileges of their gender" and they "challenged courts to justify a system that would require a woman of color paying first-class fare to accept accommodations no similarly situated white woman would be required to accept."[18] If as Edward Ayers notes, "segregation became, to whites, a badge of sophisticated, modern, managed race relations," Black women used the courts to disrupt that "polite" management.[19] By reading the lawsuits and contemporaneous newspaper accounts of Jane Brown's and Sallie Robinson's ejections, we learn the legal and social efforts of Black women to shape the perception of their class and gender identities and how concepts regarding mobility and train travel impacted those perceptions. These women actively fought, at times quite literally, to be included in the category of "lady" and to enjoy all of the privileges granted to that group.

"A Kept Woman": Sexualizing Black Female Mobility

Jane Brown, a twenty-seven-year-old woman described in court records as "mulatto," lived in Corinth, Mississippi, located in the northeast corner of the state. On January 22, 1879, Brown purchased a first-class ticket and boarded a first-class Memphis and Charleston Railroad car to travel north to Memphis, a trip she made frequently. A white conductor, James Hall, forced her off and she sued. Brown claimed that the conductor used unnecessary force, including choking her, in order to remove her from the train. In court she displayed a dislocated thumb and abrasions on the back of her neck, the conductor having "use[d] force enough to lift her from the seat around which she had clasped her feet."[20] The railroad's lawyers claimed Brown was "a notorious courtesan, who was addicted to lascivious and profane conversation and immodest deportment in public places."[21] The railroad argued that although Jane Brown acted "decently" at the time she first entered the car, her local reputation in Corinth was such that the conductor felt compelled to remove her from the other passengers sitting in the ladies' car or first-class compartment. As its defense, the railroad company argued that the conductor removed Jane Brown not because she was colored, but because she had a base reputation and bad character, and "nothing could be more repulsive to ladies, and their fathers, husbands and brothers, than to know that whores may be seated beside them in railroad cars."[22] The railroad claimed that Brown's reputation justified her expulsion from the first-class car and that the conductor forcibly ejected her only as a response to Brown's adamant refusal to leave; Hall's force was not unnecessary and only strong enough to overcome Brown's own resistance.

I am interested in the company's persistence in arguing this defense—the company lost the original trial as well as two subsequent appeals—and the methods by which the company tried to prove Brown's allegedly "repulsive" presence.[23] Having solicited for the original trial the conductor and the most recognizable figure who happened to be in the first-class car on that day, Mississippi governor John Marshall Stone, the railroad appealed, claiming it had located additional witnesses, not only to the altercation but also to Brown's behavior in Corinth and her reputation for virtue. Dozens of Corinth residents, even those called by Brown, testified to Brown's alleged lack of chastity and her sexual relationships with men. The railroad's defense depended on community knowledge—or gossip—of Corinth residents who assumed facts about Brown's chastity, not only because of her color but also, in ways more decisive, because of her itinerant presence in the town. The railroad company's approach to proving Jane Brown's unsavory reputation depended on the testimony of community residents who formed links between Jane Brown's mobility—on the streets of Corinth, particularly on and near the railroad—and her sexual immorality. Jane Brown's movements were sexualized because of her very visible mobility, particularly near the train depot.

Throughout Reconstruction and the post-Reconstruction South, African Americans found their activities regulated in public space. After the Civil War, the Black Codes of Mississippi monitored African Americans' public actions. To obtain the labor to work Mississippi's war-torn crops, the codes defined "idle freedmen" and punished "all freedmen, free negroes and mulattoes in this State, over the age of eighteen years . . . with no lawful employment or business, or found unlawfully assembling themselves with freedmen, free negroes or mulatoes."[24] It unfairly identified both nonworking African Americans as well as African Americans working for themselves as "vagrants." Although the Black Codes were removed by 1870, concern still existed about Blacks' public activities. Historically, women of any race or ethnicity have been criticized for having a highly visible presence in public space. In her "social history of walking," Rebecca Solnit points out the unsettling way in which "women's sexuality [has been] a public rather than a private matter. It equates visibility with sexual accessibility."[25] There has been and still is a consistent concern about Black women in public space. Michele Mitchell analyzed conduct manuals published in the late nineteenth and early twentieth centuries and written for an African American audience. Such books as *Golden Thoughts on Chastity and Procreation* (1914) and *Don't: A Book for Girls* (1891) tutored African American women to protect their chastity, maintain a decorous appearance, and instruct their "movement through public space."[26] Scholars of African American women's history such as Kali Gross and Cheryl D. Hicks have examined how Black women, particularly in the urban North, had their sexuality criminalized, since "evidence of sexual expression and behavior outside of marriage and outside the parameters of prostitution eventually constituted criminal activity."[27] Hazel Carby further identifies Black and white organizations at the beginning of the twentieth century and well into the 1920s that were concerned about African American women who migrated North.[28] Although we can distinguish between the disciplining of Black women from within the community, as analyzed by Michelle Mitchell, from the disciplining of Black women that occurs in a broader white society as described by Hicks, all of these works contend in some way with the assumed hypersexuality of African American women, particularly Black women who traveled.[29] This context of the unseemliness of Black female mobility, particularly for an unmarried Black woman, helps explain how and why Jane Brown's movements throughout Corinth could have led her to be perceived as a prostitute. Jane Brown's frequent walks through the town, repeatedly remarked on by witnesses in the trial, challenged ideas of "becoming conduct," and her character was conflated with her visibility and mobility. It was not just riding on a train without a chaperone that was transgressive but the larger action of mobility itself.

Walking the Streets of Corinth

The town of Corinth, originally called Cross City, has a storied Civil War history. As the convergent site of two railroads—the Memphis and Charleston (M&C) and the Mobile and Ohio (M&O)—Corinth was a pivotal location for both Union and confederate troops during the Civil War. The town's depot lay at the intersection of the two railroad lines in the northwestern part of Corinth.[30] Additionally, the Memphis and Charleston Railroad was, according to one postwar business magazine, "one of the most important lines of transit in the States south of the Ohio River."[31] In the 1880 U.S. census, Corinth had a population of 2,275, less than half the population of the Mississippi state capital, Jackson.[32]

Jane Brown and her family's livelihood depended on the railroad. Dorcas Brown, Jane's sixty-year-old mother, operated a lunch house in Corinth, at the corner of Cruise and Jackson Streets, within a short walking distance of the passenger stations for the M&C and M&O. Jane's eldest sister, the thirty-two-year-old Lizzie Brown, operated a boardinghouse for African Americans in the same location, and Jane herself, as one witness stated, "peddled lunches at the train station."[33] Other family members who lived in the Brown household included Jane's elder sister Julia, frequently mistaken for Jane, and Julia's two children.[34]

Jane Brown's movements about the town of Corinth, particularly near the depot, her travels inside and outside of the state of Mississippi, and her associations with women in other states collectively condemned her, in the railroad's lawyers' view, of being a prostitute. Her "reputation for virtue" was on trial just as much as, if not more than, the actions of the railroad, and a large number of residents were called to testify about her character, testimonies that may have been shaped in part by Jane Brown's very visible presence throughout Corinth. Witnesses testified to having seen Brown frequently on the city's streets. The railroad employee who sold the first-class ticket to Brown noted that he had known her for a least a year and "saw her frequently almost everyday when she was in town." J. R. Brady, the Corinth town marshal, stated that he had known Brown for ten years and had seen her almost daily: "I never saw her guilty of any indecent act in any public place and I have frequently seen her at the trains when I went there."[35] Other witnesses cited Jane Brown's visibility specifically on or near the train depot or railroad, noting her work selling food at the train station. B. F. Williams claimed that "I have seen her frequently at the train laughing and talking with men. She was a huckster selling lunches at the train."[36] Even Governor Stone's testimony suggested a surprising familiarity with Brown, or at least some general knowledge of who she was. A resident of Corinth for at least five years preceding the incident, he was acquainted with Jane Brown from "having seen her frequently about the trains at Corinth." He acknowledged knowing Jane Brown, at least by sight, remarking "I never saw her guilty of lascivious conduct in the streets or in public places. She was fond of talking and that was all."[37]

The rumors about Jane Brown's personal relationships traveled as extensively as Brown herself did within the town. Two phrases to describe unchaste women were extrapolated from the lawyers' questions and were repeatedly used by trial witnesses to define Brown's character: a kept woman and a public whore. Although witnesses testified that Brown conducted herself properly in public, they continually qualified Jane Brown's virtue using these terms. B. F. Williams, for example, noted that "it was generally said that certain parties could have intercourse with her. But she was not what is termed a common prostitute."[38] Jane Brown's own doctor, after testifying to the bruises she received from the altercation, claimed that Brown was "a kept woman, not a common prostitute. She has not the reputation of being a common prostitute in the community."[39] When asked about her virtue, J. R. Brady, the man who claimed to have known Brown for ten years, stated the comparison more baldly: "She is not regarded as a public whore but a kept woman." The statement of J. L. Wofford, a past superintendent of local schools, was telling in what it was supposed to *not* say. Partially crossed out—but still fully legible in the trial transcript—his testimony read, "She has not the character of being legally virtuous. The general impression is that a man keeps her and that she is as true . . . as any married woman is to her husband."[40]

Implicit in the witnesses' statements is a clear distinction between public and private, a distinction made noticeable when witnesses continually described Jane Brown as "not a prostitute but a kept woman." Under the railroad's lawyers' questioning, the residents formed moral distinctions between public dalliances and private liaisons. So long as a woman had one relationship with one man that was kept discreet, the woman was likely to face less public condemnation.[41] Also implied in the phrase was the *race* of the man who allegedly "kept" her. Would the town have made it their business to know if Brown was kept by an African American man? Given the ways in which mobile and self-sufficient African American women have been perceived by whites in the past, one cannot discount the fact that the salacious public knowledge assumed of Jane Brown's private relationships, that she may have been "just another mulatta concubine," may have been influenced by her literal and figurative independence.[42] Solnit concisely states the relationship between a woman in public space and the assumptions made of her sexuality: "Women's presence in public becomes with startling frequency an invasion of their private parts."[43] Using the language of the court, residents cast Jane Brown as a private whore and built up the railroad's defense.

Brown v. Memphis and Charleston Railroad highlights the extent to which public travel could influence a person's reputation: Both men and women could obtain a questionable character by frequently traveling on the railroad; and working on or for a railroad appeared to invite speculation about one's sexual relationships, regardless of the marital status of the parties. It was notable, for example, that just as the railroad questioned Brown's chastity, Brown's lawyers interrogated the behavior of the conductor, for the man "had been seen talking familiarly in the 'ladies' car' with white women known in the town where the plaintiff lived, and all along the road, as belonging to the denounced class."[44] Brown's lawyers brought in Thursday McKinney, a white woman who admitted that Conductor Hall would often sit and talk with her on the train—even while she was sitting in the first-class car; and they brought in additional witnesses who testified to McKinney's status as "not a virtuous woman." Further, the railroad's lawyers explained a lack of witnesses in the original trial because "such testimony must [in] general come from young men or men who frequent houses of ill fame and keep the [same] of such lewd characters."[45] Most of these male witnesses had some association with the railroad.

Perhaps the best example of how Brown's notoriety and rumors contributed to assumptions of her chastity occurred in the *St. Louis Globe Democrat*:

> The plaintiff, it seems, is well-known as a vendor of lunches, confectionery, etc. at Corinth, and is well known also as being a woman who has fallen very far below the standard of purity and virtue that the friends of Caesar's wife claimed for her. It is admitted, however, that she is good-looking and has been received into the best families as a servant. The Governor of the state, judges, lawyers and merchants, in and about Corinth, testified in open Court that her reputation for chastity was not first-class but that her conduct in public was unexceptional, and particularly so when ejected from the car.[46]

Punning on Brown's lack of a "first-class reputation" and being ejected out of a first-class space, the newspaper offered readers salacious interpretations about Brown's background, while rendering its own judgment about Brown's virtue. The paper also suggested how the trial became a communal affair. Resident after resident of the town of Corinth, Mississippi, testified about Jane Brown's visibility and character. Store owners, town leaders, peddlers, a doctor, a telegraph operator, women, and men created Corinth in microcosm. In the process, they implied what a single African American woman frequently seen walking by herself on and near the train signified to other residents. Sexuality and criminality were attached to Brown's movements within the town and outside the state. Mobile independence signified lax morality.

Jane Brown's case depended on proving "respectability," a problem common to most women of color in court. Her lawyers presented evidence of her work for prominent white women of Corinth, proving that she served "all manner of social gatherings among the most refined and elegant women of Corinth."[47] Brown also had the testimony of an eyewitness who supported her claim of proper deportment during the time she was on the train, Governor Stone, who was also a former station agent for the railroad.[48] But his testimony was not all in Brown's favor. Called by the defense, the governor claimed Hall did not use force to remove Brown, nor did Hall choke Brown. According to the governor, when Jane Brown entered the car, "she took a seat facing [him]," even though the car had several empty seats and "was not at all crowded." Aware of some issue between Hall and Brown, he was particularly attentive when he saw Hall approach Jane Brown, since "I expected to see some trouble and was careful in noting what occurred, having heard before that on a previous occasion she had been refused admittance to the ladies' car." The governor stated that Hall ordered Brown out of the compartment, using language the governor himself did not want to repeat in the courtroom. One cannot help but wonder if the presence of this political figure contributed to the violence wielded by Conductor Hall. Did the conductor respond violently because of the sight of Jane Brown talking familiarly with the governor? In this moment of situational riding, did Jane Brown violate the assumed protocols of space and race for African American women, particularly when in the presence of a significant political figure?

A trial with a jury, "composed entirely of white men of the very highest character and intelligence," took place in the fall of 1880.[49] Both the lower and appeals courts ultimately ruled in Jane Brown's favor, finding that the conductor performed a "wrongful exclusion."[50] The lower court awarded Brown $3,000 in damages, stating that if a person is of a reasonable deportment and pays for a first-class ticket, she should be allowed to ride in the first-class car. Although legal scholars have argued that a form of "judicial paternalism," or "the efforts of white male judges to protect middle-class Black women from the indelicacies of male riders of both races," contributed to the decisions when Black female litigants won their cases, it is also notable that the judge in this case was annoyed with the railroad and its determined defense.[51] With a sharp wit, Judge Hammond castigated the railroad and the railroad's lawyers for their relentless attempt to avoid paying punitive damages to Jane Brown. His ruling for the second appeal, for example, noted the railroad's meticulous efforts to place "the case again before me," "aided by lengthy oral arguments, and an elaborate printed brief for defendant of unusual earnestness and exhaustive research."[52] Moreover, as Joan R. Tarpley notes, "It was not the Black woman plaintiff's rights for a neutral charge to the jury that concerned the trial judge. His concern was the possibility that 'all' women, including white women, would be affected by the jury charge."[53] That is, any future female passenger would be susceptible to a conductor's estimation of her reputation and virtue. The judge refuted the idea that "the common carrier . . . shall become a censor of individual morals by assuming to classify his passengers according to his own idea, more or less fastidious, of their character or conduct, as established by their private lives."[54] According to Judge Hammond, one woman cannot have exclusion from other women "whose private lives, perhaps, are not what they should be." There is some tacit acknowledgment here that Brown's personal life was not as virtuous as expected of a single woman of the late nineteenth century, but that that should not exclude her from the ladies' car, if she is willing and able to pay a first-class fare. Establishing a more rigid line between public deportment and private affairs, Judge Hammond ruled "the mere presence of persons of immoral character in a public car, where the immorality is of the kind alleged in this case, and is confined to the private life of the individual, and does not affect her habits and conduct in public places, is no more a sufficient ground for exclusion than their presence in the streets, horse cars, omnibuses, or other such vehicles would be."[55]

Perhaps the most perceptive element to the judge's decision was the acknowledgment of just how much lexical imprecision influenced the case. The legal rulings from the first trial and the railroad company's two appeals demonstrate the extent to which "ladyhood" and "ladies' spaces" were artificial and subjective constructions, a fact pointed out dryly by the judge when he noted that the railroad's defense was "based upon a strained construction of the word 'ladies,' as applied to 'ladies' car,' used in the parlance of railroad people."[56] The subjective constructions were, in particular, dependent on the judgments of one individual, the conductor, revealing the power the conductor had in affecting the Black female train passenger's experience. Whether a company's segregation policies were unspoken or written down or dependent on the passenger's reputation, the act of categorizing passengers forced conductors to be detectives or phrenologists by "reading" the class, race, and character of a passenger.[57] According to the judge, the proper way to perceive the "ladies' car" was not as a space only for women and the men who accompany them but for anyone who travels and "whose habits and behavior are modest, genteel, and irreproachable." The judge offered a more expansive definition of who could occupy a first-class car that was not properly called a "ladies' car."

Despite the coverage of the lawsuit in the press, questions about the lawsuit and the parties involved remain. Who, for example, was the man alleged to have "kept" Brown?[58] Also absent in the archive: Jane Brown's activities and location after the legal win seem to have disappeared from the historical record. Where and how did Jane Brown walk out of Corinth for good, leaving behind one or more of her sisters?

Brown v. Memphis and Charleston Railroad demonstrated the lengths to which a railroad would exploit the deeply racialized and gendered space of the first-class train compartment in order to keep an African American woman out of the ladies' car. Unfortunately, the ruling in Brown's favor would not establish a legal precedent for other women of color. Two incidents reflect just how much Brown's legal success did not provide an example for others. In 1904, Jane's sister Lizzie experienced a remarkably similar form of ejection on the M&O, by then renamed the Southern Railway.[59] Lizzie "resisted like a wild cat" but was still brought off the train. Unlike her sister, Lizzie did not sue.

Jane Brown's successful win also did not affect a lawsuit an African American woman filed against the same railroad. Unlike *Brown v. Memphis and Charleston Railroad*, *Robinson v. Memphis and Charleston Railroad* depended on the Civil Rights Act of 1875 that, in part, prohibited discrimination in public accommodations. Heralded by Radical Republican Massachusetts senator Charles Sumner, the bill was passed in 1875 after Sumner's death the year before. As Reconstruction formally ended, the Civil Rights Act was targeted in attempts to limit African American rights obtained during the period. One of the more significant rollbacks occurred with Robinson's lawsuit, part of the *Civil Rights Cases of 1883*. Four other lawsuits constituted the *Civil Rights Cases*. *United States v. Ryan*, from California, and *United States v. Singleton*, from New York, both involved African Americans being refused admittance into theaters. *United States v. Nichols* involved discrimination in a hotel in Missouri, while *United States v. Stanley* involved a restaurant in Kansas.[60] Given its inclusion as one of the five cases that made up the *Civil Rights Cases of 1883*, *Robinson v. Memphis and Charleston Railroad* has received significant discussion by a generation of legal scholars.[61] My interest in the case involves the assumption of the conductor that compelled him to remove Robinson from the first-class car: African American women, when riding on a train and in the presence of white men, signified improper sexual activity.

Four months after the altercation between Conductor Hall and Jane Brown on the Memphis and Charleston Railroad, Sallie Robinson and her adult nephew Joseph purchased first-class tickets to travel from Tennessee to Virginia on May 22, 1879. They sat in the first-class car, but when the conductor approached them to get their tickets, he made aunt and nephew switch to the second-class car. The reason for their exclusion was their appearances: Sallie Robinson, formerly enslaved and a married woman, was described by the conductor as a good-looking mulatto woman, and her nephew Joseph C. Robinson was light-skinned and appeared white. The conductor assumed that Joseph was a white man traveling with an African American prostitute. As the conductor, C. W. Reagin, stated during the trial, based on his experience as a conductor, when "young white men traveled in company with young colored women it was for illicit purposes."[62] The conductor's statement suggests that it was not just Robinson's color but the larger concept of Black female mobility, particularly on a train and when in the presence of white men, that was the basis for exclusion. During the trial, Robinson's lawyer questioned the assumptions of the conductor, particularly when he referred to Robinson, an adult woman, as a "girl." The conductor stated, as an explanation, that it was "not a term of opprobrium . . . it is customary in this country to call young colored women girls and I did it from force of habit." Conductor Reagin continued, "I do not think every colored woman wanting in virtue, and I want you to know that."[63] If one believes the conductor's statement, he did not consider all African American women to be possible prostitutes but primarily those African American women in a particular situation: those traveling with white men. The conductor was guilty of misreading Joseph Robinson's race as well as Sallie Robinson's character. The conductor's assumptions of Black female mobility recall the "punch lines" of the visual images that started this chapter and the suggestion of illicit interracial intimacy between white men traveling with or near Black women. It is not the presence of white men generally that is problematic for Black traveling women but the presence of a "single" white man, that is, those who are not accompanying a white woman.

The U.S. Supreme Court ruled 8:1 against the four defendants and the one plaintiff in the *Civil Rights Cases*. The Supreme Court's majority ruling depended on the interpretation of the equal protection clause of the Fourteenth Amendment. Justice Joseph Bradley stated in his majority opinion, "It is State action of a particular character that is prohibited. Individual invasion of individual rights is not the subject matter of the amendment."[64] The court reasoned that Congress cannot act in cases in which the state was not responsible for the alleged act of discrimination. The Civil Rights Act of 1875 passed by Congress prohibited states from discrimination against citizens of those states, requiring that the state, not Congress, legislate and punish discrimination taking place between citizens of the state. The decision was interpreted as a refusal of the nation to protect African Americans from discrimination by private individuals or businesses. The ruling further emphasized state citizenship rather than national citizenship, at a time when southern states were increasingly limiting the rights of African Americans. Thus while Jane Brown successfully prosecuted her exclusion against the Memphis and Charleston Railroad, Sallie Robinson's legal loss further solidified the ill-treatment of not just African American women but African Americans in general in public accommodations—it would take nearly six decades, until *Brown v. Board of Education of Topeka, Kansas* (1954) to begin to eradicate it. The *Civil Rights Cases of 1883* effectively gutted the Civil Rights Act of 1875.

The majority decision of the *Civil Rights Cases* reflected the general attitude about African Americans and the Reconstruction amendments by the early 1880s. In an analysis of the decision along with other "great cases" in U.S. Supreme Court history, the *Civil Rights Cases* were deemed "a great case but not a hard case for the Court at the time. The public had lost enthusiasm for the civil rights agenda of the Reconstruction Congress, which probably never had widespread public support to begin with."[65] In addition to the turn against the larger objectives of Reconstruction, another common belief was the assumption of the promiscuity of African American women, so much so that, as noted earlier, the conductor could assert his claim about mobile Black femininity in court.

There are, unfortunately, other examples of African American women who did not win their lawsuits. Such defeats could be attributed to a variety of reasons, and plain racism cannot be discounted. One of the most well-known women to sue for racial discrimination on a train was Black female activist Ida B. Wells, who twice sued a railroad line for discrimination in Tennessee. In 1883 Wells attempted to ride in a first-class car on the Chesapeake, Ohio and Southwestern Railroad. On that day Wells, according to her biographer Paula Giddings, was "dressed for the first-class car . . . [she] carried a parasol—a 'lady's accessory that complemented the customary hat, gloves, and full-length dress corseted and cinched tightly at the waist."[66] Wells won her case in the local courts, but the state supreme court overturned the verdict, a decision celebrated in a local newspaper with the headline that called Wells a "darky damsel."[67] For Wells, the negative legal decision signified a larger belief about African Americans and their status in the United States: "I feel . . . utterly discouraged, and just now, if it were possible, would gather my race in my arms and fly away with them. O God, is there no redress, no peace, no justice in this land for us?"[68] A solution was available to Wells, if only through metaphor, by moving to some alternative space outside of the United States where African Americans might have full rights under the law. Wells retrospectively realized the significance of her second lawsuit, as it was one of the first cases "in which a colored plaintiff in the South had appealed to a state court since the repeal of the Civil Rights Bill," and solidified the belief that Black men and women were "not wards of the nation but citizens of individual states."[69] The nation, in essence, denied protection to African Americans.

Justice John Marshall Harlan offered the lone dissent in the *Civil Rights Cases*, and, just as Harlan's ruling in *Plessy v. Ferguson* was heralded by African Americans, so too was his dissent here. In an editorial praising Harlan's decision, Frederick Douglass noted how the Supreme Court's rejection of the 1875 law sent African Americans and the nation back to a period before the Civil War. Douglass likened the 1883 judgment to the reversal of the Civil War outcome, as an "act of surrender almost akin to treachery. If any one thing was settled by the Rebellion it was that allegiance was, first of all, due, not to the States, but to the nation and that protection and allegiance go there." The nullification of the 1875 law was not only a retrenchment; it was a signal to the white South that African Americans could be denied their constitutional rights and the law would be on the white Southerners' side: "Well may the newspapers all over the South laud and magnify this decision. Well may they gloat in triumph over the negro citizen and declare they have now got him just where they want him. They can put him in a smoking car or baggage car, take him as freight or as a passenger, take him or leave him at a railroad station, exclude him from inns, drive him from all places of amusement and instruction, without the least fear that the National Government will interfere for the protection of his liberty."[70] By ruling the 1875 law as invalid, the court further stifled Black social progress.

Analyzing the Black woman's contested right to ride in a lady's space dramatizes how a form of transportation impacted the lived experiences of African Americans and the haphazard chances an African American, particularly a woman, took when riding on a train. It reveals not only the contingent nature of Black female train travel but also the socially constructed nature of the interior space of the train compartment, reflected in the imprecision of railroad language, especially as applied to the ladies' car. As the 1880s went on, more states instituted tougher segregation laws that applied to all African Americans.[71] By the 1890s, Jim Crow laws were on the books in several southern states and would receive legal sanction with the *Plessy* decision in 1896. Two U.S. experiments—the ladies' car and Reconstruction—ultimately failed to protect the interests of Black middle-class women, a failure that betrayed Black women, and, by the end of the nineteenth century, locked in practices of racial segregation.

3 Platform Politics

The Waiter Carriers of Virginia

> When the automobile had not even reached the inventor's drawing
> board stage, when railroad passenger coaches were wooden and
> heated by pot-bellied coal stoves, when soot, smoke and ashes were
> spewed out of smokestacks by locomotive engines, when most
> overland transportation was by railroad—an institution was born
> in Gordonsville that was destined to survive almost three-quarters
> of a century before it succumbed to the onrush of progress.
>
> —*Charlottesville Daily Progress*, November 18, 1955

Only a handful of items clearly depict the group of women who
are the subject of this chapter. Consider a photograph that accompanied a
newspaper article in Virginia in 1955 (fig. 3.1). Likely taken between 1910 and
1915, the sepia-colored image portrays six Black women standing alongside
two railroad cars, with trays of food balanced on their heads or on small
stands. The dusky, grainy photograph is often reprinted in the few discussions of "waiter carriers," the African American women who sold chicken
and other food items at the Chesapeake and Ohio train depot in Gordonsville, Virginia, about twenty miles northeast of Charlottesville. Before train
cars had the capability of serving food to passengers while the train was in
motion, travelers had to either bring food with them or purchase food when
the train stopped at a station. Waiter carriers, so called because the women
carried the food on large, "waiter" platters that they transported to the station
on their heads, sold food to these passengers.[1] Known by a variety of other
names—peddlers, vendors, even chicken ladies—the women had a thriving
business in the southern town between the 1860s and 1925. Although some of

Fried Chicken and Hot Coffee—Scene at C. & O. Depot, Gordonsville, Va.

Figure 3.1: Postcard, Fried Chicken and Hot Coffee, Scene at C. & O. Depot, Gordonsville, VA, likely taken between 1910 and 1915. Left to right: Maria Wallace, Francis Taylor, Lucy Washington, Laura Swift, Adeline Downs, and Mary Vest. Virginia Museum of History and Culture (2001.586.14).

the women's backs are to the camera and none of the women's faces are fully visible, the women can be identified. They are named by Hattie Edwards, a younger waiter carrier who identified them in the course of an interview.[2]

This chapter begins with this photograph and Hattie Edwards because, together, they perform an important act. By naming these women—specifically, concretely, precisely—Edwards ensures the women remain identifiable for future spectators of the image. She secures the past, positioning the women into a disembodied archive that time and technology, the twin engines of "progress," would otherwise erase from the historical record. Although Edwards is not physically present in the photograph, her cultural and community memory installs her as part of the image. She maps the Black women into coordinates of time and space, women who would otherwise remain anonymous ghostly figures on the side of the railroad tracks.

I also begin with Edwards and the photograph of the six women she can accurately name because of where the photograph takes us—*outside* of the American train compartment. Previous chapters have detailed the racial, gender, and class drama within the train car enacted when Black women ride the rails. To ride Jane Crow, an African American woman had to contend with the feeling of abeyance while "in the break," a period of gendered double consciousness. While traveling within a train compartment that felt outside of space and time, African American female travelers, such as Mary Church Terrell, redefined themselves in that moment of simulated stasis. I studied the blueprints of segregated train depots and the interior design of the train car and the dynamics that informed the insular environment for African American women. But what happens when train cars are stationary, for whatever period of time, at a depot and passengers are stalled, temporarily, in a larger social and communal environment? What kind of trackside interactions, however brief, occurred between long-distance white passengers and local African American residents?[3] How did a Black female community interact with, and how was it shaped by, a town's railroad, a business and a site that was economically important for the town? This shift in focus, from the interior environment within the train car to the social world outside it, enables a deliberation on that most marginal of railroad spaces, the train platform, and one of its most precarious and liminal regions, the railroad tracks.

This chapter studies the politics of external railroad spaces, the seemingly innocuous activities—and people—who occupy the overlooked areas people must traverse in order to travel by rail. Train travel affected not only the passengers who could afford a ticket or those passengers who were compelled to leave one environment for another. Equal attention should be paid to service providers such as the waiter carriers, who may have never stepped inside of a train car yet relied economically on the railroad's mobile network. Studying waiter carriers offers a way to further complicate Black women's relationship to the train and the train compartment by examining a group of women who worked past the boundaries of that compartment. Examining waiter carriers and looking beyond earlier investigations of them in the field of food studies, the field that helped bring waiter carriers to wider public attention, enables us to understand how residents and passengers may have experienced the social spaces of the railroad depot, platform, and tracks. Instead of a single, individual woman navigating the train car, as we saw with Anna Julia Cooper or Jane Brown, here we see how the train economy fostered a community of Black women. This chapter, then, has two aims: to study how women financially dependent on the presence of the railroad made use of the physical, material space available to them; and to understand the role of local community politics that shaped the waiter carriers' ephemeral status in the archives of U.S. railroad history. My research uncovered an unsettling symmetry to what archivally remains of the waiter carriers and the physical space under consideration here. Both waiter carriers and the platform have, unfortunately, not garnered as much attention as other aspects of railroad studies, perhaps because of their seeming insignificance to travel. But to attend to what appears innocuous, what seems so banal as to not need analysis, is one way to expose the unarticulated assumptions that determine what is and is not included in the archive.

We can see how much the platform has been overlooked by noting that even railroad historian Wolfgang Schivelbusch glosses over its presence. Scholarship on railroad depots only tangentially discuss the platform and the people who worked on or near it.[4] Numerous books have been published examining the architecture of train depots as well as their refurbishment for new uses such as restaurants or museums.[5] There is a vibrant study of renovated train stations and a related tourist economy, as well as architectural studies on waiting rooms, restrooms, even ticket counters—notably, those areas of the depot familiar to forms of segregation. The lowly platform, and the people who formed a business there, escapes detailed analysis.

As a continuation of the depot and as the last external area before boarding the car, or the first space encountered when exiting from it, the platform is usually unexamined space. The platform, as I define it, is an interstitial space and consists of that area immediately outside of the train cars and adjacent to the depot, the space for waiting and watching, departing and arriving passengers.[6] The platform was a place of market exchange, particularly in the early years of the train depot's existence, and extended the social and economic activities of the building. In addition to providing access to and from the train compartment, the platform performed a more communal purpose. One nineteenth-century resident of Gordonsville, the place where the six women were photographed, notes the socializing function of that space: "Surrounding the [railroad passenger station] was a platform of wide, rough planks that was like the boardwalk at a public beach. Some of our residents made a habit of parading there everyday."[7] Just a few feet from where the photographed women stand, the Gordonsville train platform was a dynamic part of the community. Late nineteenth-century newspapers and journal articles similarly remarked on the activity arriving and departing trains engineered on the Gordonsville stage. A writer for *Scribner's* in 1874, for example, departed from a train one night, stood on the depot's platform and was "speedily lost in a whirlpool of English and Scottish emigrants, surrounded by their wives and children." In addition to this crowd of émigrés, another group captured the reporter's attention, a group of waiter carriers, "stout colored damsels, flitting to and fro with platters of cold and antiquated chickens, and blue-looking eggs—the lamps on their provision-trays appearing like monster fire-flies as they glanced hither and yon."[8]

In terms of railroad spaces, the platform was unique. It required an accessibility and informality that contrasted to other areas of the railroad. Unlike other areas of the train station, for example, the platform escaped definitive racial boundaries and seemed to defy identifiable demarcations such as "first-class" and "second-class," the descriptors that weighed so heavily in my earlier chapters. It was, by nature and design, more expansive than the compartment; and because in some locations, one did not need a ticket to justify one's presence there, it was more receptive to diverse others. In her reading of the significance of railroads to southern race relations, historian Grace Elizabeth Hale points out the perplexity of the platform, a confusion enabled by its openness: "The railroad platform seemed to 'baffle' southern white 'ingenuity.' . . . No structure had been devised to separate white and black as they crossed the distance between the building and the train."[9] This 1875 drawing by well-known illustrator J. Wells Champney also depicts a heterogeneous group of people on a southern railroad platform (fig. 3.2). In addition to a young boy, a likely waiter carrier, selling items to train passengers on the left, the top center of the illustration shows a well-dressed white couple, a white man in a top hat and a woman wearing a bustle, near two young African American boys and an African American man gesturing toward them.[10] At first glance, then, the platform appears immune to restrictive segregatory practices. In its openness—and in its need for an unobstructed passage in order to function well—the platform would seem to be egalitarian.[11] Here, it seems at least, the "democratic" potential of the U.S. railroad may have finally been achieved.[12]

"The railroad depots are everywhere crowded with negroes, immigrants, tourists and speculators."   [Page 114.]

Figure. 3.2: "The railroad depots are everywhere crowded with negroes, immigrants, tourists and speculators." King, *Great South*, 113.

And yet, the story of the Virginia waiter carriers' popularity and eventual disappearance from a larger archival record—and the reason why Hattie Edwards's act of naming them is so significant—complicates this democratic narrative of horizontal space. Early in the waiter carriers' approximately sixty-five-year history, the women sold from the Gordonsville depot platform. However, newspaper articles and interviews reveal that, by the early twentieth century, the women were displaced from that location. Instead of the platform, the women had to sell on the very railroad tracks. The photograph in figure 3.1 captures the women during a period after that displacement. I am interested in the local community politics—platform politics—that forced the African American women to move where they sold food, from the platform adjacent to hotels and the depot to the more precarious position on the very tracks of the railroad. By 1925 women who carried waiters were banned entirely from the tracks.[13] The movement—from platform to tracks to banishment—resulted not just from technological improvements associated with train travel but also, I argue, from the town's desire to craft a collective memory. The waiter carriers were caught in this desire for technological and civic progress. Like the question W. E. B. Du Bois asked in "Of the Meaning of Progress"—"how shall man measure progress there where the dark-faced Josie lies?"—the question of Gordonsville's progress would seem to revolve around the location of African American women.[14]

By occupying a marginal space, that is, the area between the train depot and the train car, the waiter carriers are overlooked in most studies of railroad culture. But their seemingly invisible presence is important because they exhibit a concept of "progress" that resonates throughout this book. As railroad technologies improved and as Gordonsville became concerned with its legacy or reputation, Black women were displaced, even as they themselves may have, briefly at least, benefitted from the newer technologies. Rather than moving Black women forward, railroad and civic improvements had the (unintended?) effect of inhibiting Black female movement. The rise and eventual "demise" of the waiter carriers illustrate how "progress," so often identified with forms of technology like the railroad, erases, or despatializes, Black women.[15] Only a cultural memory like that of Hattie Edwards, who at the time of her interview was a "living archive," can ensure the women stay identifiable.

The decision to displace the women from one location to another involves economics and memory: As others saw the profitability of the waiter carriers, more formal businesses tried to acquire the trade. As Gordonsville became known for its African American female food vendors, white residents attempted to reshape the town's fame. Ironically, as I discuss at the end of the chapter, the early twentieth-century efforts to enforce a homogenous cultural memory of Gordonsville backfired. The town now has an annual Fried Chicken Festival as well as a 5K Chicken Run, commemorating the African American female food vendors and the food they sold.[16] The history of southern women engaged in commerce and economic enterprise is also the story of spatial, racial, and gender politics, shaped by the economic possibilities of the railroad.

Gordonsville and the Waiter Carriers

Before the 1890s, most railroad lines did not have dining cars. When a train stopped at a station, passengers had to run out of the train car onto the platform to obtain something to eat. Illustrations such as those by Currier and Ives parody the sight of passengers running from the train to obtain food before the train departed (fig. 3.3). In his history of railroad dining, James D. Porterfield notes that twenty to thirty minutes were usually allotted for passengers to purchase and to consume food. Newspaper and magazine articles regularly described the spectacle of passengers running frantically

A "LIMITED EXPRESS."
"Five seconds for Refreshments"!

Figure 3.3: Lithograph, Thomas Worth, for Currier & Ives, "A Limited Express: Five seconds for Refreshments!" ca. 1884. Library of Congress, www.loc.gov/item /97507578/.

to fill their stomachs: "All the doors are thrown open, and out rush all the passengers like boys out of school, and crowd around the tables to solace themselves with pies, patties, cakes."[17] Until the Pullman Company improved the existing dining cars in 1868, with its well-known Delmonico train, most U.S. railroad passengers had to bring their own food—or buy it from food vendors or peddlers, such as the waiter carriers, at train depots.[18]

Although train food vendors likely existed in most towns that had scheduled railroad stops, two particular towns have a strong and recordable presence of African American female waiter carriers: Gordonsville, Virginia, and Corinth, Mississippi. Jane Brown, as noted in chapter 2, was the daughter of a "colored proprietor" of an eating house and, as the witnesses in her trial pointed out, she could be seen frequently walking around the Corinth train depot, selling her mother's food to train passengers.[19] Both of these small southern towns were literal crossroads, locations in which two or more railroad lines met, designations both locales highlighted in tourist information.[20]

Maps of Gordonsville offer a visual archive of the town's racial and spatial politics. Named after an eighteenth-century tavern owner, Nathan Gordon, Gordonsville was and is a distinctive small, southern town. An 1878 map illustrates one of Gordonsville's unique features: the triangular intersection of three sets of railroad tracks, in the southwestern part of the town (map 3.1).[21] This map is also significant because it identifies the "colored section" of Gordonsville—notably, outside the official corporation limits. While the homes that line a prominent street near the depot, South Main Street, are named, the few homes in the "colored" section (identifiable by the "colored churches") are anonymous, except for one—T. Lovelock, a white English landowner who rented out homes in the African American area.[22] Map 3.1 gives an indication of the distance some waiter carriers had to travel to get to the depot with all of their supplies. In the 1880s, Gordonsville had nine hundred residents. Despite the presence of a vibrant transportation network, the population would not exceed one thousand until well in the 1950s.

The town's success was shaped by the railroads. When the Gordonsville Depot was a lively passenger depot, several railroad lines came into the town, such as the Virginia Central Railroad (later renamed the Chesapeake and Ohio Railway) and the Orange and Alexandria Railroad, enabling an active trade and commerce industry. Passengers arriving into Gordonsville on the Virginia Central usually had a half-hour layover, and businesses sprang up that contributed to passenger comfort, such as hotels and restaurants. At various times in Gordonsville's history, there were at least two to three hotels open in the area, businesses that, along with the waiter carriers, provided food to travelers. In 1873, for example, three hotels competed for the travelers

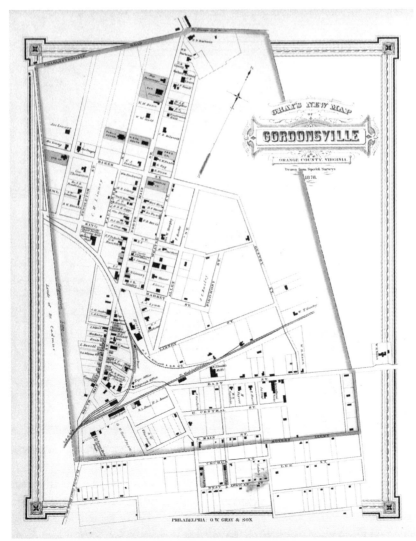

Map 3.1: "Gray's New Map of Gordonsville, Orange County, Virginia. Drawn from Special Surveys, 1878." South Main Street is on the lower left side, and the "colored" section is at the bottom middle. David Rumsey Map Collection.

arriving or departing from Gordonsville: the Exchange Hotel, the St. John's, and the Magnolia. The hotels used available space to provide convenience to railroad passengers. Both the Magnolia House and the St. Johns had "doors opening directly onto the railroad tracks," "passengers alighting from the cars, therefore, could walk directly into either establishment."[23]

Map 3.2: Detail of map 3.1. Note that the two churches labeled "Colored Bap. Ch." and the house labeled "T. Lovelock," all between Church Street and West African Street, are south of the town limit. "Gray's New Map of Gordonsville, Orange County, Virginia. Drawn from Special Surveys, 1878." David Rumsey Map Collection.

A Sanborn Insurance map of Gordonsville in 1908 provides additional geographic views of the platforms and the railroad depot's central location (map 3.3).[24] Over time, Gordonsville's maps show not only the growth of the town but also the growth and expansion of the platform, from the two planks of 1878 to the four in 1908. The platform was so significant that when a new one was in the process of being installed at the depot, the local paper made note of it.[25]

A postcard dated 1904 offers one of the best views of the Gordonsville platform at the passenger depot (fig. 3.4). By the time of the 1908 Sanborn map, there was another platform behind the depot, adjacent to the pumping station and the water tower.

Traveling from the south of Gordonsville, from such streets as West African Street (at the bottom of map 3.1), the waiter carriers carried their food, coffee, platters, and stands to the depot. When the women heard the sound of the train coming, they would gather up their belongings in preparation to sell to passengers.[26]

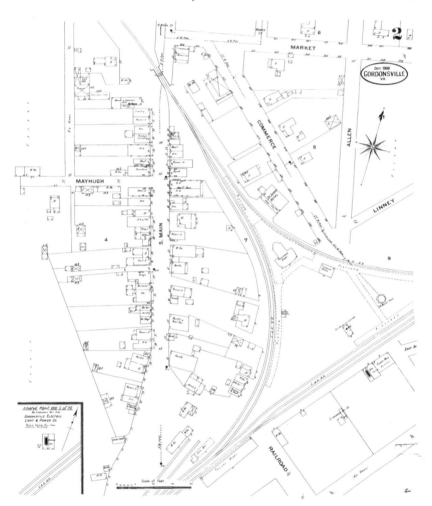

Map 3.3: Sanborn Fire Insurance map of Gordonsville from 1908. Note the extensive station platforms. Sanborn Map Company, October, 1908. Library of Congress Geography and Map Division Washington, DC, www .loc.gov/item/sanborn09025_001/.

A definitive timeline of the waiter carriers' existence is difficult to chart, but a general outline of their history can be traced. References to African Americans selling food, specifically fried chicken at southern train stations, occur before and during the Civil War. A reporter traveling on the Virginia Central in 1868 noted that university students in nearby Charlottesville referred to Gordonsville as "Chicken town. Come when you will, in war or

Figure 3.4: This postcard of 1904 shows the train tracks, the platform, and the Gordonsville train depot. From a postcard in the collection of Larry Z. Daily.

peace, a gang of colored women swarm around every train."[27] Although it is not clear when waiter carriers first had to buy "snack licenses" to sell food near the train depot, Gordonsville Town Council records list the names of people who purchased the license in 1877, just seven years after the town was incorporated. In that year, these licenses cost an individual vendor $5.00.[28] What did their chicken taste like? The *Butte Weekly Miner* of Montana published a description by a traveler to Gordonsville in 1899: "it was so tender it fairly melted in your mouth, while the crispy browned outside imparted a delicious tang to the taste."[29] By 1905 some white residents expressed concern about the image the waiter carriers created of the town and questioned how Gordonsville would be remembered. Interviews with the surviving waiter carriers in the mid to late twentieth century indicate that waiter carriers stopped selling in a widespread practice and were banned from selling at the train station in 1925.

Psyche A. Williams-Forson details the experiences of waiter carriers, noting that the African American women gained a measure of financial independence by selling fried chicken and other food items at the station, enabling them to "build houses out of chicken legs."[30] While Williams-Forson studies the complex associations chicken has in African American culture and the entrepreneurial skills of an early Black female business community, I am interested in the geographic and spatial precarity of these women—that is, their transition from selling on the platform to the railroad tracks to not selling at all. Specifically, I am interested in what this progressive displacement reveals about the politics of communal social networks dependent on the railroad and the power of such networks in shaping the cultural and communal memory of the women.

Two types of sources have been important for tracing the historical memory of women who "carried waiters": nineteenth-century newspapers, journals, and books, and mid to late twentieth-century newspaper articles that provide more firsthand accounts of the waiter carriers' experiences. The two sets of writings reveal tensions the presence of the waiter carriers created for others: a tension between the women and representatives of more formal businesses such as restaurants and hotels, as well as an unease from white residents concerned about the visual and aural impact the women had on visitors to Gordonsville. Reading the sets of sources collectively suggest the waiter carriers' unusual relationship to time and progress: they are remembered more accurately as their historical image disappears. "Progress"—in the form of the town's improvement and better railroad technologies—displaced the women, even as a more contemporary nostalgia, evident in the more recent publications, helped to "recover" the women in a disparate archive.

Descriptions of waiter carriers occurred in prominent post–Civil War journals or well-disseminated books designed to inform readers about the conditions in the postwar South and to help soothe the tensions between the North and South. One of the more prominent journalistic tours through the South was written by Jedidiah Hotchkiss, the cartographer for Stonewall Jackson during the Civil War.[31] Hotchkiss was convinced that postbellum Virginia could contend with the economic upheaval of the war if the state government, residents, and business investors concentrated on Virginia's natural resources, which he highlighted in the articles that also "emphasize[d] Virginia's readiness to forget the past and adapt to the new order."[32] Hotchkiss's lengthy 1872 "New Ways in the Old Dominion" article in *Scribner's* is notable—the article contains one of the earliest published visual images of the waiter carriers (fig. 3.5).[33]

The illustration, by W. L. Sheppard, solidified the image of the waiter carrier as an African American holding a large tray of food and coffee up to railroad passengers leaning out of train windows. Depicting Gordonsville's first passenger-only depot (in contrast to a freight or combination depot) built in 1870, the image reveals that the station eaves provided some protection from the weather to the passengers and the carriers serving food on the platform and near the tracks, while a motley crowd sits or stands on the platform. The illustration indicates that men also occupied the role of waiter carrier, a suggestion confirmed by a description of Gordonsville in the 1873 travel book, *The Pine and the Palm*, edited by N. J. Watkins, a northern reporter who toured the postbellum South. When Watkins departed from a train car and stepped onto the Gordonsville platform, he and his colleagues were "surrounded with a swarm of old and young negroes of both sexes, carrying large servers upon

Figure 3.5: This W. L. Sheppard illustration from Hotchkiss's "New Ways in the Old Dominion" is one of the earliest visual depictions of waiter carriers. *Scribner's*, December 1872, 146.

their heads, containing pies, cakes, chickens, boiled eggs, strawberries and cream."[34] Significantly, Watkins identifies both women and men as waiter carriers, although women appeared to have been predominant at the station. Watkins's *The Pine and the Palm*, like Hotchkiss's article, was part of a larger design to encourage travel to the war-torn South and to promote travel on the country's rail lines. The inclusion of waiter carriers offered "picturesque" visions of the locale. The waiter carriers made a second appearance in *Scribner's* in April 1874, in an article by Edward King. As part of his "Great South" articles for the journal, King "rambled in Virginia" and provided a brief glimpse of the food vendors. The fact that the waiter carriers appeared in *Scribner's* twice annoyed the editor of the *Gordonsville Gazette*, enough for him to remark on their doubled appearance: "Surely [King] is going into minutiae when he stops to pay Gordonsville chicken legs a passing tribute."[35]

Like the railroad itself after the reach of the 1869 Transcontinental Railroad, the image of Gordonsville and the waiter carriers traveled throughout the nation. In addition to these three national representations of waiter carriers, more frequent, albeit brief, references to the food vendors appeared in newspapers throughout Virginia between 1867 and the 1910s.[36] Known as "scribs," the reportorial, atmospheric travel anecdotes jocularly highlighted the food readily available at the Virginia stop. Reading these short reports collectively reveal what chicken legs may have signified to passengers and visitors to Gordonsville.

Papers as varied as the *Richmond Times Dispatch* to the *Alexandria Gazette* regularly invoked chicken legs to suggest the close association that particular food item had to Gordonsville for train passengers entering and leaving the town. When the *Richmond Daily Dispatch* announced the change in the Virginia Central's schedule, for example, the modification was registered in terms of the reduced opportunity to eat fried chicken: "the long detention there [in Gordonsville] for a change of cars . . . will now be abolished; but, alas, we fear the public must bid good-bye to the familiar and welcome fried chicken."[37] Other brief newspaper references captured the oral presence of the waiter carriers and their efforts to attract passengers' attention. A Presbyterian missionary recounted traveling by train through Gordonsville and "seized ten cent snacks as he flew by Gordonsville, and other ('hot coffee!' 'nice fried chicken' and 'fine lemon pie!') stations," while an anonymous train passenger noted, in the *Richmond Daily Dispatch*, the relative quiet of passing through Virginia soil "until the cry of 'fried chicken' . . . at Gordonsville interrupted the jovial flow of the party."[38]

Correspondents found eclectic ways to depict the large number of chicken legs offered at this one location. A reporter for the *Alexandria Gazette* vividly captures the scene of chicken available for purchase: "We never pass through Gordonsville without being lost in amazement at the wilderness of chicken legs which encompass us. They are like the leaves of the forest or sands of the sea. They are thrust at you through every window; they besiege all doors of the cars; they infest the platforms, they are everywhere. Turn where you will, they meet your gaze."[39] But a reporter for the *Richmond Daily State Journal* focused not only on the large number of chicken legs but also on the considerable amount of other animals interested in the food: "At Gordonsville, where fried chicken and hard-boiled eggs do muchly abound, we found a thousand, more or less, slobbering dogs, watching the car windows to greedily catch the falling bones, as they dropped from the mouths of the passengers into their own."[40] Waiter carriers at Gordonsville were so conspicuous that their *absence* from the station was striking as well, as one reporter noted: "Our journey to Gordonsville was uninterrupted by any unusual occurrence. At that important station of snacks, we found the retailers of chicken legs scarce, but soon discovered the cause: the circus having drawn them off and held them with a sort of enchantment."[41]

Multiple brief references to Gordonsville link the town to fried chicken legs, with that part of the chicken's anatomy becoming a metonymic shorthand for the Virginian town. The representational force of the Black women becomes apparent when perusing news reports about Gordonsville. The women's heightened visibility—they were often the first image to greet arriving train passengers—and this visual greeting contributed to the memorable impression they made to visitors to the town. Newspaper articles create and reflect the "imagined community" of Gordonsville, one deeply conscious of—and defensive about—its fried chicken associations.[42] The repetition and the brevity of the references assume, if not create, a feeling of communality in the newspaper readers. Or, as the WPA visitors' guide to Virginia stated much more succinctly, "Gordonsville to travelers meant fried chicken."[43] Although the *Scribner's* image and the editor of *The Pine and the Palm* identify male waiter carriers, it is the Black women who come to represent this occupation, and it is a negative representation, according to some residents.[44]

While the scribs repeated here are generally innocuous, merely recounting the sense of the unusual image the waiter carriers presented to people unfamiliar to Gordonsville, other representations of waiter carriers hint at the discomfort the sight of Black women may have had on white residents concerned about Gordonsville's image.

An antebellum drawing of a waiter carrier indicates how an outsider may have perceived the women. Created by the English doctor Sir Henry Wentworth Acland, the drawing merges the visual and aural "vulgarity" visitors to Gordonsville may have attached to the African American women (fig. 3.6). In the fall of 1860, the Prince of Wales (later King Edward VII) toured Canada and the United States. Virginia was the only southern state the royal visited, and Acland was a member of the entourage, serving as the prince's personal doctor.[45] Known for his watercolors and drawings, and for his concern about hygiene, Acland drew an image of a waiter carrier at a train station in Richmond.[46] Although the drawing depicts an elegant Black woman in a majestic profile, the handwritten caption below the woman sutures her to commonality: "Negro girls in the most tawdry [dress?] and of extreme vulgarity offer at the station rolls and chicken's legs." However, nothing in this image, or in the others discussed in this chapter, stands out as "vulgar." It is not clear what Acland perceived as "extreme vulgarity" (the woman's dress? her calls to passengers to purchase her food?), but the caption clearly indicts the woman for an assumed profane presence and impropriety.[47] Acland's drawing is important not only because it confirms the presence of the waiter carrier at Virginia train stations before the Civil War but also because it suggests what the sight and the sound of the waiter carrier may have impressed on new

Figure 3.6: In 1860, Sir Henry Wentworth Acland drew
this scene of a waiter carrier in Richmond, Virginia, and
captioned it: "Negro girls in the most tawdry dress, and
of extreme vulgarity offer at the station rolls and chicken
legs." Sir Henry Acland Collection, Library and Archives
Canada, accession C-128473.

visitors to those train stations a classic example of how "visible blackness is
forced into the historically assigned role of the negative and devalued."[48]

Acland's drawing, as well as the brief newspaper articles, suggests the
discomfort the sight of waiter carriers may have provoked in white residents concerned about Gordonsville's image. Indeed, the *Native Virginian*
remarked with some defensiveness about the "contemptuous" comments

residents and travelers made about the town as early as 1870, "when Gordonsville appeared to the railroad passenger to consist of a few unhappy houses water-logged in an agitated ocean of fried chicken legs, coffeepots and hardboiled eggs."[49]

Acland's image has significance when read with an early twentieth-century newspaper article, "Gordonsville and Its Future." It is the concern about the image—and the sound and the gender—of the waiter carriers that distresses the white residents quoted in the *Richmond Times Dispatch* article of 1905. Printed in two columns and subtitled "The Town has Many Good Things in it Besides Chicken and Hot Coffee," the article opens with the sound of waiter carriers hawking their food. Using an amalgam of tropes from the plantation literature tradition, including the requisite "chicken thief" joke, the reporter positions the waiter carriers as part of Gordonsville's colorful, well-known, and "antiquated" past. The article registers the public anxiety of the town becoming associated with chicken and Black women and hints at the tension between waiter carriers and more formal businesses like the hotels and restaurants: "The people of Gordonsville would like to see the selling of fried chicken and hot coffee come to an end. Several of them told me rather plaintively they believe the people who knew Gordonsville from a distance thought there was nothing else sold in the town." The article details those other businesses, including general merchandise stores and banks. The report made distinctions between past and present: Will the residents be able to take advantage of the rich geography and natural resources of Virginia or will "this section [go] to waste"? Will Gordonsville, in other words, progress toward a more industrial future or will it remain rooted to "antiquated old mammies," that is, to the image and sound of the Black female body? The article presents waiter carriers as inhibitors of the town's progress. If investors, business leaders, or potential residents could just get past, literally and figuratively, the Black women they meet on first entering the town, opportunities for growth and development would be possible through banks, hotels, and the transportation enabled by the presence of the railroad lines that enter Gordonsville. By positioning Black female waiter carriers as representatives of Virginia's obsolescent past, the newspaper article suggests that the town's progress, its claim to the future, will depend on the erasure of the "old aunties" at the train stations.[50]

Although "Gordonsville and Its Future" was only one reporter's opinion, it does provide some insight into how community members concerned about the images of the town may have perceived the waiter carriers.[51] Within twenty years of that article's publication, by 1925, waiter carriers would cease to sell on the platform or on the train tracks. The Black women were placed in a temporal framework that emphasized a nostalgic appearance and an anachronistic market exchange. A more telling example of how waiter carriers were perceived in opposition to technology and the future occurs in a short story.

Working on the Tracks: "Aunt Sanna Terry"

Some Gordonsville residents positioned waiter carriers as anachronistic images at the site of an industry that could help propel Virginia into the future, a depiction that also occurs in a 1918 short story. Landon Dashiell's story "Aunt Sanna Terry," published in Hampton University's *Southern Workman*, complicates and extends the analysis of Black women and railroad space.[52] On the surface it is a story of Black and white female interactions, of a white woman coming to a Black woman's aid, but the tale also reveals the othering of railroad space and details the Black female waiter carrier's relationship to technology and progress. The Black female waiter carrier is perceived in opposition to "progress" or, at least, in need of instruction on how to capitalize on technological improvements.

"Aunt Sanna Terry" is narrated by an African American woman, Leah Heber Jenkins, one of several women who work as waiter carriers in an unnamed southern town. During one of the train stops, a young white woman, Honey, or as Leah calls her "Miss Honey Chile," obtains fried chicken and coffee from Leah through the train window. Honey disembarks from the train, telling Leah: "I want to be your fren' an' give you a few sirgestions." Honey enjoys the chicken, but the coffee is, in Honey's words, "vile, puffickly vile." She also is disturbed at the lack of hygiene surrounding Leah and her food. She tells the Black woman: "jes' now you had to slap dat po', hungry, yeller dog away fum yo' waiter an' dat ain' neither clean nor sannerterry." Miss Honey makes several "sirgestions" to Leah that she feels will increase Leah's business. One of the most important suggestions concerns Leah's appearance: "I want yer ter wear here at de depot a white cap, a large white ap'on an' white cotton gloves an' a lovely white han'kerchief folded ercross dis way,' smiling an' crossin' her little white han's over her puitty front." Miss Honey mails the described outfit to Leah and, after some hesitation, and accompanied with ridicule from the other food vendors, Leah dons the clothes. Her new uniform makes her appear like a mammy and cleaner, more "sanitary," compared to the other food vendors—or "Aunt Sanna Terry." To Leah's surprise, her new appearance nearly doubles her business. Passengers look approvingly at her white clothes out of the train window: "Some uv 'em look at me and wave dey hand' an' one say, 'Don' she look sweet?'"[53]

Much like the schedule of a train, the short story depends on sequence and seriality: Miss Honey's stops at Leah's food stand progressively improve Leah's business. In a sequence of three visits on the tracks, Miss Honey offers both advice and products that increase Leah's sales. The second time Honey stops at that station, she surprises Leah with a gift: a coffee percolator that can replace the "vile coffee" Honey tasted earlier. The third and last time Honey stops at Leah's town, she has another surprise for Leah: she has gotten married. When Leah laughingly asks the newlyweds if they need a new cook, Honey says no, but her husband "standin' behime her wave a chicken leg at me an' noddin' his haid, say, 'Yes!'"[54]

Dashiell's story displays the economic importance of space, property, and location. The entire narrative takes place outside the train compartment, in a space adjacent to, but not on, the railroad platform. Indeed, Leah's informal food vendor business is located on the least desirable, and most dangerous, railroad space—on the side opposite the hotel, on the tracks. The local railroad has purchased the hotel near the train station and has forced Leah and other waiter carriers to conduct their business off the platform. As Leah explains in the white Dashiell's version of Black dialect, the move affects their business: "Dere was a time when we-all colored women folks could sell we-alls' eatin's fum de flatform, but dat done been stopped a long an' a merry ago. De railroad done bought de hotel an' dem black boys, callin' deyself waiters fum de hotel, sells fum de flatform an' we all has ter sell fum de yuther side uv de train."[55] Instead of a space of cross-race sociality, the platform here is a segregated space and gendered male, the place where newly hired African American male waiters from the hotel congregate and ridicule Leah.[56] The few existing postcards of waiter carriers, such as the one in figure 3.1, illustrate the hazards of Leah's move from hotel/train platform to "de yuther side uv de train," on the tracks, perhaps the most dangerous area near the train depot. Dashiell's short story, then, takes place during an important transitional moment, after the displacement of waiter carriers from the platform and as they navigate alternative locations because of the local power of hotels and restaurants.

Food studies scholar Elizabeth S. D. Engelhardt reads "Aunt Sanna Terry" as an example of "narrative texts as cookbooks," recipes conveyed to the reader in a nondidactic, entertaining fashion, and a tale that instructs female readers how to cook, prepare meals, and have better hygiene. "The surface discussion of hygiene, taste, and efficient cooking technologies is on a deeper level an exploration of racial hierarchy, market-based capitalism, and gendered activism."[57] But because Leah remains on the periphery of the train car and has to be instructed on how to use the percolator, the story also reinforces stereotypes of Black knowledge and spatial belonging. "Aunt Sanna

Terry" demonstrates clear but problematic demarcations of space, gender, race, and technology. Leah never enters the train but maintains "her place" on the outside of the compartment and on the railroad tracks as a server to the white passengers. Moreover, even when Leah and Honey interact, racial hierarchies persist. Leah is careful to note that when the two women discuss food and business, Miss Honey is the one who sits on Leah's stool; Leah sits on an upturned box, maintaining hierarchies of race and respectability.

"Aunt Sanna Terry" presents the meeting of white and Black femininity outside the train car. It is a positive interaction that ends with benefits for both parties: Leah adopts a more sanitary image with her handkerchief, apron, and gloves, and Miss Honey possibly gets a new cook. But Dashiell's short story leaves the reader with unanswered questions: Will Leah herself travel by the train to reach Miss Honey's domestic space? Will there continue to be such positive interactions *inside* the train car? Indeed, will Honey and Leah occupy the same train car? Will Leah leave her business, her house that she is "only two tickets away" from paying off, and her son, who has stopped drinking alcohol?

In addition, there are competing forms of "progress" operating in the short story. Like the "Gordonsville and Its Future" article, "Aunt Sanna Terry" reveals a tension between embracing new forms of technology and maintaining a link to an older way of life. Two developments contributed to the end of waiter carriers: the competition to sell food from hotels and inside of train stations, and the developments in the dining capabilities of train cars. These advancements helped to improve the travel experience for passengers but in the process displaced the Black female waiter carrier. There is a third, more elusive reason for the waiter carriers' eventual disappearance: white residents' desire to amend the town's reputation and their concern about the visual and aural impact of food vendors on train passengers, hinted at in the newspaper articles. Dashiell's short story presents a similar "updating." By dressing Leah in white, "sanitary" clothing, Honey sanitizes Leah's visual appearance and thus increases her sales. But her appearance as a mammy is a commercialized nostalgia that appeals to white passengers. Leah sells more chicken, but by drawing on a romanticized image of Black femininity—one based on an antebellum past. The nostalgia implicitly invokes a subservient attitude of a past time that makes Leah successful. Like Quaker Oats' use of Nancy Green to sell Aunt Jemima pancakes at the 1893 Columbian exposition, Leah merges the plantation past with improved consumer technologies like the percolator.[58] The short story reveals competing forms of "progress" and nostalgia, the issues that similarly wrap around the waiter carriers and the collective memory of them.

The photograph of waiter carriers in figure 3.7, likely taken around 1915, presents another aspect of the waiter carrier's relationship to time. One woman lifts a large platter to two passengers, a white man and a white woman. The Black woman's arms are held in an awkward position, holding a tray of food up to the man. While the white woman keeps her body inside the train, merely placing her elbows on the train window's frame, the man's arm extends crookedly outside the window frame, his wrist up to his face as he peers at his watch. The waiter carrier's and the male passenger's actions are not synchronized: a wide gulf exists between the waiter carrier's tray and this figure who checks the railroad's time, the latter apparently more important than the former; time appears to be on one person's side more than the other. The photograph depicts two contrary relationships to time. The man appears time-conscious by staring intently at his watch while the waiter carrier waits for the passenger to select his food. The image suggests Harold Schweizer's theories about waiting, not only the "gendered implications of waiting," but also the "marginal social position . . . of the person who waits. Time is synchronized only for those who have pocket watches."[59]

The passage of time does, in fact, nearly erase the Virginia waiter carriers. The invention of train cars with sealed windows, air-conditioning, and dining compartments made waiter carriers such as Leah unnecessary.

" Fried Chicken and Hot Coffee."—Scene at C. & O. Depot, Gordonsville, Va.

Figure 3.7: Waiter carrier with tray, ca. 1915. From a postcard in the collection of Larry Z. Daily.

Moreover, long-distance trains ceased to halt at the station, instead going straight through the town, and fewer "local" trains stopped at the depot, making the waiter carriers less necessary for the hungry railroad passenger.

Tracking the Archive

And yet—this is not where their stories end. Curiously, after the women disappeared from the Gordonsville tracks, there was a kind of "afterlife" of the waiter carriers: their disappearance propelled a series of newspaper remembrances during the late twentieth century that more accurately recorded the character of their experiences. Here, then, is the waiter carriers' complex interaction with time: decades after they disappear as visible workers on the Gordonsville platform and rails, there is a nostalgic desire for recapturing their presence. Ironically, the waiter carriers are remembered only after they have ceased to exist, after local politics displaced them from the profitable train tracks. The mid- to late twentieth-century accounts of the women shape what we now know about them. Only in interviews, when their own stories are reported, do the waiter carriers emerge from two-dimensional drawings, defeat stereotype and problematic nostalgia, and form a counter-archive.

Previous discussions of the presence—or absence—of African American women in the archive concentrate on slavery. Scholars such as Michel-Ralph Trouillot, Saidiya Hartman, Simon Gikandi, and more recently Marissa Fuentes detail vexed efforts to identify and narrate the lives of African-descended people enslaved in the Americas. All four scholars remark on feelings of frustration when encountering archival gaps, and on the risks present when a scholar fills in those gaps.[60] These are scholars of transatlantic slavery between the sixteenth and early nineteenth centuries, a period in which first-person accounts of the enslaved individual transported across the Atlantic are rare, and in which archives of recorded "history" occlude information about Black diasporic women from ready perception. Yet my study of women who lived during more "recordable" moments warns us that archival absences occur throughout the African diaspora. Because the lives and activities of women of color have so often been undervalued, archival absences shape most histories of African American women. The rich, though disparate, alternative archival resources on African American women and railroad travel reveal that "silences [in the *recent*] past" also deserve attention.[61]

How the waiter carriers of Virginia are represented in the archive cannot be divorced from their encounters with the spatial politics in the town in which they lived. Only after the women have been banned, after they have served food at the station and have passed away, do more individualized images of the women come into view through the newspaper interviews. There is a persistent irony in the waiter carriers' history: the African American female food vendors signified the Gordonsville railroad but resided on the outskirts of the town. Their presence offered the first sight to passengers arriving in the town, so much so that their images were captured, verbally and visually, in major journals and periodicals of the nineteenth century, but they were continually displaced from around the town's railroad tracks in order to accommodate other businesses. The waiter carriers' history, like the waiter carriers themselves, resides outside formal or institutional settings. An alternative archive of the waiter carriers develops from the mid to late twentieth-century newspaper articles.

Newspapers disclose some reasons—and individuals—at the root of the ban that displaced the women from the Gordonsville platform and tracks; and Gordonsville Town Council records cryptically hint at biased practices. Both sources indicate that one Gordonsville resident bears some responsibility for the end of the waiter carriers' careers. In the same newspaper article in which Hattie Edwards identifies the six women in the photograph, she also names a white resident responsible for banning the waiter carriers. According to Edwards, in 1925, a resident named Robert Watkins "bought from the railroad a concession to establish a depot restaurant and forced the Negro women to discontinue their selling at the trains."[62] While searching for more information about this concession, more questions than answers are revealed.

Gordonsville Town Council records reveal that Robert Watkins had deep ties to the town council and with the Chesapeake and Ohio Railroad. His father, George Miller Watkins, was a member of the town council in the late 1890s, and the younger Watkins once worked as Gordonsville's sheriff.[63] In 1925, the same year in which the ban started, Watkins was one of the seven trustees of the town. This was also the time in which Watkins started a restaurant near the depot, as noted in a local newspaper announcement in February 1925.[64] Moreover, Watkins had previous interactions with the C&O Railroad, as mentioned periodically in the town records; and, notably, his brother-in-law was the assistant secretary of the line.[65]

Trouillot identifies several moments during a historical event that can form silences in the archive. The Gordonsville Town Council records create a silence "at the moment of fact creation," for when researching the Gordonsville council records of 1925, there is, indeed, a remarkable silence in those records about the events that led to the ban against the waiter carriers.[66] Two opaque references in the 1925 Gordonsville Town Council record book provide some limited information on Watkins and his interactions with the waiter carriers and illustrate the power of the silence formed "at the moment of fact creation." Watkins is one of the seven town councilmen in

a meeting held on September 15. The secretary of the town council records
the following lines, at the conclusion of regular business, regarding Watkins
and William H. Swindlinger, another prominent white resident of the town:
"licenses against W.H. Swi[n]dlinger for boarding house, and ticket against
RG Watkins for two waiters were also ordered cancelled." A vote was called
on what was apparently a motion, and all present, including Watkins, voted
yes. Then on November 10, 1925: "On motion it was carried that Mr. Watkins
be requested to communicate with the C and O Ry official regarding block-
ing the Ry crossings."[67] The opaqueness in the Gordonsville Town Council
records, whether by happenstance or design, prevents a full understanding of
the interactions between Watkins and the anonymous "two waiters," or two
African American female food vendors. Without additional context for the
second reference—the request that Watkins "communicate" with a railroad
representative about blockings at railroad crossings—one can only speculate
about the possible meanings of this phrase and about the implications this
consultation may have had for the women who sold food on the tracks, and
by doing so, "block[ed] the Ry crossings."

What the records show then is that sometimes even "official" records can
occlude or lead one astray. Indeed, an archive of the waiter carriers' engagement with the town council and railroad representatives exists outside of
official knowledge production and dissemination. Important communal
information is located not in the town records but in the alternative archives
of living people, such as Edwards, in 1955. Local Virginia Black family gene-
alogist Gloria Gilmore and her friend Doretha Taylor Dickerson also offered
a wealth of information about the waiter carriers.[68] The images of the waiter
carriers that emerge from these living sources are more complex than those
presented in newspapers or recorded so briefly and opaquely in town council
records. Conversations with these "living histories" are important for a variety of reasons, most significantly for correcting misreadings of or absences
within the archive.

The newspaper interviews compete with the omissions in the archive, shaping what verifiable knowledge can be obtained about the women. The newspaper articles of 1948, 1955, and 1970, in newspapers such as the *Richmond
Daily Dispatch*, the *Charlottesville Daily Progress*, and the *Orange Observer*,
evoke a past time of southern life, but in the process, the waiter carriers'
experiences reveal the fraught racial and spatial politics complicating the
space surrounding the depot.

We can return once again to Hattie Edwards and her act of naming the
women. Because Hattie Edwards functions as an archival source and provides some of the waiter carriers' names, for example, the names can be
compared to those women who are recorded in nineteenth-century town

council records as having received snack vendor licenses. Following the faint traces in this archive gives us some specificity: without this article, the picture of women on the tracks would remain one of nameless, unknowable figures. The newspaper interview with Edwards ensures that the women in the photograph, their backs to the viewer, do not remain anonymous, but instead are included in a traceable history.

Additionally, living sources reveal that the hotels and restaurants were not exactly in "competition," as the businesses tended to draw different clientele. Transactions depended on how much a passenger was willing or able to pay. The waiter carriers were more economical than the restaurants and hotels. As one individual familiar with the vendors' history told me about hungry passengers, "the wealthier people would just walk to the hotel." And yet, despite the difference in cost, there was still some concern about the women's business being in competition with the more formal restaurants.

Spatial politics impacted where and when the waiter carriers could sell food. According to the three last surviving women who worked as waiter carriers, the women sold in the least favorable spaces: the "outside" of the tracks, or the "back side" of the train or platform—that is, the nonstandard spaces that one would consider to be valueless or inferior—"to avoid interfering with the transfer of baggage and passengers." On Sundays and weekends, presumably when train traffic was lower, waiter carriers were allowed on the platform to sell. This was not necessarily a privilege. According to one of the surviving waiter carriers, "I believe we had more sale[s] on the back side than on the front." By being on the tracks, the waiter carriers had more immediate access to those passengers who, not partaking of the comparatively higher-priced meals at the St. John's or one of the other two nearby hotels, wanted to purchase ready-to-go meals and food items. Additionally, railroad porters would open the train doors for the passengers, enabling them to buy from the waiter carriers.[69]

In 1948, the former waiter carriers who were still alive were interviewed, and they discussed their past experiences; they described the system of "gestures" that offered some form of protection from the state health inspector. As Mrs. Bella Winston stated, "you could buy [the inspector] with a bag of chicken—and he wanted the best, too. But I said to myself, 'Let him send me home. God promised me a living.' And I kept on and never gave him any chicken."[70] The health inspector, from Richmond, made a decided impact on Mrs. Winston. Interviewed again in 1970 about her past experience as a food vendor, Mrs. Winston recalled that this inspector "used to make me so mad that I would cuss and I would cry."[71] She believed he just wanted to determine the women's recipe for frying the chicken. Perhaps Mrs. Winston was herself aware of the power of record creation. In both interviews, she refuses to reveal the health inspector's name.

There were unintended consequences of forcing the women to stop selling. Those local merchants who depended on the waiter carriers for their own business suffered when the women were banned. The waiter carriers did not raise the chickens they cooked ("us waiter carriers didn't have time to raise our own chickens, cook and meet the trains, all!") but instead bought cooking supplies in the town and purchased flour, lard, and nearly "1,000 chickens each week." The economic exchange, however, ended with the ban: "It sure did knock Gordonsville when we had to stop. Them merchants used to sell out."[72] All of this information comes out only through the interviews, which offer a more vivid depiction of the waiter carriers and describe their daily experiences.

Comparing the versions of progress presented in "Gordonsville and Its Future" with the lived experiences of the waiter carriers captured in print, perhaps here, one can posit a different definition of "progress," one that, rather than centering technological ingenuity or the railroad's speed and efficiency, instead includes such considerations as a researcher's ability to identify and individualize subjects like these women, so that they do not remain unknown.[73] Progress, then, occurs when African American women can be identified in an otherwise evanescent archive. This "progress," is not engendered by their forced obsolescence but is a more accurate, firsthand recounting of the women's experiences. Progress lies in the information conveyed in the newspaper articles that helps individualize and identify the women with the kinds of details that earlier records disregarded.

The erasure of waiter carriers from the train platform corresponds to their similar displacement in the archive of American railroad history. How do we come to know these women who provided services to the railroad? How, in other words, is the past remembered in the archive? Country depots are now gone, remodeled as museums or renovated into entirely different kinds of eating establishments. But the historical trace of waiter carriers remains in a diffuse collection of ephemera such as the newspaper articles that celebrate their cooking, in the images that emphasize how they occupied a marginal space, in the minds and memories of once and still living archives such as Hattie Edwards and Gloria Gilmore, and even in the tourist information that the town of Gordonsville now uses to attract visitors to the annual "Fried Chicken Festival" every May.[74] Ironically, the most forgotten of Black railroad women are the ones who summon most effectively the relationship between the train and the archive: The "archive" of the waiter carrier is open, amorphous, much like the space of the platform itself.

4 Handmaidens for Travelers

Archiving the Pullman Company Maid

Interviewer: Was there just one maid to a train?
Albrier: One maid to each train.
. . .
Interviewer: So there were many porters—
Albrier: Yes.
Interviewer: And many waiters and cooks, and the one woman.
Albrier: One woman, yes.

—Frances Albrier, Pullman Company maid,
  Interviews of the Black Women Oral History Project (1977)

The Newberry Library in Chicago holds a collection of employee cards in nondescript gray and brown boxes. Approximately four by six inches, the cards document the performance of the people who worked for the Pullman Palace Car Company. The cards, some with small ID photographs attached, list the biographical information and brief work history of people long associated with the railroad and romanticized in books, on film and television: the conductors, the white men who organized and collected passenger tickets; the engineers, the white men who drove the train; and the porters, the African American men who interacted with passengers and who, in addition to the many other services performed on the train, shined shoes for tips to supplement their wages. Several cards form an unexpected group: interspersed among the cards for porters are a few with women's names, having the job of "maid," African American women, some identifiable with the small photographs. Who were these Pullman maids? Why did Black women decide to work for the Pullman Company? What kind of experiences did they have on the railroad? And why, when the Pullman employee or when

Figure 4.1: A Pullman Company maid with Pullman Company porters (Hooks Brothers Photographers, Memphis, TN). Photograph courtesy of Dr. Earnestine Jenkins, Department of Art, University of Memphis.

African American railroad labor is discussed, is the figure of the Pullman maid so infrequently mentioned?

The story of the African American Pullman porter resonates powerfully in African American culture. In 1867 George Pullman hired formerly enslaved African American men to work in his railroad sleeping cars. The men were ideal as porters because, as noted by a company historian, they were "trained as a race by years of personal service in various capacities."[1] Pullman sleeping compartments contained special berths that could be used as seats during the day and transformed into small beds at night. Preparing the beds was an important part of the porter's job, and porters supplemented their modest wages with tips. They were constantly abused—both by the company and by passengers. After several failed attempts to unionize in the early twentieth century, the porters found a leader with A. Philip Randolph. As the head of the Brotherhood of Sleeping Car Porters and Maids (BSCP), Randolph obtained recognition of the BSCP by the American Federation of Labor (AFL) in 1937, becoming the first African American–led union to do so. The efforts of the BSCP to organize enabled Randolph to secure better working

conditions for porters and prepare the groundwork for the civil rights movement of the 1950s and '60s. These political successes complemented the high
social status most porters enjoyed in African American neighborhoods and
communities. The Pullman porter was a standard bearer: numerous prominent Black men had worked as a Pullman porter or in some other capacity
in a train compartment, including the cowboy Nat Love, author and film-
maker Oscar Micheaux, the poet Claude McKay, U.S. Supreme Court Justice
Thurgood Marshall, the BSCP organizer C. L. Dellums, photographer Gordon
Parks, and Malcolm X.[2]

    This is a familiar narrative of an important group in American and African
American labor history, but it is a chronicle that occludes the women who
worked as Pullman maids. Rather than continuing to repeat the customary
story of the African American porter, a narrative that has its own striking
mobility in American culture,[3] I analyze the experiences of the women who
worked for the Pullman Company and the way they have been archived in
Pullman Company files.[4] In chapters 1 and 2, I examined the first-class train
compartment as a travel space only reluctantly granted, if at all, to middle-
class African American women as a "ladies' space." Here I complicate the
spatiality of the train compartment, viewing it as not just a travel space that
confirms or contests class identity or a space within which Black women
measure the progress of the nation, but also as a work site in which the travel
needs of white passengers and the customer service concerns of white managers conditioned the labor of African American women. Simultaneously
a leisure travel space and a worksite, the Pullman sleeping car complicates
my earlier discussions of travel and Black female mobility by studying the
enclosed area from a Black female worker's perspective. How does inhabiting
the space of the train car change when the traveler is a worker, not a passenger, and when the space is a not a Jim Crow car but a luxurious Pullman
Palace Car? How does the gender and racial analysis of the compartment
space change when the site of *leisure* is based on the Black woman's *labor*?

    Although the historical record is not complete, some elements of the
women's experiences do become apparent within the massive Pullman Company archive. Two types of documents, when read against each other, give
some indication of the experiences of Pullman Company maids. The Pullman Company's *Instructions for Maids* pamphlet and the document used
to note any deviations from the high standards for good service, the maid
employee card, hint at the maids' complicated interactions in a predominantly white space. These company documents, when read in light of the
larger history of corporate communications, provide an alternative archive of
those women who, for a variety of reasons departed from Pullman Company

rules. Employee cards tell the limited narratives of women who worked in a Pullman compartment. By reading these materials, I demonstrate both the maids' attempts at autonomy in a space that was highly surveilled and the complicated intersections of race, space, gender, and power in the Pullman train car, perhaps the most fraught of all the travel spaces discussed in this book. By reading the Pullman maid through two spaces, the space of the train compartment and the space of the archive, her neglected narrative comes into view, showing yet another aspect of African American women and American railroad history. Who enters—and can maintain an uncontested presence—in either space shapes what we know of the African American female travel experience, just as the way in which the company archived the records of maids structure what we can now know, or not know, about these African American women.

This chapter benefits from George Pullman's conscious efforts to determine how he and his company would be remembered and the documents the company used to ensure quality service and productivity from those workers who had the most contact with the traveling public. Evidence of the Pullman Company's efficiency and modernization can be found in the meticulously detailed records for nearly all aspects of the business, in some-times mind-numbing minutiae: construction of cars, when and where cars were built and for whom, when the cars entered and went out of service, the names of each car and its routes. George Pullman also maintained a series of scrapbooks while he was alive, large bound volumes that recorded every mention of the company in the newspapers in his city of Chicago and across the United States. These records are held at the Newberry Library, which obtained the business files when the Pullman Company began to disband in the late 1960s.[5] The Newberry's plain brown or gray boxes, a library's own version of portable compartments, record Pullman's corporate efficiency and determination to develop "corporate memory."[6] With its own printing and photography departments, the Pullman Company generated reams of paper and information on its employees, especially African American workers. Because the company was in the late nineteenth and early twentieth centuries one of the largest employers of African Americans in the country, its archives have become a valuable repository for African American genealogy.[7]

Here, near the end of this book, is a tantalizing paradox. Having contended earlier with Black women's absence in the historical record, here at last is a searchable, and sizable, archive of documents, reports, facts. The Pullman Company's inquisitive desire to know, to categorize, to itemize, as well as its emphasis on tracking service quality among porters and maids, generated a wealth of material on African American workers.[8] And yet the quantity of porters' records makes the search for maids more difficult: one must pore through the massive number of documents, always on the lookout for a brief reference or citation to a maid. In some cases, it is necessary to read in and through the margins. A look at several pages from the Porter Application Register explains this method (fig. 4.2). The register is a bound volume that contained the names of each Pullman Company porter who applied for and received a position, the date he began service, and the area of the country in which he served or was anchored.[9] The researcher glances through the register and reads page after page of men's names, until, sometimes in parentheses,

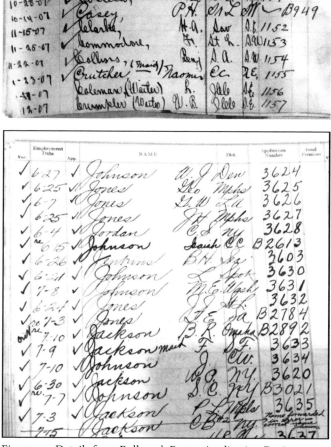

Figure 4.2: Details from Pullman's Porter Application Register. Pullman Company Archives.

the word "maid" demurely sits, between columns of other information. The company did not systematically document maids in its records.

The way the Pullman maids have been recorded in the Pullman Company Archives, then, almost ensures their erasure, dispersed as they were within the larger archive of porters. This dispersal is just one of the many reasons to highlight when trying to explain the omission of maids in the standard histories of African American Pullman workers. A more pragmatic reason is the fact of sheer numbers: there were always far more porters than maids. Where there may have been anywhere from two to five porters on one line of a train with Pullman compartments, there was usually only one maid for the entire train, as depicted in the photograph that opens this chapter.[10] In addition, Pullman porters framed their narrative for improved economic conditions as a story of the acquisition of their "manhood rights." A position with the Pullman Company, for example, was a rather lucrative job for African American men, but it enforced subservience in exchange for tips. Porters were able to enjoy travel, but it also required long hours and for them to work off the clock. Before the AFL recognized the BSCP, porters were not paid for the time they worked preparing the berths assigned to them. Their paid workday started not when they boarded to prepare a compartment but hours later when the train departed a station.[11] One of the more common complaints porters had was being called "George" by passengers, after George Pullman. These and other demeaning interactions between white passengers and Black porters impacted Black masculine selfhood. There were important benefits to presenting the porter's labor challenges in terms that supported the development of racial manhood. Historian Beth Thompkins Bates argues that by categorizing labor issues in this manner, the BSCP earned "buy-in" from the African American middle class in Chicago, where the largest number of Black Pullman workers resided.[12] But as both Bates and Melinda Chateauvert note, because women involved with the BSCP "defined their gender interests mainly in racial terms as they worked with black men to improve the place of black Americans," the emphasis on manhood rights did not draw attention to the issues specific to African American women workers.[13]

This chapter on the Pullman Company maid has been difficult to write because of several archival and ethical considerations. Not only did Pullman's recording practices make it harder to find information on maids compared to conductors and porters, but if I looked at employee cards as compressed biographies of these women, how do I also take into account the possible biases of their anonymous supervisor?[14] How was I to interpret the hierarchies that appear in the employee cards, the statements from supervisors that are less concerned with objectivity than with the maid's value in relation to the Pullman passenger? How can the researcher use the archived business document to shift the perspective from that of the supervisor or passenger to that of the employee?[15]

Go Pullman: An Overview of the Pullman Compartment

Pullman cars were leased from Pullman by a railroad line. To ride in a Pullman, the passenger paid a fare in addition to the cost of the ticket. Pullman sleeping cars were distinguished not only from standard train cars but also from sleeping cars created by such rivals as the Buffalo, New York–based Wagner Car Company and the southern-based Lucas Car Company. In many ways, the Pullman sleeping car was even better than the first-class ladies' spaces described earlier. A description of the Pullman compartment, archived in one of George Pullman's scrapbooks, highlights some of its amenities: "The woodwork in the interior is mahogany throughout, handsomely decorated and embellished with inlaid work of different colored hard wood. The seats are upholstered in crimson plush. In the forward-end of the car is a dressing-room for ladies, which is fitted up with every convenience. Adjoining this is a small drawing-room . . . which is handsomely furnished and so arranged that it can be cut off entirely from the main saloon."[16] Pullman offered leisure for the long-distance railroad passenger. Before the Pullman sleeping car, U.S. train passengers bemoaned the discomfort of cross-country travel. The Pullman compartment was different from standard train cars, as noted in one of the earliest news reports on George Pullman's improvement on the sleeping car design. Pullman's design allowed the passenger "to *enjoy* a night's rest on the cars, proceed on your journey with all the speed of flying wheels, the while you recline upon a comfortable couch."[17] Pullman's design success can be measured by the rapid growth of the company into a national corporation. In railroad history, the development of the Pullman sleeping car stands as a notable advancement—"progress," for the long-distance train traveler. There was something imperial about the Pullman Company, its reach symbolized by the multiple uses of the name "Pullman." By the end of the nineteenth century, the company was so pervasive in U.S. culture that Pullman was a noun (Pullman Company), an adjective (Pullman porter), and a verb (to "go Pullman").[18]

Although there was distrust between the Pullman Company and Black Pullman workers, the Pullman car itself was an important resource for the African American traveler. For the late nineteenth- and early twentieth-century African American train rider, the Pullman Car was less a luxury than a safety precaution. By paying more to ride in a Pullman car, Black travelers could avoid hostile or even violent passengers who opposed their presence in first-class railroad spaces. Yet white riders challenged even this privilege. In 1903, when the governor of Tennessee initiated a law prohibiting African Americans from traveling in southbound Pullman cars, Booker T. Washington campaigned against it. Working with W. E. B. Du Bois, Washington wrote to Robert Todd Lincoln, President Lincoln's son and the president of the Pullman Company since George Pullman's death in 1897: "You have no idea what a great injustice will be done our people and what suffering will be caused if your company were to yield to the wishes of some of the more prejudiced and narrow-minded people."[19] Although Washington claimed to have "found no trouble in securing accommodations in the Pullman palace cars," his statement was in stark contrast to another African American traveler who, responding to Washington's request that he give a speech at Tuskegee, "enquire[d] as to whether [he] can come through to Tuskegee on a Pullman Car, and escape both the Separate Car Law and the roughs who, judging from reports, sometimes invade the Pullman and take passengers out, and force them into the 'Jim Crow' car."[20]

The Pullman Company's profitability hinged on the people who provided quality service: the porters—and maids—who catered to the traveling public in the company's upholstered compartments. These service workers interacted with passengers and were vital to the Pullman Company's success, especially in the 1920s. Two documents that track how the maids provided service within the compartment—the Pullman maid instruction pamphlet and the Pullman maid employee card—together demonstrate how the Pullman maid contributed to the company's success. Progress in the form of luxury or better conditions for travelers came at a high cost to these women.

Handmaidens for Travelers

The Pullman Company's porter service was important in making its sleeping car the favorite of the traveling public. One late nineteenth-century Atlanta newspaper, for example, distinguished the Pullman Company from its rivals by noting the difference in the quality of each company's porters.[21] Wagner Car porters were "offensively familiar and inattentive to business. The sleepers are stuffy and unwholesome with the same remark true for the porters."[22] The best service was anonymous and quiet, as performed by the Pullman porter. Similarly, the company marketed its maid service as distinguishable from other rail lines and an example of the refinement and luxury available on the Pullman car.

Present on Pullman cars as early as 1901, maids serviced the most exclusive train lines.[23] The *Pullman News*, the official in-house journal for the company, highlighted the women who worked as "Handmaidens for Travelers."[24] Maids worked on "all the celebrated limited trains" between Chicago and New York "to the Florida East Coast, from Chicago to the South and to the Pacific Coast and the Northwest," and trains charted for special occasions by organizations or companies (fig. 4.3).[25] Ads suggest how the maids created a sense of opulence for female passengers.[26] To demonstrate "some of the comforts found in the new Pullman Car," the *Pullman News* included several images of a maid attending to female passengers.[27] Just as Pullman porters received tips by doing favors and by shining shoes, the Pullman maids earned tips by performing manicures and styling hair (figs. 4.4 and 4.5). Applicants for the position of a Pullman Company maid indicated these beauty skills by writing "beauty culturist" on their application form (fig. 4.6).[28] The company provided curling irons to the maids and trained them in first aid so that they could take care of "children, babies, and elderly people."[29] Other images showed the maid entertaining white children by reading the newspaper to them. The addition of maid to the long list of amenities available on a Pullman helped to distinguish the company from other sleeping car businesses. "Progress" and luxury on the Pullman car came in the form of Black female assistance. Throughout the 1920s and early '30s, Pullman maids, along with porters were mentioned in a column in the African American newspaper, the *New York Age*. There readers learned about "Things Seen, Heard, and Done Among Pullman Employe[e]s," such as a maid's suicide or a maid being shot

Figure 4.3: "Twelve New Efficient Maids on Florida Limiteds." *Pullman News*, January 1924, 288. Pullman Company Archives.

Figure 4.4: A Pullman maid gives a female passenger a manicure. Great Northern Railway Collection, Minnesota Historical Society.

Figure 4.5: A Pullman maid styles the hair of female passengers. Great Northern Railway Collection, Minnesota Historical Society.

several times.[30] The women working as maids were furloughed in the 1930s as a result of the Depression and their numbers continued to dwindle into the 1940s; maid service ended on Pullman cars and trains by 1958.[31]

Frances Albrier, one of the few women to be interviewed about her time as a Pullman maid, offered some insights about the job. Many of the women

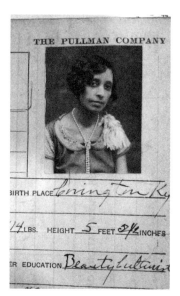

Figure 4.6: The applicant notes her education as a "beauty culturalist." Detail from a Pullman maid application. Pullman Company Archives.

Figure 4.7: A Pullman maid reads to two white children. Great Northern Railway Collection, Minnesota Historical Society.

who became Pullman maids learned about the position by word of mouth. Albrier had heard about the post from another maid who noted that Albrier's nursing skills would be valuable to the company.[32] The application and selection process for porters, and eventually for maids, was rigorous and intrusive; the company even inquired into the living arrangements of its Black employees. The company's application procedures considered their suitability for work in the train compartment as well as the tidiness of the prospective workers' homes. Investigators were sent to porters' and maids' homes to see how clean and orderly their residences were. The company required references from neighbors and former employers for the past three years of employment, preferably at least five employers and preferably from white employers, with the race of the referent noted in the application file with a small "w" or "c." Because of concerns about the sanitary conditions of the compartment space, Pullman porters also had to undergo a physical examination to ensure they were not ill or contagious; by 1927, maids also had to complete a health screening and an examination in which they were asked about their menstrual cycle and any pregnancies.[33]

Most Pullman maids had some form of education. Frances Albrier had a nursing background and degrees from Tuskegee Institute and Howard University. Having worked as a Pullman maid from 1926 to 1931, she recalled: "That was a very nice position. I call it position because I met so many fine people."[34] She spent her first year working as an emergency maid "running wild." "Wherever there is a need for a maid, you were to go." On one "running-wild" trip, Albrier met Governor Franklin Roosevelt and Eleanor Roosevelt. Albrier obtained a permanent position as a maid on the Sunset Limited, running from San Francisco to New Orleans; on one of those trips, she met her future husband, a porter. Although Albrier helped organize the BSCP in California and invited the porters' wives to hear A. Philip Randolph when he spoke in California, she noted that some maids on the East Coast were worried that joining the union would cost them their jobs. In order to conceal her union membership, she paid her dues out of New Orleans, "because they couldn't see my name on a list." Significantly, Albrier credits her work with the BSCP as preparing her for her later organizational and political work in the Bay Area. Albrier's interview is remarkable because there are few firsthand accounts of Black women who had worked on trains, and her interviews from the 1970s are among the few interviews with a former Pullman Company maid. In a telling indication of the lost history of this occupation, Albrier revealed her Pullman maid experiences offhandedly while discussing her work in Bay Area women's clubs and as a politician.[35]

The Material Culture of Maids: Employee Cards

Pullman's emphasis on exceptionally high standards of service, especially by those who came into frequent and close contact with the paying public, required careful oversight of those employees' interactions. An early historian of the company, Joseph Husband, notes that "such standards of personal service cannot be quickly developed; they can be achieved only through years of experience and the close personal study of the wide range of requirements of those who are to be served"—and one could add, close accounting of those who are to do the serving.[36] For the Pullman Company, the employee card was one such method of evaluating good, or bad, service.

JoAnne Yates and Lisa Gitelman detail the relationship among bureaucracy, authority, and "paper knowledge," and they provide some context regarding how to read the Pullman documents. Yates traces the history of business communications, noting how business discourses were forms of managerial control and representation. The dissemination of documents helped the business entity to both inform employees about company protocols and to instill a type of corporate memory that facilitated the transmission of knowledge from employee to employee. This "control through communication" increased a business's efficiency. In *Paper Knowledge*, Gitelman studies four types of documents. I am most interested in her discussion of the "job-printing" document with numerous blanks to be filled in by a supervisor or some other person, facilitating rapid and verifiable information and enabling "corporate speech proper to the conduct of businesses of every sort." Gitelman states more succinctly that "blanks make bureaucracy, directing and delimiting fill-in entries that form the incremental expressions of the modern, bureaucratic self."[37] While Gitelman's description of the "modern, bureaucratic self" describes the manager, a type of mediator between an executive-level administrator and an office worker or laborer, I am interested in using employee documents to trace the activities of the worker, specifically, the Pullman maid. Although Yates and Gitelman do not extend their analysis to the evaluation of the employee, "paper knowledge" embodied in the job-dependent document usually also enabled knowledge of the employee, information about mistakes or errors that could be taken down to mark, punish, or reprimand. If the Pullman Company employee cards were a type of "corporate speech," what did they say and to whom?

The Newberry Library's vast Pullman Company files detail the ordinary communications about and recordings of the Pullman Company worker. What can we learn about maids from the company documents? I examine employee cards, not to learn about the corporation but to ascertain the "identity" of the employee, as recorded by the Pullman supervisor. I place "identity" in quotation marks for a variety of reasons, not least of which is the highly contingent presentation of an individual by an employer or supervisor. The character of an employee is even more open to fabrication, as recorded, observed, or complained about by the Pullman supervisor or passenger, particularly in a company in which there was chronic tension, if not outright hostility, between white management and African American service workers. The benefits of the job-related document for a business as identified by Yates—objectivity, efficiency, reproducibility—could work against the Pullman maid or porter. Indeed, Pullman Company documents indicate how the "paper knowledge" that enabled efficiency for supervisors may have compromised the autonomy of Black female maids.

The Pullman employee cards enabled a segmented assessment of the service qualities of the Pullman maid, offering compressed, biographical facts, or problematic employee histories. Collectively, these items and the women's personal accounts of working on the train complicate Pullman's advertised sense of leisured domesticity. The appearance of the Pullman maid employee card reveals just how much the status of the maid was, at times, a bureaucratic oversight. Approximately four by six inches, on white cardstock, the cards were printed with a Pullman employee's role stamped in the left-hand corner. Perhaps most illuminating about the Pullman maids is the fact that the company did not print cards specifically for the maids. Instead, two of the most significant positions in the company—porter and conductor—had printed employee cards. To document a maid's service, Pullman supervisors or others scratched out "porter" and "conductor" and wrote in "maid" (fig. 4.8). Not printing employee cards for Pullman maids may have been a cost-saving measure and provides further evidence of the relatively low number of maids employed by Pullman compared to the other occupations.

The card detailing the maid's labor in the train car is itself compartmentalized, with her service to the Pullman passenger and her compliance to Pullman rules logged for commendations or penalties. The largest sections of the card, the area with the most space, were the sections that recorded those activities. There was a duality to the Pullman Company's employee card, literalizing what Lisa Gitelman has called the "know/show" function of a document: factual information on one side, contested information on

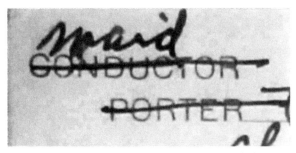

Figure 4.8: Pullman did not print employee cards for maids. Pullman Company Archives.

the other.[38] On the front of the card, basic biographical information was listed, such as the employee's name, birthdate, birthplace, contact information, and next of kin. These data were important for those maids working as "emergency" personnel, filling in for someone who failed to report for an assignment. The front of the card also detailed the person's hiring date and company property, such as curling irons, the maid had to return on departure from the company (fig. 4.9, top). Some cards indicate whether or not the maid signed a "loyalty pledge," an assurance made to the Pullman Company in 1927 that the employee would abide by the company's union representation.[39] Any special ability that the maid possessed, such as nursing or manicuring skills, along with any "distinguishing marks," were also noted.[40] The bottom

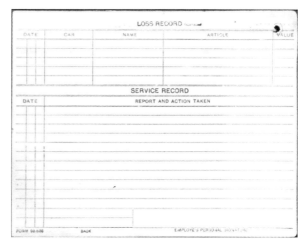

Figure 4.9: Front and back of a Pullman employee card. Pullman Company Archives.

of the front of the card and the top of the back were dedicated to the "loss record": a list of items that a passenger reported as lost during the trip (fig. 4.9, bottom).

Also on the back of the card were comments on the employee's interactions with passengers or comments from supervisors or conductors. Significant space was devoted to the "service record," permitting more subjective evaluation of the maid's performance. Positive encounters appeared to have been acknowledged with a "credit letter" and the name of the passenger making the commendation. Warnings and reprimands were listed here as well, such as the one of a maid who had an "extremely insolent and insubordinate attitude" toward the conductor and a "failure to benefit [from] previous warnings."[41] Reprimands were given for not reporting into work on time and suggests the Pullman Company's reach into its employees' personal lives: one maid was reprimanded several times, for example, for not calling in to see if the company needed her services, even though she explained that she was traveling to see her mother, on Christmas Eve.[42] The loss record and infractions written on the cards raise several questions. How did the passenger know that the conductor, porter, or some other passenger did not take the missing item? What happened if the lost object was "found" later but not in the maid's possession?

As Yates's history of business communication reveals, railroads and related businesses were some of the first in the United States to use "communication as a tool of management."[43] Railroads, because of their wide geographical operations and need for accurate information to ensure passenger and worker safety, systematized internal communications.[44] Although the Pullman Company was not a railroad but a manufacturer of sleeping cars, it also developed methods to relay company and employee information up and down the company ladder. An important element of business communications was what Yates calls "corporate memory," the writing down of rules and protocols to create an institutional memory. But how does corporate memory interact with the kind of information collected on Pullman employees, particularly the Pullman maid? How did corporate communications, such as the employee card or an instruction manual instill authority and control? Scholars have argued that the Pullman Company instructed average Americans on how to enjoy mobile luxury. Sara Blair, in her reading of Henry James' experiences in a Pullman compartment, notes that porters "train[ed] white America . . . in the freedoms of managerial and social mastery."[45] For the price of a ticket, middle-class white Americans could experience the comfort of a Pullman car. One could argue that Pullman was perhaps an even better, if not more rigorous, instructor of its Black employees, particularly Black women.

Pullman regulated both the physical space of the Pullman car and the bodily movements of its Black workers with the card and instruction pamphlet.

Perhaps the best texts to highlight the management of Black bodies within the Pullman compartment are from the Pullman Company itself: the Pullman rule books, issued to all employees. As Amy Richter notes, these books "marked the transformation of courtesy from a personal attribute of gentlemen" into "a list of tasks to be mastered."[46] Conductors, porters, and engineers each had their own job-specific manuals. The manuals were small enough to be placed in a pocket, as if a tangible, constant reminder of the service the employees were expected to perform. A porter, for example, would be expected to know, in detail, everything in the rule books for porters and conductors, on handling Pullman linen, and on safety and sanitary regulations. The rule books provided for "the codification of politeness" and "the regimentation and predictability of service."[47] This Taylorization of subservience and etiquette standardized the interactions among people located in a space that, other than the hoped-for punctuality of the train itself, could be susceptible to the unexpected.[48] Detailed rules enabled Pullman service to be replicated in train compartments all across the country. The guidebooks listed the functions porters and maids were expected to perform, any deviation from which could lead to infractions for failing to provide service "the Pullman way." Rule books and manuals were forms of what Yates calls "downward communication" that also helped to establish corporate memory. I would argue that the rule books were more; they were Pullman imperatives controlling Black movement and spatial politics.

In his "sensory history of race," Mark M. Smith identifies the white anxiety that was a cultural paradox of racial segregation in the South: "Whites relied upon black labor, and that dependence often allowed for a degree of intimacy and physical proximity that collapsed racialized space."[49] What were interactions like in the "collapsed," insular space of the Pullman car, that necessitated frequent contact between passengers and workers? How did collapsed space intersect with gendered isolation? The rule books were one way to manage and regulate the insularity in a Pullman compartment, regimented instructions to placate a traveling white public and remove any possibility of conflict from interactions with Black employees. Issued at the peak period of maid service in 1925, the four-page *Instructions for Maids* contained seventeen rules that covered nearly every aspect of Pullman maid service, from the appearance of uniforms to the way they should assist female passengers (fig. 4.10).[50] The Pullman Company rule book for maids constructed and organized social hierarchies. The pamphlet shaped not only the maid's actions but also her interactions with other railroad employees and

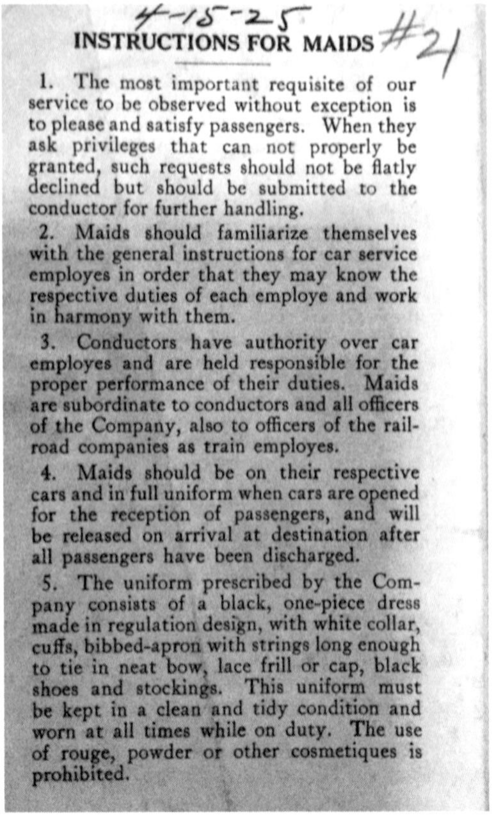

4-15-25

INSTRUCTIONS FOR MAIDS #2/

1. The most important requisite of our service to be observed without exception is to please and satisfy passengers. When they ask privileges that can not properly be granted, such requests should not be flatly declined but should be submitted to the conductor for further handling.

2. Maids should familiarize themselves with the general instructions for car service employes in order that they may know the respective duties of each employe and work in harmony with them.

3. Conductors have authority over car employes and are held responsible for the proper performance of their duties. Maids are subordinate to conductors and all officers of the Company, also to officers of the railroad companies as train employes.

4. Maids should be on their respective cars and in full uniform when cars are opened for the reception of passengers, and will be released on arrival at destination after all passengers have been discharged.

5. The uniform prescribed by the Company consists of a black, one-piece dress made in regulation design, with white collar, cuffs, bibbed-apron with strings long enough to tie in neat bow, lace frill or cap, black shoes and stockings. This uniform must be kept in a clean and tidy condition and worn at all times while on duty. The use of rouge, powder or other cosmetiques is prohibited.

Figure 4.10: Page 1 of Pullman's four-page *Instructions for Maids* (1925). Pullman Company Archives.

passengers. Read in conjunction with employee cards, and an anonymous grievance letter, the Pullman Company's *Instructions for Maids* demonstrates how Pullman circumscribed Black female mobility within the compartment space.

The first rule suggests the delicate position any service employee occupied, whether Black or white, in a Pullman car, and appears in other Pullman Company instruction books: "The most important requisite of our service without exception is to please and satisfy passengers. When they ask privileges that can not properly be granted, such requests should not be flatly declined but should be submitted to the conductor for further handling."[51] There is some tension in this first rule. Although it recognizes that some requests cannot be reasonably fulfilled, the assumption is that a Pullman employee should not immediately deny such requests. While the rule acknowledges the burden of making difficult decisions regarding passengers' requests, such decisions reside primarily with the conductor, limiting the decision-making abilities of porters and maids.

In their pointedness, the rules betray the hierarchy of racial and gender power in the confined space of a compartment and the organization of mobile bodies therein. The pamphlet makes clear where maids are in the chain of command of the train car and among Pullman employees. As noted in rule 3: "Maids are subordinate to conductors and all officers of the Company, also to officers of the railroad companies as train employees" (1). The *Instructions for Maids* pamphlet makes clear that the African American maid was the lowest employee on the train car. The pamphlet also identifies the Pullman maid's main role as caretakers for women and children. The maids were especially important when, as highlighted in the *Pullman News*, bathrooms for women were installed on Pullman cars. Rule 7 required maids to keep bathrooms "scrupulously clean."

Reading *Instructions for Maids* helps to decode certain aspects of the maids' employee cards, offering a context for the reprimands written on the back. The "instructions" become another kind of "guide," not only for training maids but also on how to decipher the cards. In her essay on female absences in a transatlantic archive of slavery, Saidiya Hartman notes that it is the female figure who departs from or refuses to abide by established protocol who makes herself known in the archive. Girls or women are recorded only when "an act of chance or disaster produced a divergence or an aberration from the expected."[52] African American women who diverged from the detailed *Instructions for Maids* stand out in the Pullman archive.

Some identifiable qualities of individual maids become apparent through their employee cards. I was interested in the departures from standard protocols of one maid in the Western Division of the Pullman Company. The backs of Maid P.S.'s employee cards, for example, document common infractions, such as "failing to keep the women's restroom clean" and complaints of "indifferent service" from a female passenger (fig. 4.11). Several entries reveal that this maid tended to use her time on the train to read. Typed entries note that the maid was "disinterested in work . . . spends about 50% of time in women's lounge reading." Another entry is a report from a conductor who "found maid sitting in car working puzzles"; a later entry states that "she was seen sitting in section giving herself a manicure." The repeated infractions raise the question of why she was not fired or suspended from service; her card indicates that, despite all of the reprimands, she was not fired but furloughed along with most maids in the 1930s. Although it is dangerous to speculate about these partial, fragmented work histories, one finds in this employee card the possibilities available for a maid who created her own breaks in not-so-subtle defiance of the *Instructions for Maids*.

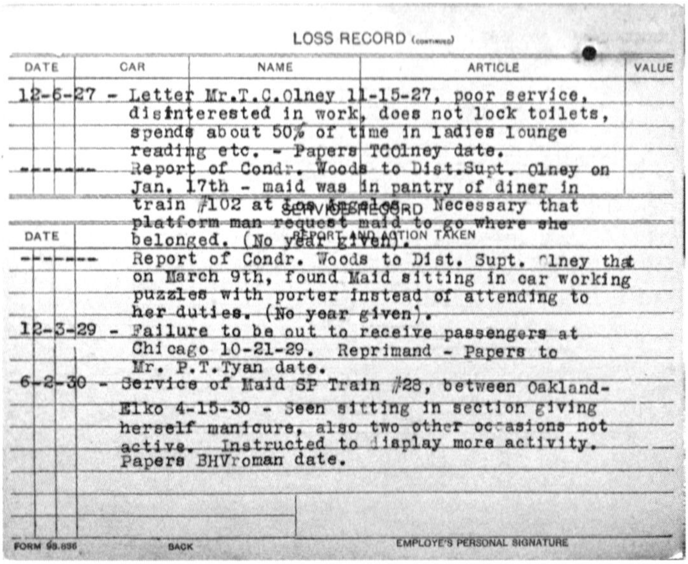

LOSS RECORD (continued)				
DATE	CAR	NAME	ARTICLE	VALUE

```
12-5-27 - Letter Mr.T.C.Olney 11-15-27, poor service,
          disinterested in work, does not lock toilets,
          spends about 50% of time in ladies lounge
          reading etc. - Papers TCOlney date.
------- - Report of Condr. Woods to Dist.Supt. Olney on
          Jan. 17th - maid was in pantry of diner in
          train #102 at Lynchburg Necessary that
          platform man request maid to go where she
          belonged. (No year given)
```

| DATE | | | REPORT AND ACTION TAKEN | |

```
------ - Report of Condr. Woods to Dist. Supt. Olney that
          on March 9th, found Maid sitting in car working
          puzzles with porter instead of attending to
          her duties. (No year given).
12-3-29 - Failure to be out to receive passengers at
          Chicago 10-21-29.  Reprimand - Papers to
          Mr. P.T.Tyan date.
6-2-30 - Service of Maid SP Train #23, between Oakland-
          Elko 4-15-30 - Seen sitting in section giving
          herself manicure, also two other occasions not
          active.  Instructed to display more activity.
          Papers BHVroman date.
```

FORM 98.696   BACK   EMPLOYEE'S PERSONAL SIGNATURE

Figure 4.11: A Pullman Company maid received several reprimands for such violations as "reading," "working puzzles," and "giving herself a manicure." Employee card of Maid P.S. Pullman Company Archives.

Aberrations: Maids N.P. and E.W.

Some documents in the Pullman maid's archive are at odds with the others. Maid N.P. submitted a handwritten work history. Census records reveal that N.P. was born in Duvale County, Florida, in 1888. To be hired as a Pullman maid, N.P. had to account for her past work experiences, explain why some of her references were hard to contact, and detail why there was a gap in her work history, or "an aberration from the expected."[53] In a six-page letter to her supervisors written in pencil in cursive, on lined tablet paper, N.P. explains her background and her circumstances.[54] N.P. details that she moved frequently, making the location of her past employers hard to determine. Her past work, in fact, consisted of helping other people pack up and move, the reason she gives for the difficulty of providing references. Because she was the only single (female?) in her family, she was also responsible for taking care of her ill mother in her married sister's home. An unsigned evaluation written on the top of the first page of the letter, in a different hand than hers, and likely written by a supervisor, states "Just fine Best we had Clean and smart and does good work." When N.P.'s references were contacted, all of them spoke highly of her. On its own, N.P.'s autobiographical work history is explanatory, credible, and ordinary, striking only in how it may have reflected the circumstances of many African American women during the Great Migration.

But N.P.'s employee card tells a contradictory tale. In March 1926, someone notes on her card: "3-31-26—Complaint of Cond. J.P. Kennedy relative to [N.P.] failing to abide by rules in instruction book and acting sulky and insubordinate. Warned."[55] One is left wondering which one of the seventeen rules N.P. "failed to abide," since the complaint states nothing aside from "acting sulky and insubordinate." What was the form and manner of insubordination? Did Maid N.P. have any recourse to contest this complaint? Or was the conductor's reproach final? This note on N.P.'s card also implies how much authority conductors had over maids, as stated in rule 3.

Instructions for Maids regulated the maids' appearance. Rule 5 stipulates: "The uniform prescribed by the Company consists of a black, one-piece dress made in regulation design, with white collar, cuffs, bibbed-apron with strings long enough to tie in a neat bow, lace frill or cap, black shoes and stockings. This uniform must be kept in a clean and tidy condition and worn at all times while on duty. The use of rouge, powder or other cosmetiques is prohibited." The lack of makeup may have intended not only to maintain uniformity in maids' appearances but also to prevent their physical enhancement. Perhaps this rule also explains the specificity with which one supervisor records the sartorial infractions of one Pullman emergency maid. The reprimand was recorded with unusual detail on the back of a card. The emergency maid worked on the Century Limited, based out of the New York Division, and, instead of putting on the uniform described in the pamphlet, this maid donned her own set of clothes: "while oper'g on Cen'y Maid wore silk dress, grey shoes & stockgs and short sleeves[.] Maid claims just before arr'l of Cent'y Chgo she took off her unfm and put on grey shoes and stockgs and a black canton crepe dress with ¾ sleeves[.] Maid warned[.]" Several things stand out here. First, there is the detail with which the writer notes the maid's clothes—it is not a simple "out of uniform" note but a concise rendering of her fashion infraction. Why does the supervisor, or whoever typed in this reprimand, offer so much specificity about the maid's clothes but abbreviate certain words while noting the violation? There is also a question regarding the sequence of the maid's actions: before the train arrives, she puts on her gray outfit that so offends the supervisor, so why get out of uniform *before* the train arrives? The conciseness of the information hints at a history of disagreement between employee and supervisor, some tension that may explain the imperative written in a large scrawl on the front of the maid's employee card: "Do not re-employ under any circumstances."[56] The maid's "aberration" from the instructions issued to maids was not so much an act of chance but rather a studied deliberation. This employee card, then, appears to record dueling intentions: the intentionality of the emergency maid's actions and the intentionality of recording her departure from the expected. Although Lisa Gitelman argues that there is no "author" of the business document as the term is conventionally understood, the personality of both the writer and the employee come through, as clearly as the maid's clothes.[57]

Rule 5 also stands out while looking at the identification photos attached to some of the cards. What first resonated with me when I encountered the maids in the archive were their ID photographs, what art historians have called "vernacular photographs," defined by their emphasis on use value. The photos are "efficient, cheap, and simple."[58] They are "not made for an artistic context," rather "the aesthetic or expressive considerations of image making are secondary to their functional uses."[59] Even though the photographs are black-and-white images of the women, usually in their Pullman uniform, individuality and difference come through in some of these photographs. While some women seem to be wearing the Pullman uniform, others are highly stylized and fashionable, suggesting that some women may have sent in their pictures as part of the application, while other photos may have been taken before the uniform was issued. Take, for instance, the ID photograph for Maid N.B.C. (fig. 4.12).[60] She smiles confidently into the camera and not only wears makeup but also has her hair textured or finger curled. When we recall the specificity of rule 5 in *Instructions for Maids*, women like maids

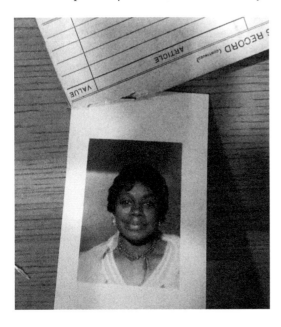

Figure 4.12: Photo ID for a Pullman maid. From the employee card of Maid N.B.C. Pullman Company Archives.

N.B.C. and E.W. (the maid who wore a silk gray dress) appear to be "an aberration from the expected." The ID photos are important because they individualize the faceless number and statistics of earlier discussions of Pullman maids, when they did occur, and bring to life the information on the employee cards.

The Maid's Letter

The spatial hierarchy of the Pullman compartment, outlined in *Instructions for Maids* and recorded on the employee card, also appears in an anonymous maid's grievance letter, one of the more unusual documents in the Pullman Company maid's archive. The letter concerns rule 11, regarding when maids should aid the conductor in collecting female passengers' tickets. The rule directs the maid's actions and movements: when needed, maids were to walk ahead of the conductor, to ensure that all passengers, even women, paid their fare. Only another woman, the Pullman maid, could enter a female passenger's space such as the women's bathroom, to do so. In a missive dated March 31, 1928, a maid on a southern line wrote to R. J. Ruddy, the Pullman Company's Chicago District superintendent, to voice her complaint about the behavior of a train conductor as she performed this task:

> Leaving Miami, Florida March 23, 1928, line 530 enroute to Chicago, Illinois Central, on the night of March 25, as was the usual custom, I was preceding the conductors in collecting the tickets. A passenger in the compartment car in which I was passing, stopped me and asked for a hat bag. While I stopped to give this passenger this service, the train conductor and Pullman conductor got in front of me. In an effort to pass them—get in front of them again where I should have been, I started forward and the Pullman conductor stepped aside to let me by, but knowing the disposition of the train conductor, I thought I would wait until he was ready, before attempting to pass him. While I was standing there, the train conductor, without any provocation, turned very suddenly and in the most bitter and angry manner, hollered, "Well, you or I one will have to clear out of here."[61]

The maid and conductor continued to have disagreements during the trip, with the conductor wielding his authority—within the compartment and outside it, with other railroad officials—over the maid. A Pullman inspector was on the train at the time and the maid reported this incident, as well as a "previous incident," to him. When the inspector departed the train, the conductor retaliated and, as the letter writer details, "came to me very roughly, using many curse words and informed me that he stood very strong in Fort Pierce, Florida and that he was going to have me taken off." That night, after the maid retired to a berth, the conductor pulled the curtains of her berth open. The maid hid in one of the rear cars, but the conductor made good on his threat. At Fort Pierce, "the sheriff and several of his men and the station master came through the train to take [her] off." The letter closes with a request: "on account of the above happenings, to me, I would prefer not to run south any more."[62]

There is much about this letter that is odd. There is no evidence, for example, to determine if, in fact, the letter was mailed or received.[63] There is precision in the opening lines—almost as if the letter writer were trying to conform to the expectations detailed in *Instructions for Maids*. It confirms, that is, that the maid did precisely what was expected of her. The letter provides just enough concrete information to corroborate the train, the route, and the date but lacks the names of the two conductors and the porter. Finally, there is no signature or name on the typed letter. Where the maid's name would appear there is instead an empty line, a blank—who, if anyone, alerted the superintendent to the conductor's behavior?[64] And why, finally, was this incomplete letter kept, preserved—archived? A fugitive letter of grievance, did the document even reach Pullman's Chicago office? How was it decided which archive would be the letter's termination point? Why the BSCP archive in the Chicago History Museum and not the Pullman Company archive at the Newberry?

The concisely formulated protocols in *Instructions for Maids* place the letter into context. The anonymous letter details the practical applications—and implications—of the maids' instructions, not only rule 11, but also rule 14, which states that "maids will sleep in accommodations designated by the conductor." With only *Instructions for Maids* as a guide, and without any additional context, the anonymous letter documents the deep psychic costs of being the only Black female worker in the Pullman car. The letter renders palpable a racialized and gendered anxiety, a letter demonstrative of a counter-archive, a letter perhaps suggesting a story the Pullman Company didn't want known.

A Marginal Archive

Some questions are not answered within the archive or in the finding aids associated with the Pullman Company records. Did the maids, for example, have access to their cards after they filled in the biographical information? A card that instructs someone *not* to inform a maid about a pension ("No advice concerning her retirement should be given to her") suggests that the cards were not routinely shown to them after the basic information was entered.[65] In addition, there are maids who are even more difficult to locate than the African American Pullman maid: the Asian American maids who primarily worked on the western lines. Here, again, this group of maids becomes apparent by chance: in this case, through a disagreement between a Black maid and a Chinese American maid. The dispute between the Asian and Black maids was recorded on the Black maid's employee card: The Black maid, according to a supervisor, wrote a "letter criticizing Chinese maids," using a false name, perhaps that of a passenger. The maid "denied writing this letter, of course, but handwriting corresponds exactly with her time slips." The Black maid was "dropped" from service.[66] Although names of Chinese American women appear in the porter register, I did not locate photographs, employee cards, or applications of these women in Pullman's voluminous Newberry records. The Chinese American woman may be the most absent figure in the Pullman maid's archive.

Fully placing Pullman maids into the larger story of the Pullman Company and its relationship with Black workers presents a counter-archive of Black women and railroad history. Trouillot illuminates how the production of history depends on many elements: not only the material objects or documents that are collected and saved as part of a historical event, to be included in an archive, but also the narratives that are then constructed from those artifacts. Both moments of origination—the initial moment of the collection of artifacts and the inaugural narrative told from those artifacts—are open to rereading. Trouillot's point is evident with the Pullman Company archive. The fact that the women of this chapter lived during the twentieth century is telling of the still difficult work of filling in the lives of "ordinary" Black women, during a period more conducive to recordings than earlier periods. Of course, it is not possible to know the "real" stories of these women, not only because of archival absences but also because of the women's dissemblance that may have protected them while they were alive but renders them obscure in the present.[67]

One final reason for the Pullman maid's previous obscurity involves a coincidence of timing. Just when the BSCP, which advocated for better working conditions for the Black Pullman worker, enjoyed its most important success, recognition by the AFL in the 1930s, the BSCP changed its name from the Brotherhood of Sleeping Car Porters and Maids to the Brotherhood of Sleeping Car Porters. The elision of this part of the organization's name, occurring during a period in which an increasing number of maids were furloughed in the late 1930s, cements what would become the cultural amnesia of the Pullman's "handmaidens for travelers."[68]

Terminus

Pauli Murray, Pete, and Jane Crow

> I knew nothing would stop [Pete] from trying for that train. . . . He
> had always had a secret ambition to do some expert train-nabbing
> and cop-dodging. He wouldn't be satisfied until he could boast of
> nailing a freighter on the fly.
> —Pauli Murray, "Three Thousand Miles on a Dime
>   in Ten Days" (1934)

By centering the Black female subject in transportation history,
Riding Jane Crow tells an alternative story of the American railroad imaginary—the collective memory of and sustained narratives about the railroad
that have been fundamental to conceptions of U.S. national identity. Placing Black women at the center of the train's imaginary within U.S. national
consciousness forces a revision of the familiar story of U.S. ingenuity and
progress. Indeed, as the various women in the previous chapters illustrate,
Black women's experiences on the railroad question the mythology of progress that has become so embedded in the narrative we tell about the United
States. *Riding Jane Crow* creates a counter-archive of the American railroad
by broadening our perspective of the American train, showing how African
American women experienced this technology and engaged with its symbolic meanings. In relating this counter-narrative, the existing archive, in
its literal and metaphorical versions, is as significant a structure as the train
compartment. Both are contested spaces of memory and identity, problematic
spaces with a history of denying full and unconditional admittance to African
American women. By telling the alternative stories—ejected from the space
of the compartment or occluded within the space of the archive—*Riding*

Jane Crow fills in the gaps and reveals another narrative of the railroad in American culture.

To conclude *Riding Jane Crow*, I continue probing this relationship between archive and travel, identity and space. This terminus, the final stop in the book, explores the implications of the knowledge found within the archive, the identities constructed within or adjacent to the train compartment, and the relationship between the two. That the individual most responsible for coining the term "Jane Crow" also embodies the engagement of travel, identity, and the archive offers one of the most fitting conclusions to this counter-archive of Black women's travel narratives.

So many of Black women's encounters on the railroad have been fraught with anxiety. One claim I make throughout *Riding Jane Crow* is that women of color, especially African American women, have been denied the "feeling of forgetfulness" so routinely celebrated in men's real or fictional travel narratives. Although this book contends with the railroad's delights and dangers, for African American women the dangers far outweigh the delights. Pauli Murray, however, had some joy on the train, and, notably, a divergent gender identity contributed to it. A figure now more readily discussed, particularly in light of several books on Murray's life, career, and friendships, Pauli Murray developed the concept of Jane Crow in a variety of contexts.[1] *A Song in a Weary Throat* (1987), Murray's posthumously published autobiography, details how and why she came up with the term and how she in particular experienced the restrictive elements of Jane Crow. Murray's first awareness of how sexism limited women came as a student at Howard University Law School in the 1940s. There, in a predominantly Black male space, "the factor of gender was fully exposed" (237). Murray was one of two female law school students in her first-year class, an experience that revealed Jim Crow's "twin evil of discriminatory sex bias" (236).[2] More legally informed analysis of Jane Crow appeared in Murray's scholarly writings, such as a 1965 law review essay Murray cowrote with Mary Eastwood, "Jane Crow and the Law: Sex Discrimination and Title VII." The article detailed "the ways in which the Fifth and Fourteenth Amendments and the sex provisions of Title VII could be interpreted to accord women equality of rights" (472).[3] Murray continued criticizing the effect of Jim and Jane Crow in legal work for the Presidential Commission on the Status of Women and as a cofounder of the National Organization for Women (NOW).[4]

Recent scholarship on Murray has tried to expand the term Jane Crow from its legal usage. Tracing the long genealogy of Black female intellectual thought, Brittney Cooper redefines Jane Crow as "a sociospatial race and gender formation," as a way to discuss the strategies Black women use to navigate inhospitable spaces. According to Cooper, the term describes how Murray "reasoned from race, through American peculiarity, toward a profoundly queer and embodied conception of what it meant to be Jane Crow."[5] As I've shown, Black female intellectuals and activists repeatedly drew on their travel experiences to theorize about Black femininity in the United States, to critique the limitations to their literal and figurative mobility, and to demonstrate the lack of respect accorded to them, compared to white middle- and upper-class women. Read in this alternative formation, Jane Crow is not only a legal term used to expose the gender dynamics of racism and systemic oppression; here, at the end of the line, Jane Crow also describes a queered form of mobility, specifically, a queer, pleasurable form of travel that Murray experienced while presenting as male and that is preserved in Murray's private papers.

My interest in Murray, then, lies not only in the term Murray defined but also in Murray's travel experiences as archived in published writings and personal papers. Before Murray embarked on a remarkable legal career and before an ordination as an African American Episcopal priest, Murray had several notable travel experiences. Three railroad incidents from Murray's early life, all recorded in Murray's published writings, foreground the anxiety of Black female passengers on trains and the performative component of safe travel. In contrast, Murray's private accounts of travel experiences with women to whom Murray was sexually attracted, preserved in personal photos and scrapbooks, materialize the embodied interiority of the train compartment and the triangular matrix of travel, identity, and the archive. Murray's private writings, photographs, and scrapbooks are one of the few places where we find pleasurable Black (fe)male train riding. By reading the public and private travel accounts together, the significance of Murray's male identity while traveling becomes apparent.

An explanation is needed about my use of pronouns to refer to Pauli Murray in this conclusion: The discussion of which pronouns to use when writing about Murray has arisen in recent scholarship. It did not escape me that, much like first-class, second-class, and Jim Crow passenger cars, pronouns confine an individual's identity into comfortable and familiar categories, with limited abilities for degrees of difference. Earlier scholarship on Murray used the female pronoun, with perhaps the unintentional effect of portraying Murray as a cisgender woman, as Naomi Simmons-Thorne notes.[6] Scholarship on Murray's private papers reveal that Murray may have had a gender expression that was female and a gender identity that was male.[7] In that case, had Murray remained alive to witness the growing acknowledgment of nonconforming gender identities and the success of hormone treatments to help people fully live their gender identities, Murray would have likely adopted male pronouns. I have adopted a hybrid method of pronouns when discussing Murray, guided by Murray's choices in public and private writings: I use female pronouns for both the young and mature Murray and as indicated in the autobiography, but masculine pronouns when discussing Murray's travels, particularly when Murray crossed the country by train riding, as Murray's personal papers indicate that Murray actively identified and presented as male during these trips. Admittedly, this makes talking about Murray's train riding as a pleasurable "female" travel experience a paradox, but this seeming contradiction is my larger point, as I believe Murray's masculine identification contributed to the moments of pleasure we see in his travel episodes.[8]

Much about Murray's early train trips echo the experiences of the women described in this book. Like nearly every figure discussed in *Riding Jane Crow*, Murray details the intentional infliction of hurt and humiliation from others while traveling and the lack of national courtesy away from home. When Murray was nine years old, she traveled by train from Baltimore to Durham, North Carolina, with Aunt Pauline, Murray's surrogate mother. The two were going to visit her ailing grandfather. Murray and her aunt had to carry their luggage almost a mile to the station. On the way, Aunt Pauline fell on the pavement and broke her glasses; some of the shards cut into her cheeks. As Murray writes: "Two white men sat on the curb nearby, watching us passively. They continued to sit without moving, and when we turned toward them they looked the other way" (*Song*, 38). Like Anna Julia Cooper, who experienced "the old whipped-cur feeling" of "wounded sensibilities" when she was denied travel courtesy as a Black woman, Aunt Pauline was also injured.[9] Murray continues: "I knew how deeply she had been hurt in another way when she sighed, 'To think, those two white men saw how helpless I was and sat right there. They never made a move to lend a hand'" (*Song*, 38).

Train travel also strengthened the young Murray's racial consciousness. After arriving at a train station in Norfolk, Virginia, Aunt Pauline left her to get tickets to continue their trip south. In an episode reminiscent of "the first time the Race question was brought home" to Mary Church Terrell, a "red-faced white man" approached and stared intently at Murray who, in fear, could only stare back. Without her glasses, her aunt could not tell that she had left Murray in a whites-only waiting room. Although there was no confrontation, the aunt and niece later sat in the Jim Crow car "tense through the night" and unable to sleep. Like Terrell, Murray was indelibly affected: "The incident awakened my dread of lynchings, and I was learning the dangers of straying, however innocently, across a treacherous line into a hostile world" (*Song*, 38).[10]

The most significant period of Murray's train riding, and gender questioning, occurs in the 1930s, the period of Murray's multiple hitchhiking and cross-country trips and an early publication of an account of those trips.[11] In 1931, at the age of twenty, Murray and an acquaintance drove from New York to Vallejo, California. This transformative cross-country adventure showed Murray "the changing face of the vast United States. . . . Each hour was filled with wonderment over the miles of flatland" (*Song*, 101).[12] Unfortunately, Murray was in California for only a few days when Murray received a telegram stating that Aunt Pauline was sick. With no money, Murray had to return east by hopping freight trains. Murray recounts that return trip in two works: "Three Thousand Miles on a Dime in Ten Days," published in 1934, and *Song in a Weary Throat*, published in 1987.[13] The version in Murray's autobiography is straightforward: Murray travels by freight train, finding comfort and safety in being able to pass as a boy: "No one questioned me about my gender and I soon discovered that my boyish appearance was a protection" (*Song*, 102). Murray links the ride by freight trains to the experiences of hobos, the thousands of boys, girls, and young adults who survived the Great Depression by hopping trains.[14] The cross-country trip gave Murray a temporary sense of freedom and independence; Murray concludes the episode in the autobiography with the feeling that the event "had satiated my wanderlust" (*Song*, 82).

The adventure is also recounted, with significant changes, in "Three Thousand Miles on a Dime in Ten Days," where an unnamed male narrator and his friend Pete hop freight trains from California to New York so that Pete can return to his ailing mother.[15] The danger that Pete and the narrator encounter consists of both possible dismemberment by falling under the train when trying to jump aboard and the threat of train cops. Other freight hoppers told stories about Black men who had been lynched on the very lines they were riding. In the compartment, situational riding lost its potentially divisive force as all the hobos in the freight car faced the same deprivations. Outside the freight car, however, class, racial, and age-related hierarchies remained. The thrill of adventure common in early accounts of train travel is finally apparent here, romanticized, with the train personified as female: "Pete leaped the fence. I followed. . . . I jumped [the train] on the fly—she threw me. I hung on desperately with one hand. . . . I felt myself going, my hand was slipping. If I let go, it was sure death" ("Three," 69). The boys finally reach the Jersey Yards and, with their single dime, pay their way past the turnstiles of the Seventh Avenue New York City subway.

Questions abound in Murray's brief, curious narrative. He experiments not only with identity and gender but also with genre and form: is it a short story or an essay? The tale appears in Nancy Cunard's magisterial anthology, *Negro* (1934), with a photograph of "Pete"—who is, it turns out, Murray in a Boy Scout uniform. As explained by Rosalind Rosenberg in her biography of Murray, "Pete was Pauli's fearless twin, her daredevil foil."[16] Although the narrative was published in *Negro*, the tale does not explicitly disclose Murray's or "Pete's" race. Cunard herself remarked in a letter to Murray that "Three Thousand Miles" was the only contribution in the volume that was not a "purely racial piece of writing."[17] As Doreen M. Drury notes in her analysis of the different recountings of Murray's trip from the West to the East Coast, the fictional version—the one in which Murray is Pete—is "the richer story."[18] Like a twentieth-century Ellen Craft, Murray travels safely while presenting as masculine, but, unlike Craft and the other Black women discussed earlier in this book, Murray also manages to "satiate" a feeling of "wanderlust."

The Private Murray

The two public accounts of Murray's west-to-east movement are illustrative of how Murray edited details to create less controversial accounts of an intimacy with women and to modulate a male identity. Murray is more forthcoming about an attraction to women in private papers, scrapbooks and photo albums, places where Murray's masculine identity is foregrounded and a desire for women acknowledged. There is a distinction between the public-facing presentation of Murray, the Pauli Murray who emerges in published writings, and the private Murray that is assembled in the scrapbook pages. Murray's private papers and scrapbooks tell an even more candid narrative of wanderlust, facilitated in part by Murray's identification as male.[19]

It is perhaps expected that the private papers reveal a different side of Murray. But this acknowledgment is important because of what Murray discloses in those papers. Two aspects of Murray's identity that he worked to conceal publicly are apparent in his personal archive: Murray's repeated hospitalizations for "breakdowns after each love affair has become unsuccessful" and Murray's identification as male.[20] In a careful reading of Murray's diaries, notes, and papers written during these hospitalizations, Drury demonstrates how Murray did not consider the terms "homosexual" or a "lesbian" for himself but rather a "latent heterosexual male," primarily attracted to feminine women.[21] During the hospitalizations, Murray investigated the possibilities of being injected with hormones to more fully inhabit a male identity. The private papers show a frank acknowledgment of maleness, also revealed in the private accounts of travel.

A photograph album in Murray's archive at the Schlesinger Library pre-serves and displays Murray's love of travel and Murray's identification as male. In the album, "The Life and Times of an American Called Pauli Murray," Murray documents eight different "Moods and Facets," helpfully illustrated with photographs of a young Pauli.[22] One of these personas, "The Vagabond," is the same photo that had been published with "Three Thousand Miles on a Dime in Ten Days" and identifies Murray as "Pete."[23] He wears the clothing that biographers have identified as a Boy Scout's uniform—short leggings tucked into long socks that allowed for easy movement—Murray's clasped hands over a bent knee suggesting his confidence and comfort.

This album also memorializes Murray's friendship with Peggie Holmes, a young white woman that Murray met at the Camp Temporary Emergency Relief Administration (TERA).[24] Located in upstate New York and developed as part of a federal New Deal program, Camp TERA provided exercise, art,

Figure 5.1: This image appeared with Murray's narrative "Three Thousand Miles on a Dime in Ten Days" and in a photograph album as one of Murray's "Mood and Facets." The Vagabond, Pauli Murray Papers, Schlesinger Library, Radcliffe Institute, Harvard University. © by the Estate of Pauli Murray, used herewith by permission of the Charlotte Sheedy Literary Agency Inc.

and outside activities to unemployed women. Murray arrived at the camp in November 1934 and departed the camp after three months in early 1935, forced to leave because of a "personality clash" with the camp director.[25] While there, Murray became close friends with Holmes, who shared Murray's interest in poetry. Murray and Holmes traveled together in April and May 1935 and again in 1937, and he recorded the 1935 trip, publicly, in the autobiography, and privately in a diary and with photographs in "The Life and Times of an American Called Pauli Murray." When Murray discusses the outing with Holmes in *A Song in a Weary Throat*, Murray is somewhat nonchalant about the trip. In a mere two paragraphs, the reader learns about the young adults' journey from New York to Nebraska and back again, an innocuous adventure of two friends who wanted "to see the country as inexpensively as we could live in one place" (*Song*, 127). The diary entries, however, reveal some "problem" that they have at the start of the trip and that the trip was supposed to resolve: "Still scared about the trip. Wondering if we're doing the right thing. Have no way of knowing yet. At least we're trying to solve our problem in the best way possible." Murray is sometimes oblique about their encounters with racism during the trip in the diary: "Refused service in small town of Roseville, Ill. Held and questioned next morning. One armed sheriff. Race again." Trains provided both shelter and transportation for them. They slept in boxcars (though Murray notes one night that "the trains woke us all in the night"), and occasionally either one or both travelers fell "off the roof" of a boxcar or freight. Significantly, the train cars Murray and Holmes rode were freights and not the passenger cars that were overdetermined by class considerations. Here, the negative element of travel away from one's home community—"white people think their Negro is the fairest," as a character in Terrell's short story states—works in Murray's favor. Lack of familiarity with the people around them when traveling enabled Murray to present as male. The diary entries note, with some sense of pride, how he was sometimes perceived to be a boy during the trip.[26]

The freedom symbolized by the freight car is even more evident in the photographs taken on their 1937 trip. Two snapshots placed side by side in "The Life and Times of an American Called Pauli Murray" show Murray and Holmes, important images because they are active subjects, physically climbing the side of the freight (figs. 5.2a and 5.2b). The images highlight the contrast between travel within a first- or second-class passenger car and travel by a freight car. Just as Pete and the narrator in "Three Thousand Miles on a Dime in Ten Days" find themselves on the top, on the side, behind, and inside freight cars, the photographs of Murray and Holmes show them climbing over train cars. With the two wearing pants, actively jumping up or leaping down the car, class considerations are not evident in these moments, and there is a playfulness in the pictures. The freight car, as a mobile stage, enabled Murray to live out a masculine identity in ways that may have been easier than in the fixed spaces where Murray lived or went to school, such as North Carolina or New York. We can read the freight cars, and Murray's enjoyment of riding them, as one form of the "black women's geographies" articulated by Katherine McKittrick.[27] Murray's queered form of train travel offers some control over the otherwise highly contingent act of Black (fe)male train riding.

Other material in Murray's private archive link the mutability of a gender identity with the condition of travel. A scrapbook page titled "Toni's Sketchbook," named after Murray's friend Dorothy Hayden, displays elements of collage and assemblage. The page celebrating "Hobo Life" is filled with

Figures 5.2a: "Peggie [Holmes] on a coal car." From "The Life and Times of an American Called Pauli Murray" album, Pauli Murray Papers. © by the Estate of Pauli Murray, used herewith by permission of the Charlotte Sheedy Literary Agency Inc.

Figure 5.2b: "Pauli catching the old freight." From "The Life and Times of an American Called Pauli Murray" album, Pauli Murray Papers. © by the Estate of Pauli Murray, used herewith by permission of the Charlotte Sheedy Literary Agency Inc.

ephemera from Murray's and others' travel adventures. The brief clippings all appear to comment on Murray's understanding of himself as a vagabond who experiments with the presentation of his identity.[28] The page contains a short notice of a "Girl, 22 Years Old Dresses as a Boy," placed alongside a paragraph about U.S. Texas representative John N. Garner, who would later become Franklin Roosevelt's vice president, hitchhiking for eighty miles in Texas. The scrapbook page also contains an article describing yet another Murray travel escapade: in March 1931, Murray and Hayden hitchhiked throughout New England disguised as boys. "Slip Brings Halt to Tour of Two Girls" describes how Murray and Hayden hitchhiked from New York City to Rhode Island to visit Hayden's family (fig. 5.3). The trip ended early at the railroad station in Bridgeport, Connecticut, when Hayden entered the women's bathroom, while Murray "walked boldly into the men's room" in order to "put her disguise to the supreme test."[29] A traveler's aid representative stopped Hayden, identified her as a girl, and became concerned about "the propriety of a boy and a girl hiking around the country together." When they were eventually identified as two girls, Murray and Hayden laughed off the deception, with Murray telling the reporter, "it was real good fun while it lasted. It'll make great material for the book we are going to write."[30] We could, perhaps, think of the book Murray refers to as not one of her published books but the uncensored scrapbook.

Murray's archive is the material embodiment of an imaginative interior life. One of Murray's biographers, Troy R. Saxby, considers Murray's large archive a "crowning success" in a life of achievements. Consisting of "over 135 boxes of correspondence (sent and received), diaries, short stories, photographs, medical records, school reports, legal cases, newspaper clippings, interviews," the records were a type of companion for him as Murray "lug[ged] the ever-accumulating boxes with her through a rarely settled life."[31] Due to Murray's peripatetic life, Murray's papers, photograph albums and scrapbooks were literally a mobile archive.

Murray wrote about the importance of archival research to tell an alternative story that may be overlooked in the usual history books. Having conducted extensive archival research, not only for legal scholarship but for Murray's 1956 family biography, *Proud Shoes*, Murray's comments on the archive are illustrative: Murray notes the thrill of finding items related to the family: "the past merged into the present in a continual drama of ordinary people who, although not found in textbooks, nevertheless illuminated the history of an era" (*Song*, 391). The information presented in *Proud Shoes* was available only in the "living histories" of his aunts. Although Murray recognized the importance of preserving archival material, when it came to his own life, Murray was much more cautious. Aware of the possibilities and

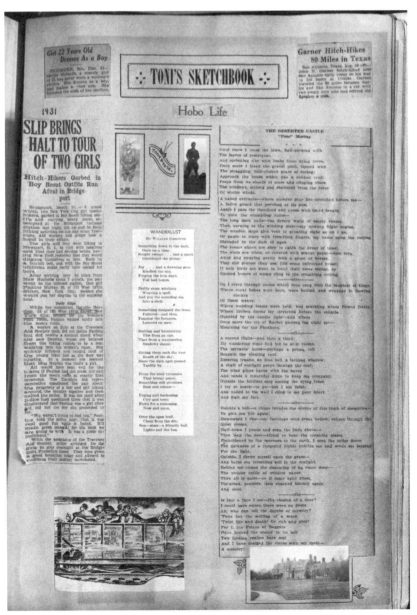

Figure 5.3: A page from Pauli Murray's "Vagabond" scrapbook with the article "Slip Brings Halt to Tour of Two Girls" on the left side of the page. Pauli Murray Papers. © by the Estate of Pauli Murray, used herewith by permission of the Charlotte Sheedy Literary Agency Inc.

limits of the archive, Murray expressed some anxiety over how he would be perceived when other people read about his life, and he had some ambivalence about the stories that would be constructed about him and his family from the material left behind. In one diary entry, for example, Murray wrote "one is apprehensive that all of the details of one's intimate private life will be spread on the record to be read, sifted, weighted, evaluated and judged by strangers."[32] Drury notes that much of Murray's archive "survived her own efforts to 'sanitize' her files in the mid-1970s and again close to her death in 1985."[33] If Murray did expurgate personal papers, it is significant that he kept the records of hospitalizations, the investigations into the usefulness of hormone therapies, and the trips taken with Holmes. One can read the photo album and the scrapbook, then, as deliberate acts of self-presentation memorializing Murray's enjoyment of travel and Murray's male identity, testifying to Murray's efforts to become more congruent with a male identity.

At the risk of romanticizing not just the pleasure of travel but also Murray's active self-fashioning, the self-presentation of travel in Murray's scrapbook, photograph album, and short story offers a more compelling insight into Murray's masculinity as linked to the joy of travel. By archiving the experience, Murray's private archive becomes a material embodiment of the freight compartment where Murray can live out loud an identity as male. Although the personal archive can be performative or fictive, Murray reveals multiple selves in the scrapbook, a very personal archive of Murray's travel experiences. Scrapbooking does not have to follow the linear storytelling one assumes in the autobiography—the straight line of rising attainment and progress that mirrors the train's rigid rails. The permanence associated with a print book gives way to the possibilities of collage and assemblage exemplified in scrapbooking. Murray's travels enabled him to present and live out the male identity that was more congruent with his own self-image. Perhaps we can even consider Murray's scrapbook, especially the vagabond pages, as an embodiment of the "stilled yet moving" quality of Black women who rode the rails.

But not even a masculine identity can fully protect Murray from danger. As stated earlier, the diary of Murray's 1935 trip with Holmes notes that they were stopped and questioned by law enforcement several times. Moreover, just one day after Murray and Hayden, dressed as boys, were stopped in the Bridgeport railroad station in 1931, nine African American boys and young men were arrested in Alabama on a Southern Railway freight train, accused of raping two white women.[34] The horror of the Scottsboro episode clashes with the image at the bottom of Murray's scrapbook page: a drawing of what

Figure 5.4: Detail in scrapbook, Pauli Murray Papers. © by the Estate of Pauli Murray, used herewith by permission of the Charlotte Sheedy Literary Agency Inc.

appears to be young boys, the wind blowing their hair away from their faces in a visual image of enjoyment, pleasure, satisfaction (fig. 5.4).

Not many accounts of train riding depict the pleasure of the Black female subject. Pleasure is occluded here in Murray's public-facing travel representations. It is significant, then, that in one of the few episodes in which an African American publicly identified woman finds excitement, risk, and adventure on the locomotive, in lines that echo the familiar American narrative of freedom and resourcefulness, the "woman" presents as a boy or a man. Both in the short narrative, "Three Thousand Miles on a Dime in Ten Days," and in the scrapbooks and photos, the more pleasurable forms of Black female travel are also the ones that are more self-constructed, nonlinear—*private*—and suggests why gratifying Black female railroad experiences are so rare—an unsettling but telling fact of the delights and dangers of riding Jane Crow.

Notes

Introduction

1. "Gourmet Express," Napa Valley Wine Train, www.winetrain.com/content/uploads/2020/09/20180822_WT_GourmetExpressMenu_2-1.pdf, accessed August 18, 2021.

2. "Our Route," Napa Valley Wine Train, www.winetrain.com/the-wine-train/our-route/, accessed August 27, 2018.

3. *Johnson, Neal, Neal, et al. v. Napa Valley Wine Train, Inc, et al.*, 2016 U.S. Dist. LEXIS 16502 (U.S. District Court for the Northern District of California, February 9, 2016, filed).

4. "Wine Train Woes Hit Close to Home," *Sonoma (CA) Index-Tribune*, August 27, 2015, www.sonomanews.com/news/4398250-181/wine-train-woes-hit-close, accessed August 27, 2018.

5. Ibid.; *Johnson v. Napa Valley Wine Train*. The book club members consisted of eleven African American women and one white woman. Since this incident, the company has changed ownership.

6. Perata, *Those Pullman Blues*; Amy Richter, *Home on the Rails*.

7. Goldsby, *Spectacular Secret*, 48.

8. See, for example, Isabel Wilkerson's discussion of the Illinois Central in *The Warmth of Other Suns*, 189–92, and Marcia Chatelain's *South Side Girls*.

9. Houston Baker, *Blues, Ideology, and Afro-American Literature*; Carby, "It Jus Be's Dat Way," 234. For Davis's discussion on this topic, see *Blues Legacies and Black Feminism*, 66–90, and especially 71–74.

10. Anecdotes of pleasurable train travel may also be found in Zora Neale Hurston's works. During her first ride on a railroad, Hurston became "crazy about the train. . . . The inside of that train was too pretty for words. It took years for me to get over loving it" (*Dust Tracks on a Road*, 113).

11. Hartman, "Venus in Two Acts"; Gikandi, "Rethinking the Archive"; Trouillot, *Silencing the Past*; Fuentes, *Dispossessed Lives*.

12. The early 1830s were an important time for railroad travel in the United States and England. In the 1830s, the Baltimore and Ohio Railroad first offered passenger travel in the United States, and in 1831 the Liverpool and Manchester Railway opened in England.

13. For more critiques of Marx's text, see J. L. Bryant, "Usable Pastoralism." Bryant claims, among other criticisms, that the book makes "broad generalizations [that] also over-simplify American history and literature" (69). For a measured critique of the significance and the shortcomings of *The Railway Journey*, see George Revill, "Perception, Reception, and Representation."

14. Marx, *Machine in the Garden*, 15, 12, 192. Marx tells the story of the appearance of the new technology in the United States and the development of a language to help describe and reflect that appearance.

15. See Erbacher, Maruo-Schröder, and Sedlmeier, *Rereading the Machine*. None of the ten essays in that book discusses the absence of slavery in the text, although Kirsten Twelbeck discusses slavery in her reading of Henry Ward Beecher's novel *Norwood* ("Eden Refounded").

16. William G. Thomas, *Iron Way*, 34.

17. Marx, *Machine in the Garden*, 10.

18. Martin Delany (1812–1885) is perhaps most well-known for his novel, *Blake, or the Huts of America*, a novel published serially in 1861 and 1862. Paul Gilroy in *The Black Atlantic* identifies Delany's important role in the Black diaspora (20).

19. Only the Confederate government—not the Union government—granted such patents. Enslaved persons who were inventive had no one other than the Confederate president, Jefferson Davis, to thank for this privilege. It was one of the first laws passed by the Confederate Congress after being recommended by Davis. See Henry Baker, "Negro in the Field." In a pamphlet, Delany also imagined the railroad as a way to colonize East Africa. In his plan, a train would cross the continent of Africa from east to west, providing a link to the Atlantic Ocean: "All the world would pass through Africa upon this rail road, which would yield a revenue infinitely greater than any other investment in the world." See Gilroy, *Black Atlantic*, 24, 21; Sterling, *Making of an Afro-American*, 139.

20. Revill, "Perception, Reception, and Representation," 47.

21. Schivelbusch, *Railway Journey*, 14, 104, 110, 92.

22. William G. Thomas, *Iron Way*, 22.

23. Slavery offered a unique labor advantage for southern railroads, as detailed by William G. Thomas: "If confronted with an unusually large harvest or a compressed and intense period of work on a railroad, [Southern railroads] could force work from women and children, extending their control over time and its restraints. Northern railroads, even with their extensive rule books, could not control time and space in the same way" (*Iron Way*, 54). Moreover, "the North and the South applied their free and slave labor to the same work on the railroads, and as a result created opposing labor systems in the most visible modern industry of the day" (47).

24. Schivelbusch, *Railway Journey*, 72–3.

25. It is interesting to consider here Samira Kawash's argument regarding the "moment of escape" in slave narratives. Examining the narratives of Henry "Box" Brown and William and Ellen Craft, Kawash notes that both narratives detail "the intermediate condition of escape" (*Dislocating the Color Line*, 64). For my argument, it is significant that these intermediate conditions take place within a train compartment.

26. Schivelbusch, *Railway Journey*, 110.

27. Ruchames, "Jim Crow Railroads."

28. I briefly discuss the significance of railroads in *Incidents in the Life of a Slave Girl* in chapter 1.

29. W. Craft and E. Craft, *Running a Thousand Miles*, 25–26.

30. Schivelbusch, *Railway Journey*, 101. See Matthew Beaumont, "Railway Mania," for further discussion of the railroad compartment as the site of murder and other crimes.

31. See also Kate Masur's discussion of African Americans occupying space in the United States Capitol after the Civil War (*Example for All the Land*, 99).

32. Wells-Barnett, *Crusade for Justice*, 171–72. See also Gary Totten's work on Wells's writings from the United Kingdom ("Embodying Segregation" and *African American Travel Narratives*).

33. Foucault, "Of Other Spaces," 23–24; Ellison, "Little Man," 504.

34. We can also consider here previous studies on the cultural intersections between technology and race, such as Lisa Gitelman's work on the phonograph (*Scripts, Grooves*); Mark Goble's analysis of modernism, the phonograph, and the production and distribution of Black music (*Beautiful Circuits*); and Joel Dinerstein's study of the train and American culture as a way to analyze other forms of technology and race (*Swinging the Machine*).

35. Pryor, *Colored Travelers*; Gilroy, *Black Atlantic*.

36. Gilroy, *Black Atlantic*, 111.

37. Jefferson, *Notes on the State of Virginia*, 228, emphasis added. Deborah Gray White notes that "For all African Americans, a real mark of liberty was to come and go at will—without white permission, without a pass, without fear of dogs on their trail" (*Ar'n't I a Woman*, 169). See also Stephanie Camp, *Closer to Freedom*: "At the heart of the process of enslavement was a spatial impulse: to locate bondpeople in plantation space and to control, indeed to determine, their movements and activities" (12).

38. See Masur, "Rare Phenomenon."

39. Washington, *Up From Slavery*, 41.

40. As one anonymous reader noted, mobility is important even in those legal cases in which it may not appear to be at the center. *Jones v. Mayer* (1968), for example, banned all race-based restriction of the right to buy and sell property. But it was also a ruling about mobility, stating specifically, "Negro citizens, North and South, who saw in the Thirteenth Amendment a promise of freedom—*freedom to 'go and come at pleasure'* and to 'buy and sell when they please'—would be left with 'a mere paper

guarantee'" unless Congress could empower that freedom guaranteed under the Thirteenth Amendment (Jones v. Alfred H. Mayer Co., 392 U.S. 409 [1968], emphasis added). As this Supreme Court case indicates, mobility, which has historically been a denied category for Black people, is a fundamental marker of modern subjectivity and autonomy.

41. Du Bois, *Souls of Black Folk*, 54.

42. Stepto, *From Behind the Veil*, 75.

43. Daylanne English notes that railroad scenes "recur so often in the African American literary tradition as to constitute stock scenes that encapsulate the always-potentially-violent intersection of blackness, law, and time" (*Each Hour Redeem*, 53–54). One could argue that mobility is a recurrent dilemma that appears even in late twentieth and early twenty-first-century fiction and poetry, particularly among African American postmodern writers. Consider the significance of travel in just three of Colson Whitehead's novels, *The Intuitionist* (1999), *John Henry Days* (2001), and *The Underground Railroad* (2016), and in Kevin Young's poetry, such as *Brown* (2018).

44. Camp, *Closer to Freedom*, 7.

45. Twinam, *Purchasing Whiteness*; A. Gross, *What Blood Won't Tell*; and Cope, *Limits of Racial Domination*. Twinam notes the qualities affected by situational differences include such characteristics as "appearance, clothing, occupation, wealth, and friends, rather than strictly genealogy or ancestry" (46).

46. A. Robinson, "It Takes One."

47. Both Booker T. Washington and Mary Church Terrell were criticized for traveling in Pullman cars. See "Denies He Avoided Race: Booker T. Washington Explains Pullman Car Trip in Texas," *Washington Post*, October 13, 1911, 10; Terrell, *Colored Woman*, 306; and May, *Traveling Black*, 93.

48. Although two of the more celebrated figures of the fugitive slavery lecture circuit, the Crafts did not escape via the Underground Railroad. The earliest known escape attributed to the Underground Railroad was described by Henrietta Buckmeister in *Let My People Go*: Tice Davids, a slave in Kentucky, disappeared from his owner. The owner claimed, "he must have escaped by some under ground road" (59). There is a fortunate temporal convergence: The origin of the term "underground railroad" was 1831, the same year as the beginning of the Baltimore and Ohio Railroad. See Strother, *Underground Railroad in Connecticut*, 12, and Ross, *Recollections and Experiences*, 2–3.

49. Sanborn, "Plagiarist's Craft," 909, 911.

50. Again, Samira Kawash's concept of the "intermediate escape" in *Dislocating the Color Line* (64) is relevant here. Geoffrey Sanborn also uses Kawash to explain his ideas of "theatricality" in the Crafts' narrative ("Plagiarist's Craft," 914).

51. W. Craft and E. Craft, *Running a Thousand Miles*, 28.

52. Ibid., 29.

53. Certeau, "Railway Incarceration," 111.

54. W. Craft and E. Craft, *Running a Thousand Miles*, 38. These encounters with white female passengers also indicate how female travel depended upon the woman's

age. When the two young white ladies "fall in love with the wrong chap"—that is, Ellen disguised as a man—they are accompanied by their father, unlike the older woman who boards at Richmond and who travels alone.

55. W. Craft and E. Craft, *Running a Thousand Miles*, 39.

56. McCaskill, "Yours Very Truly," 527n6; Ernest, "Representing Chaos," 480.

57. To continue with the language used by Amy Robinson in her discussion of racial passing, the Richmond woman is the one being "duped."

58. Traveling on a train, Freud has a disconcerting experience: A stranger enters his train car, but Freud, "to [his] dismay," realizes the unattractive man is himself; it is his reflection in the mirror—"the intruder was nothing but my own reflection in the looking-glass of the open door. I can still recollect that I thoroughly disliked his appearance." Freud, "Uncanny," 248n1. See also Marcus, "Psychoanalytic Training."

59. See also Foucault's description in "Of Other Spaces," 23–24.

60. As Blair L. M. Kelley notes about post-Reconstruction travel, "'proper' education, manners, and attire did not necessarily improve a person's status on the train, just as improvements in class standing did not improve Black chances toward full and equitable inclusion in southern society" (*Right to Ride*, 41).

61. The importance of space and citizenship status is obliquely revealed in the following exchange William has on a steamboat. He "went on deck and asked the steward where I was to sleep. He said there was no place provided for colored passengers, whether slave or free." William Craft, at this point a fugitive in the narrative, is neither. W. Craft and E. Craft, *Running a Thousand Miles*, 31.

62. Bay, "From the 'Ladies' Car'"; Bay, *Traveling Black*; Chateauvert, *Marching Together*; Kelley, *Right to Ride*; Richter, *Home on the Rails*; and Welke, *Recasting American Liberty*. My discussion of Black women and the American railroad has also been informed by the work of scholars who look at the railroad in other locations and with other racial/ethnic groups, such as Marian Aguiar (*Tracking Modernity*), Todd Presner (*Mobile Modernity*), and Manu Karuka (*Empire's Tracks*).

63. Tarpley, "Blackwomen, Sexual Myth, and Jurisprudence."

64. For more on how a "validated" Civil Rights Act of 1875 would have impacted *Plessy v. Ferguson*, See Charles A. Lofgren, *Plessy Case*, 132–37.

65. Williams-Forson, *Building Houses*. I appreciate Williams-Forson's comments and suggestions on the chapter.

66. Ruchames, "Jim Crow Railroads," 62. Curiously, just two months before abolitionist David Ruggles was forced out of a first-class car from New Bedford to Boston, an article on the "Origins of Jim Crow" appeared in the *Boston Transcript* newspaper. The article traced the beginnings—and appropriation—of T. D. Rice's performance and song from an African American. See "Origins of Jim Crow," *Boston Transcript*, May 27, 1841.

67. Ruchames, "Jim Crow Railroads," 62.

68. I am using the terms "gender expression" and "gender identity" as defined by the Human Rights Campaign. Gender expression is, briefly the "[e]xternal appearance of one's gender identity, usually expressed through behavior, clothing, haircut or voice." Gender identity is "[o]ne's innermost concept of self." In accounts of Mur-

ray's private notes during his hospitalizations, it appears that Murray identified as male and had a feminine gender expression in the autobiographical *Song in a Weary Throat*. Murray used female pronouns throughout that text. I discuss my decision to use male pronouns for Murray when discussing his private writings in more detail in the terminus. See Human Rights Campaign, "Sexual Orientation." I realize that this explanation may not prove satisfactory to all readers, but it is a clarification that I hope demonstrates my acknowledgment of and respect for Murray's concerns about gender, gender identity, and gender expression, although these specific terms were not available to Murray when Murray was alive. See also scholar Brittney Cooper's discussion of Murray. Cooper notes: "Murray's struggle was made more difficult by her acceptance of deeply entrenched and societally imposed heteronormative assumptions that made it nearly impossible for her to consider expressions of sexuality and gender that we would today call queer or gender nonconforming" (*Beyond Respectability*, 90).

69. I found this striking image in the Theodore Kornweibel Jr. Collection of the California State Railroad Museum, one of the more remarkable archives for scholars interested in railroad history, travel, and African Americans. Kornweibel's research was for his book, *Railroads and the African American Experience*.

70. Rosenberg, *Jane Crow*, 389–90n4.

71. Du Bois, *Souls of Black Folk*, 31.

72. Sundquist, *To Wake the Nations*, 500.

73. Du Bois, *Souls of Black Folk*, 31.

74. Ibid., 35, 36.

75. Carby, *Race Men*, 18.

Chapter 1. Ladies' Space: An Archive of Black Women's Railroad Narratives

1. Jacobs, *Incidents*, 173, 247–48, emphasis added.

2. Ibid., 248.

3. McKittrick, *Demonic Grounds*, 40.

4. Schivelbusch, *Railway Journey*, 37–38, 41.

5. Ibid., 64. This is, of course, only one among many reactions to train travel, or, indeed, any kind of travel. Marc Augé, for example, similarly details the internal change that takes place within the subject who travels by airplane, a mental weightlessness and "the feeling of freedom imparted by having got rid of [one's] luggage" (*Non-Places*, 2). The frequent appearance of freedom in association with the railroad indicates how prominent the idealized idea of leisured introspection is. For a detailed discussion of speed and its impact on modernism, see Edna Duffy, *Speed Handbook*.

6. Hunter, *Steamboats*, 391 n.3.

7. Buchanan, *Black Life on the Mississippi*, 168. Hunter also notes the boiler deck as a type of dividing line between crewmembers and passengers (*Steamboats*, 391).

8. Hunter, *Steamboats*, 23, 490–91. This necessarily brief history of the U.S. steamboat is derived from the following sources: Hunter, *Steamboats*; Buchanan, *Black Life*

on the Mississippi; Welke, *Recasting American Liberty*, 252–53, 259; and Bolster, *Black Jacks*.

9. Welke, *Recasting American Liberty*, 259.

10. Not referenced in the short story are the "emigrant cars," usually considered third class. These train cars derived their names from the large number of immigrants who traveled by rail westward across the United States. This was a single car pulled by various railroad lines to a final western destination.

11. By the early twentieth century, railroad cars, especially Pullman sleeping cars, were longer and larger, some cars being eighty feet in length. See Shrady, *Sleeping Car*, 5.

12. Ayers, *Promise of a New South*, 137.

13. Quoted in ibid., 139.

14. Ayers, *Promise of a New South*, 137.

15. The Fourteenth Amendment, which protects the rights of U.S. citizens and offers equal protection under the laws, and the Civil Rights Act of 1875, which prohibited segregation in public accommodations, were important tools in discrimination law-suits. The Civil Rights Act was repealed in 1883; see chapter 2.

16. Woodward, *Strange Career of Jim Crow*, 22. In his analysis of the "sensory dimensions of race," Mark M. Smith identifies railroads and railroad stations as one of the three spaces or issues that enabled white southerners to distill ideologies about Black racial inferiority (*How Race Is Made*, 60–63). The other two topics identified by Smith, "gender and lynching" and "nineteenth-century conversations about disease," also invoked the railroad. The railroad station was a frequent site of lynchings in order to enable white spectators to travel easily to lynching locations, as Jacqueline Goldsby points out (*Spectacular Secret*, 23). Whites' fiction that African Americans lacked basic levels of hygiene was one justification for segregation of the compact railroad car.

17. McKittrick, *Demonic Grounds*, xv, xvi.

18. M. Simpson, *Trafficking Subjects*, xiii.

19. Ayesha Hardison uses the term "Jane Crow" to describe a set of literary texts written between World War II and the 1954 *Brown v. Board of Education of Topeka, Kansas* decision in order to "reconsider the parameters of social realism" and to shed new light on several mid-twentieth-century "female-centered" Black-authored texts (*Writing through Jane Crow*, 411–19). Hardison draws on the writings of lawyer and author Pauli Murray, who used the term in several essays to describe "the twin immoralities of Jane Crow and Jim Crow" ("Liberation of Black Women," 186). My use describes the vexed valences of Black female travel and focuses on the specific spatial practices that shaped Black women's relationship to and experiences on the railroad in the United States. That the term can be used in both literary and spatial instances to describe the experiences of Black women illustrates how racial and sexual oppression change over time but are linked to an ongoing kernel of oppression and domination in the United States. The recurrences of Jane Crow—in different times, texts, and *spaces*—illustrate the adverse durability of this oppression. As I discuss

in the conclusion, Brittney Cooper uses the term as a description of a "sociospatial" paradigm (*Beyond Respectability*, 102).

20. Stepto, *From Behind the Veil*, 75.

21. Mann, "Railway Accident," 320–21. The train compartment helps Mann's character settle in for night travel, "full of contentment and good ideas," a satisfaction enabled by his well-furnished berth: "A real little bedroom, most luxurious, with stamped leather wall hangings, clothes-hooks, a nickel-plated wash-basin. The lower berth was snowily prepared, the covers invitingly turned back. Oh, triumph of modern times!" (323). Those white male figures who did experience anxiety on the train—for example, Charles Dickens, who was famously involved in a train accident and experienced aftershock—pinpointed their dis-ease as a function of the powerful machine itself, and not, as it does for Betsy and other African American women, from the other people on the train, especially male passengers. For more on Dickens's train accident see Nicholas Daly, "Railway Novels."

22. Washington, *Up From Slavery*, 120–21.

23. Notably, spatial metaphors permeate intersectionality. As James Bliss dryly pondered, should one consider intersectional identity "as lines on a plane or as streets on a map?" ("Black Feminism," 728).

24. May, "By a Black Woman," 129.

25. A. Cooper, "Woman vs. The Indian," in *Voice From the South*, 97. Subsequent citations appear parenthetically in the text. Lowell's (and Cooper's) reading borrows from Orientalist conceptions of the East.

26. As I note briefly in the introduction, Ida B. Wells makes similar distinctions between England and the United States when she compares the railcars of the two countries and the experience of traveling in them. That both women reference railcars in their comparison of the nations suggests the particular affronts African American women endure in this specific space and the vast differences of their experiences abroad compared to those in their native land.

27. Throughout the essay collection, Cooper's style and argument reflect the nuanced effect of the feminine presence, perhaps most memorably expressed by the "subtile [sic] exhalations of atmospheric odors for which woman is accountable, the indefinable, unplaceable aroma which seems to exude from the very pores" (92), the indefinable poise that marks a lady and inspires courtesy and kindness from others. Foreshadowing the kind of travel instruction imparted to African American women in *The Correct Thing to Do or Say*, Cooper emphasizes being "quiet and unobtrusive." Although Cooper's work, on the surface, appears to confirm the familiar "cult of true womanhood," the specific role and need for the African American "lady," as well as her subtle sarcasm about the "Southern lady," surpasses the type of femininity described by Barbara Welter. Cooper uses her conduct and her writings to exemplify the term.

28. Smith, *How Race Is Made*, 69. Perhaps another way of putting it, as Betsy remembers her father telling her, "every white man considers his own Negro the fairest" (Mary Church Terrell, "Betsy's Borrowed Baby," 8, Mary Church Terrell Papers).

29. Brown, *Correct Thing*, 46. Brown herself routinely experienced discrimination on Pullman train cars and sued. See for example, White, *Too Heavy a Load*, 92–93; and Gilmore, *Gender and Jim Crow*, 180, 185.

30. Hall, "What Can the Colored Woman Do," 455.

31. Here, it may be interesting to compare Helene's response to the conductor to a similar scene in a short story by Ralph Ellison, "Boy on a Train." Both scenes contain African American mothers trying to travel safely on a railroad. When the mother in Ellison's story has her breast touched by a white male vendor, she spits at him: "Why couldn't a Negro woman travel with her two boys without being molested?" ("Boy on a Train," 14).

32. This is yet another notable difference from Booker T. Washington's travel scenes. He tells us how while traveling in the South every white man in the train car came up to thank him for the work he was doing with Tuskegee Institute: "This was not flattery because each one of these individuals knew that he had nothing to gain by trying to flatter me" (*Up From Slavery*, 121).

33. Barbara Welke identifies "alighting," the movement from jumping on or off a street car as one of the most dangerous for women in the nineteenth century (*Recasting American Liberty*, 20–25).

34. One cannot help but compare Cooper's dismay at these signs with Morrison's perception of them in her essay, "What the Black Woman Thinks about Women's Lib." Writing about the segregated signs "White Ladies" and "Colored Women" of the mid-twentieth century, Morrison reads these signs as not "malevolent" but accurate: "White ladies" describes a femininity of "softness, helplessness, and modesty" while "colored women" describes women who are "tough, capable, independent, and immodest." Morrison's reading makes clear not only the race but also the class distinctions between "ladies" and "women." Morrison, "What the Black Woman Thinks of Woman's Lib," *New York Times*, August 22, 1971, SM14.

35. Alexander, "We Must Be about Our Father's Business," 344.

36. Berg, *Buildings and Structures of American Railroads*, 291.

37. See May, "By a Black Woman," 128, and Scruggs, *Women of Distinction,* 209.

38. Berg, *Buildings and Structures of American Railroads,* 291. A blues song made famous by Clara Smith, "The L. and N. Blues," invokes the racism of the L&N line: "Mason-Dixon line is down where the South begins / Mason-Dixon line is down where the South begins / Gonna leave a Pullman and ride the L. & N." The lyrics recognize that, once the traveler crosses the Mason-Dixon Line, the privilege of the Pullman car disappears. The lyrics—and the blueprints—register the fact of racial segregation. Lyrics quoted from Angela Davis, *Blues Legacies and Black Feminism,* 86.

39. No detailed information is available about this ejection. It was noted by a biographer, Lawson Scruggs, who wrote a brief profile of Cooper. The only other information Scruggs provides is that the person who ejected Cooper was "a white man who is by far her inferior in every respect" ("Mrs. A.J. Cooper," in *Women of Distinction*, 207–9). See also May, "By a Black Woman," 128.

40. "Betsy's Borrowed Baby," 1, 2, 15, Mary Church Terrell Papers. Subsequent references are cited parenthetically in the text. There are three earlier brief discussions of this short story. Historian Mia Bay examines the short story in the larger context of gender-segregated train cars. Literary scholar Elizabeth McHenry reads the story among other unpublished works by Terrell. See Bay, "From the 'Ladies' Car'"; Bay, *Traveling Black*; and McHenry, "Toward a History of Access." See also, McHenry, *To Make*, 215–19, 224–26.

41. May, *Anna Julia Cooper*, 17. Cooper and Terrell graduated from Oberlin with another African American woman, Ida Gibbs Hunt.

42. Terrell continues to talk about her travel difficulties in a later chapter in her autobiography and notes that she sometimes passes as white to ride in a Pullman. Like Terrell, author Alice Dunbar Nelson traveled to Talladega to give a speech in 1930, for example, and perfunctorily notes in her diary that she "did not travel J.C." Biographer Gloria T. Hull further explains that Dunbar Nelson "indulged in [a] bit of occasional 'passing' for white for the traveling convenience" (Nelson, *Give Us Each Day*, 354).

43. Terrell, *Colored Woman*, 45.

44. Ibid., 46.

45. Bay, "From the 'Ladies' Car' to the 'Colored Car,'" 151–52.

46. Terrell, *Colored Woman*, 297.

47. Ibid., 298–99.

48. Betsy, of course, is not seeking a job or a life free from white oppression like those who traveled during the Great Migration. She wants to get to school without being harassed or raped.

49. Curiously, this route would have Betsy traveling on the L and N Railroad, whose station depots are depicted in the blueprints.

50. McKittrick, *Demonic Grounds*, xxiii.

51. Howard Thurman, qtd. in Chafe, Gavins, and Korstad, *Remembering Jim Crow*, 1.

52. Richter, *Home on the Rails*, 86.

53. Schivelbusch, *Railway Journey*, 37.

54. This is reminiscent of Harriet Jacobs's Linda Brent who, while in the North takes her white female employer's baby with her on a trip to escape Dr. Flint. See chapter 40 of *Incidents in the Life of a Slave Girl* (1861). Betsy is not the first African American to pretend to be someone she's not in order to travel safely from one location to another. Frederick Douglass famously passed as a sailor on a railroad to Philadelphia to escape slavery. The conductor on his train did not carefully peruse the documents describing the sailor to whom Douglass's borrowed uniform and transit papers belonged. See Douglass's detailed description of his escape published in his third autobiography, *The Life and Times of Frederick Douglass* (1881). More relevantly, James Weldon Johnson passed as a Spanish-speaking foreigner, also by rail. On a train to his college, Atlanta University (now Clark Atlanta University), the young Johnson conversed in Spanish with his friend Ricardo to avoid removal from the first-class car in which they rode: "As soon as the conductor heard us speaking a foreign language, his attitude changed. . . . In such situations any kind of Negro will

do; provided he is not one who is an American citizen" (Johnson, *Along This Way*, 205). Johnson repeats this same phrase, nearly word for word, in another railroad incident that took place when he was older. This second time, however, the threat of a white mob at the next train station encouraged him and his fellow African American travelers, one of whom was a woman, to move into the Jim Crow car (*Along This Way*, ch. 8). Finally, Johnson's character, the anonymous ex-colored man, passes as white in order to ride south in a Pullman car. Betsy's disguise is different from these other examples in that she passes as a servant. If she appeared on the train as a college student, she would be hypervisible as "out of place." As a colored nanny to a white child, she fades safely into the train compartment background.

55. This comment is perhaps Terrell's oblique reference to Jack Johnson's own travel difficulties. He was convicted in 1913 for transporting his wife, a white woman, across state lines in violation of the Mann Act. Johnson was pardoned posthumously in 2018.

56. Emphasis in original. A search of *Harper's* archive at Columbia University reveals no correspondence to or from Mary Church Terrell.

57. Diary, Mary Church Terrell Papers.

58. See also Mia Bay's discussion of this issue in *To Tell the Truth Freely*, 120.

59. Bradford, *Harriet Tubman*, 46.

60. Painter, *Narrative of Sojourner Truth*, 125. See Painter's introduction to Truth's biography, for more on the highly "mediated" nature of Gilbert's biography and the subsequent iterations of Truth's life and speeches (*Narrative of Sojourner Truth*, xii). In recognition of this, Painter uses the term "(auto)biography" to describe *Narrative of Sojourner Truth*, and I borrow her usage here (xx).

61. See "Extracts from a Letter from Frances Ellen Watkins to a Friend," *Boston Liberator*, April 23, 1858, 67.

62. Indeed, both author William Wells Brown in the 1850s and abolitionist William Grant Still in 1859 noted Philadelphia's discriminatory railway policies, with Still claiming that "this severe proscription, for some unaccountable reason, is carried to an extent in Philadelphia unparalleled in any of the leading cities of this Union" (Still, *Brief Narrative*, 3).

63. S. Taylor, *Reminiscences*, 70.

64. Pike, *Jubilee Singers* 152–53. I thank Heather Cooper for bringing the Jubilee Singers' ejections from the waiting room and train cars to my attention. See also "More Counterfeiting," *New York Daily Graphic*, October 23, 1880, 870, for a brief news item about the singers' lawsuit, funded in part by a local colored convention. Another Black woman forced from a street car was Barbara Pope. See Jennifer Harris, "Barbara Pope."

65. The reasons for the Toomers' trip and Toomer's subsequent lawsuit against the Pullman Company are recounted in detail in Kent Anderson Leslie's biography of Dickson. Toomer's son from an earlier marriage fell in love with Dickson's daughter from an earlier marriage. The son planned to kidnap his stepsister, and Dickson and Toomer traveled to Baltimore to prevent that. See Leslie, *Woman of Color*, 119–33.

After Dickson's death, Toomer married Nina Pinchback and they later gave birth to New Negro poet Jean Toomer.

66. Chesnutt, "Plot Notes," in *Marrow of Tradition*, 215.

67. Chesnutt, *Marrow of Tradition*, 41.

Chapter 2. A Kiss in the Dark: Sexualizing Black Female Mobility

1. "Kissing in the Dark," *Bangor (ME) Daily Whig and Courier*, July 27, 1865. The report was originally published in the *Nashville Union*.

2. J. Richards and MacKenzie, *Railway Station*, 13.

3. The print may have been a part of Currier and Ives's bestselling, racist Darktown series. One website that studies the series states that "A Kiss in the Dark" was the first in the series of forty-one stereotypical images of African Americans. See http://www.booktryst.com/2011/02/dark-side-of-currier-ives.html, accessed October 21, 2021.

4. The scenes occur so often, in fact, that film historian Jacqueline Stewart categorizes them as "interracial kissing films" ("What Happened in the Transition?" 114). Other analyses of Porter's film include Lynne Kirby, *Parallel Tracks*, 98–9, 126–27; Gaines, *Fire and Desire*; Best, *Fugitive's Properties*; and Williams, "Of Kisses and Ellipses." The other films Stewart identifies as interracial kissing films are *Under the Old Apple Tree* (1907), *The Mis-Directed Kiss* (1904), and *Jack the Kisser* (1907). Historian Edward Ayers describes a slightly different train episode in which a white man mistakes a light-skinned Black woman as white and flirts with her. The woman's race is revealed when she exits the train in the Black section of a town and "none enjoyed the episode more than the ladies on the train." Ayers, *Promise of a New South*, 139.

5. Kirby, *Parallel Tracks*, 98–99.

6. Welke, "When All the Women," 278.

7. As I discuss later in this chapter, these perceptive words were uttered by the judge in Jane Brown's and Sallie Robinson's cases, S. E. Hammond, who was the judge of the Circuit Court of the Western District of Tennessee.

8. There are additional elements in the switching scenes that, because of space, I note only briefly here. The easy switching that the Black and white women perform denies the difficulties Black women experienced when trying to occupy the first-class ladies' car. The scenes also demonstrate a hierarchy of power relations between the Black and white women: if one assumes that in each episode, the white woman is the employer of the Black woman who serves as maid or nanny, the women switch places at the request (or order) of the white woman (although it is not clear in the lithograph if the women know each other or are traveling together).

9. Mencken, *Railroad Passenger Car*, 14. See also the brief reference to the ladies car, "On the Philadelphia and Baltimore Railroad," *Virginia Free Press* (Charlestown, VA [WV]), August 16, 1838. The B&O was first chartered in 1827.

10. E. M. Richards, "Our Western Correspondence."

11. "The Ladies' Car," *New York Times*, February 1, 1879. This article also demonstrates the widespread general acceptance of segregating based on gender, the author noting that the practice of setting aside a ladies' car is "a reasonable regulation which

carrying companies have the right to make to secure the comfort and security of female passengers."

12. "Separate Sleeping-Cars for Women Travelers," *Minneapolis Tribune*, July 11, 1876.

13. Richter, *Home on the Rails*, 68–72. Richter's larger argument is that the presence of women on trains forced Victorian Americans to revise ideas of separate spheres, with women in the private space of the home and men in the competitive, aggressive public. Richter's work is invaluable in showing how a form of transportation or technology, conventionally considered to be well-entrenched in a masculine domain, has been shaped by women.

14. Richter, *Home on the Rails*, 60. For more on this topic in the context of Victorian England, see Robin Barrow, "Rape on the Railway," 352.

15. Cooper, "Woman vs. The Indian," in *Voice From the South*, 89.

16. Richter, *Home on the Rails*, 32.

17. E. Higginbotham, "African American Women's History," 261.

18. Welke, "When All the Women," 266.

19. Ayers, *Promise of a New South*, 97.

20. "Women Traveling," *Memphis Daily Appeal*, April 27, 1881, 2.

21. *Brown v. Memphis and Charleston Railroad*, 4 F. 37 (1880).

22. *Brown v. Memphis and Charleston Railroad*, 7 F. 51 (1881).

23. I offer a detailed reading of *Brown v. Memphis and Charleston Railroad*. This reading, what some may call granular, is necessary I believe in order to make discernible the assumptions community residents had about Brown's movements and relationships.

24. Wharton, *Negro in Mississippi*, 85.

25. Solnit, "Walking after Midnight," 235. In other locales—and with other subjects—walking through a city harkened the emergence of modernity. Consider, for example, Baudelaire's discussion of the flaneur. Art historian Temma Balducci persuasively notes that "the influence of Baudelaire's flaneur has distorted theorizations of gender, gendered space, and the gaze" (*Gender, Space*, 1–2). One could add that the influence of the flaneur has, for the most part, occluded the theorizations of Black femininity and Black female spatiality.

26. Mitchell, *Righteous Propagation*, 109, 120; Hartman, *Scenes of Subjection*, 148.

27. K. Gross, *Colored Amazons*; Hicks, "Bright and Good Looking Colored Girl," 419.

28. Carby, "Policing the Black Woman's Body." Carby discusses the mobile early twentieth-century African American woman, primarily in the urban city.

29. This assumption can be seen, for example, in the lawsuit of Hattie Green against the *City of Bridgeton* steamer. Green sued when, in 1878, she was refused her request to sit in the first-class space on the upper deck and was ordered by the purser to occupy a cabin below deck, an area traditionally reserved for African Americans. The steamer's purser claimed that a passenger told him Green "was a person of immoral character." During the trial, the master of the steamboat claimed

that Green was "noisy and exhibited much passion; that she had been playing on the piano, waltzing around the cabin, and making herself generally conspicuous." As recounted by Welke, the captain of the steamer testified that Green's appearance on the boat led him to believe she was promiscuous. The captain claimed "I never have seen a woman on my boat whom I would suspect so quickly as this one." See *Green v. City of Bridgeton*, 6 F. Cas. 1090 (S.D. 1879), and Welke, "When All the Women," 279.

30. This depot was built in 1917, well after Jane Brown's lawsuit. The depot has been registered as a historic landmark and now houses the Corinth Crossroads Museum.

31. "Memphis and Charleston Railroad," 361.

32. Alcorn County, Mississippi, U.S. Census, 1880. Jackson had a population of 5,200 in 1880 (Hinds County, Mississippi, U.S. Census, 1880).

33. A brief note on the research sources for Jane Brown: I consulted the 1880 census for Mississippi, the Corinth 1875–76 Town Directory, and several newspaper articles. There are references to Jane Brown or her family in John T. Edge, *Fried Chicken*, 98, and Williams-Forson, *Building Houses*, 234n60. The Crossroads Museum in Corinth also has a folder of loose newspaper and encyclopedia articles on African Americans in Corinth and several of these items reference Julia or Lizzie Brown. Brown's lawsuit comes up briefly in a book critical of passenger lawsuits, *The Damage Suit Disease*. I also searched published county tax records for Alcorn county of 1890 but did not see the Brown family listed. See "Assessment," and "Alcorn County 1890 Tax List." Other work that discuss Jane Brown's lawsuit include Welke, "When All the Women," 271, 280, 305–6; Minter, "Failure of Freedom," 1001–3; and Mack, "Law, Society, Identity."

34. The last name of Julia Brown's children was Ware. The Brown women maintained a domestic space that, according to my census research, did not include any men.

35. *Brown v. Memphis and Charleston Railroad* (1880), C.C.W.D. Tenn 1880, no. 2611, trial transcript, 13.

36. *Brown v. Memphis and Charleston Railroad*, transcript, 88.

37. Ibid., 92.

38. Ibid., 85.

39. Ibid., 85, 88.

40. Ibid., 17. The Corinth City Directory of 1875–76 lists Wofford as the superintendent. In the trial transcript, Wofford is identified, somewhat illegibly, as "P.M. of Corinth."

41. Jane Brown also traveled outside of Mississippi to visit female friends in Chattanooga, Tennessee, and Huntsville, Alabama. Those trips were likewise up for interrogation in regards to Brown's chastity. Ann Leatherwood, Brown's African American friend who lived in Huntsville, was accused of operating "a house of assignation," an important point according to the railroad's lawyers because Jane stayed with Leatherwood for one week, seeking relief from the yellow fever epidemic of 1878. Although Leatherwood testified that nothing untoward happened at the house, several witnesses described Leatherwood's home as a place of prostitution, which Leatherwood

denied. Since hotels were not open to African American travelers, Brown likely stayed with these women when she traveled.

42. The phrase "just another mulatta concubine" appears in Victoria Bynum's essay about the mixed-race women in the Knight family of Jones County, Mississippi. See Bynum, "Negotiating Boundaries," 175.

43. Solnit, "Walking after Midnight," 234.

44. *Brown v. Memphis and Charleston Railroad Company*, 4. F. 37 (1880).

45. *Brown v. Memphis and Charleston Railroad*, trial transcript, 103.

46. *St. Louis Globe*, November 19, 1880.

47. *Brown v. Memphis and Charleston Railroad Company*, 7 F. 51 (1881).

48. Winschel, "John Marshall Stone." Stone served as governor of Mississippi from 1876 to 1882 and 1890 to 1896, thus during the formal end of Reconstruction.

49. *Brown v. Memphis and Charleston Railroad Company*, 7 F. 51 (1881).

50. *Brown v. Memphis and Charleston Railroad Company*, 5 F. 499 (1880).

51. Minter, "Failure of Freedom," 995. Kenneth W. Mack also cites paternalism as a factor as to why some Black middle-class women won their lawsuits ("Law, Society, Identity"). In her essay on Black female litigants, Janice Sumler-Edmond argues that "an African American woman's formula for legal success rested more with compelling facts than with a reliance on liberal judicial interpretations of the law" ("Quest for Justice," 109).

52. *Brown v. Memphis and Charleston Railroad Company*, 7 F. 51 (1881).

53. Tarpley, "Blackwomen, Sexual Myth, and Jurisprudence," 1365.

54. *Brown v. Memphis and Charleston Railroad Company*, 7 F. 51 (1881).

55. Ibid.

56. Ibid.

57. In *Up From Slavery*, Booker T. Washington humorously recounts how the power to classify and rank passengers was invested in this one railroad official. A light-skinned Black man sits in the Jim Crow car, confusing the conductor: "To solve the difficulty [the conductor] stooped over and peeped at the man's feet. When I saw the conductor examining the feet of the man in question, I said to myself, 'That will settle it;' and so it did, for the trainman promptly decided that the passenger was a Negro, and let him remain where he was" (82).

58. The railroad deposed a witness, Thomas A. Young, but Brown's lawyers had his deposition stricken from the record because, according to her lawyers, his testimony did not have any relevance to what took place on the train, so Young's testimony is absent from the trial records. Could this have been the man alleged to have "kept" Jane Brown? There are several Thomas Youngs listed in the Corinth directory of 1875–76, three years before Brown was forced off the first-class car. *Gardner and Gaines' City Directory of Corinth*, 257–91. One Thomas P. Young Jr. was the owner of the Corinth Hotel, "located immediately at the crossing of Mobile and Ohio and Memphis and Charleston Railroads" (291).

59. *Weekly Corinthian* (Corinth, MS), February 17, 1904, 3.

60. *Civil Rights Cases 109 U.S. 3* (1883); Fairman, "Civil Rights Cases," 138.

61. Discussions of the case revolve around Justice Harlan and the similarities of his dissent here with the dissent in *Plessy v. Ferguson*. See, for example, Tushnet, "To Enable the Black Race"; and Luxenberg, *Separate*. Earl M. Maltz looks at the issue of common carriers in relation to the *Civil Rights Cases* and *Plessy v. Ferguson* ("Separate but Equal"). Other scholarship on the *Civil Rights Cases of 1883* looks at the decision of Chief Justice Bradley and Bradley's dissent in the Slaughterhouse Cases of 1873. Additional scholarship that helped to shape my understanding of *Robinson v. Memphis and Charleston Railroad* include Leon Higginbotham, "Supreme Court's Sanction"; Woodward, *Reunion and Reaction*, especially 184 and 245; Hoffer, *Plessy v. Ferguson*; S. Robinson, "African American Citizenship"; and Sandoval-Strausz, "Travelers, Strangers, and Jim Crow."

62. *Robinson v. Memphis and Charleston Railroad* (C.C.W.D. Tenn 1880, no. 2611).

63. Ibid.

64. *Civil Rights Cases*, 109 U.S. 3 (1883).

65. Fairman, "Civil Rights Cases," 149.

66. Giddings, *Sword Among Lions*, 61.

67. "A Darky Damsel Obtains a Verdict for Damages Against the Chesapeake and Ohio Railroad," *Memphis Appeal Avalanche*, December 25, 1884.

68. Wells-Barnett, *Memphis Diary*, 20.

69. Wells-Barnett, *Crusade for Justice*, 20.

70. Douglass, "Civil Rights and Judge Harlan."

71. Mack, "Law, Society, Identity," 400; Woodward, *Strange Career of Jim Crow*.

Chapter 3. Platform Politics: *The Waiter Carriers of Virginia*

1. The *Oxford English Dictionary* provides some insight into the etymology of the term "waiter carrier." In the eighteenth century, a "waiter salver" was "a tray intended to be carried by one waiting on a table." Other versions of the term also imply an object used to transport food, such the term "dumbwaiter." Nineteenth-century newspapers referred to the women collectively as "the waiters" and twentieth-century newspapers identified the women and family members who "carried waiters."

2. Boyce Loving, "Fried Chicken, Ham Once Made Gordonsville Station Famous," *Charlottesville (VA) Daily Progress*, November 18, 1955.

3. In my research on waiter carriers I have not located any references to African American railroad passengers being served food by African American waiter carriers. Descriptions and invocations of the food vendors always involved a white passenger obtaining food from an African American vendor. This does not include railroad porters who received chicken from waiter carriers as a form of "thanks" for letting passengers disembark off of the train car near their location on the tracks. This is speculative but it may be because African American travelers were prone to prepare "fried chicken baskets," as Psyche Williams-Forson describes, before embarking on long distance trips, knowing that most eating establishments along their route would be segregated. See Williams-Forson, *Building Houses out of Chicken Legs*, 116. See also Mia Bay, who describes a "Jim Crow traveling kit," in "From the 'Ladies' Car," 167–68.

In John Edward Bruce's 1907 serialized novel, *The Black Sleuth*, when a train stops at Gordonsville, the Black character looks out of his window and sees "a number of colored women, with trays of fried chicken, home-made biscuits and pies of various kinds" (35–36).

4. Schivelbusch's chapter on railroad stations focuses primarily on the station as a "gateway" linking the "traffic space of the city and that of the railroad" (*Railway Journey*, 171–77).

5. See, for example, Grow, *Waiting for the 5:05*; Meeks, *Railroad Station*; E. Alexander, *Down at the Depot*; Grant and Bohi, *Country Railroad Station*; and Traser, *Virginia Railway Depots*.

6. The platform was also significant for Harlem Renaissance author Jean Toomer. As recounted by his biographer: "In 1926, while standing on an elevated train platform in New York City, Toomer suddenly went into a mystical trance that demonstrated to him the possibility of a 'higher consciousness' able to transform him into a 'radically different being'" (Rusch, *Jean Toomer Reader*, 31).

7. Jones, foreword, viii.

8. King, "Great South" (1874). This article was one in a series about King's travels throughout the New South, "to present to the public . . . the present social and political condition of the people in the Southern states," and later published in King's 1875 *The Great South*. As this chapter makes clear, references to Gordonsville, Virginia, in newspapers and journal articles repeatedly referenced the African American women who sold food at the train depot, so that, at times, the food vendors or a description of the women stands in for the town itself.

9. Hale, *Making Whiteness*, 134.

10. King, *Great South*, 113.

11. One literary description of the mixture of classes and races on the train platform comes from Charles Chesnutt's short story, "A Matter of Principle." The platform of the fictional Groveland's Union Depot confuses a character and the resulting plot depends on this misidentification. Notably, Mark M. Smith notes how crowds, such as the kind depicted in the drawing, became a coded term to express concerns about "social equality": "Immediately after the war, [whites] made unusually heavy use of a word that became standard in the segregationist lexicon for the next century: crowded. At war's end, whites began to use 'crowd,' 'crowded,' and 'crowding' as a shorthand for social equality, one they registered through bodily senses" (*How Race Is Made*, 54).

12. Additional insight to the railroad platform can also be gained by examining a similarly transient space, that of the hotel desk, "a margin that articulates vulnerabilities as well as dangers." Jann Matlock examines the cinematic scenes that take place in or around hotel lobbies, theorizing how the "way stations" help to form characters' identities in the films. We must note, of course, the obvious differences between the hotel desk and the platform: one is housed in the interior of an architectural space; the other is often external to a building, the train depot, and the railroad. But both are potentially economic areas of arrivals and departures, spaces for waiting for others

and for watching or observing the community and strangers. For Matlock, studying hotel desks is important because "identity takes narrative shape in the hotel lobby because it is exchanged—for space or services" ("Vacancies," 79).

13. Loving, "Fried Chicken."

14. Du Bois, *Souls of Black Folk*, 36.

15. My use of the term "despatialization" is slightly different from cultural geographer Katherine McKittrick's, who uses the word in terms of captivity and confinement, of not owning a space. She foregrounds an oppressor's captivity of the Black body in order to wrestle as much economic benefit from that body as possible, using as an example Harriet Jacobs's confinement in her grandmother's attic. But we both acknowledge how the term "assumes geographic inferiority," the ability to be displaced, to be moved from one area of economic benefit to one of lesser benefit (McKittrick, *Demonic Grounds*, 9). My use signifies not confinement but mobility in the "open" platform, showing that despatialization is not limited to one time period or form of captivity. By examining a marginal location, in both senses of the word (a space that forms a boundary and a space that is often overlooked), we get a sense of the precarious position of Black women in relation to the railroad and a different understanding of Black women in relation to railroad time and space.

16. "Community Events," Town of Gordonsville, www.townofgordonsville.org/, accessed June 3, 2018.

17. Quoted in Porterfield, *Dining by Rail*, 6–7. Railroad dining history is one other sub-genre in the larger field of railroad studies. Scholars study menus offered on railroad passenger cars. See also Quinzio, *Food on the Rails*.

18. "Excursion on Board Mr. Pullman's New Dining Room Car," *Chicago Tribune*, March 30, 1868, Pullman Company Scrapbooks, Newberry Library. See also Leyendecker, *Palace Car Prince*, 86–88. For a discussion of the dining car in England, see T.F.R., "Pleasures of the Dining Car."

19. The 1875–76 Corinth City Directory lists Dorcas Brown, "col[ored] proprietor of an eating house" (*Gardner and Gaines' City Directory of Corinth*, 265).

20. See also John T. Edge, who briefly discusses Julia Brown. According to Edge, Julia Brown was a former slave who, through her cooking, was able to establish her own eating establishment (*Fried Chicken*, 98). Based on the census and the Corinth directory, I believe the "Julia" referred to here may be Dorcas, Jane and Julia's mother.

21. "Gray's New Map of Gordonsville, Orange County, Virginia. Drawn from Special Surveys, 1878" (Philadelphia: O. W. Gray & Son), in David Rumsey Map Collection, David Rumsey Map Center, Stanford Libraries.

22. Alcorn County, Mississippi, U.S. Census, 1880.

23. William H. B. Thomas, *Gordonsville*, 65, 64. The Exchange Hotel, built in 1860 and in close proximity to the passenger depot, became a Civil War hospital during the conflict, receiving both Union and Confederate soldiers. The hotel was purchased by the Gordonsville Historic Society in the 1970s and since then has functioned as a tourist museum.

24. Sanborn Fire Insurance Map from Gordonsville, Orange County, Virginia, Sanborn Map Company, October, 1908, Library of Congress Geography and Map Division Washington, DC, www.loc.gov/item/sanborn09025_001/.

25. "Platform," *Gordonsville (VA) Gazette*, October 23, 1873.

26. Gordonsville historian William H. B. Thomas also notes that some of the carriers "cooked in little buildings near the tracks," and he credits Mrs. Isabella (Bella) Winston with this information (*Gordonsville*, 62). I have not located any other references to these buildings. The Exchange Hotel, however, did have an outdoor kitchen that was used to provide meals to passengers and guests. The breezeway between the hotel and the kitchen was called the "whistle walk" because, according to a placard in the Exchange Hotel and Museum, as the enslaved "transported the food between the kitchen to the tavern the slaves were instructed to whistle as they walked. This was to make sure that the slaves did not put food in their own mouths in transit." Placard, "Tavern Room," Exchange Hotel Civil War Medical Museum.

27. Itinerant, "Communications," *Semi-Weekly Raleigh (NC) Register*, January 10, 1868. The waiter carriers appeared in a University of Virginia reunion book in 1913. Two waiter carriers appear on the Gordonsville platform with their trays, and hand food to two alumni (Crenshaw, *History*, 61).

28. The Gordonsville Town Council Records (Richmond) distinguish a "snack license" from a fruit license. The latter license cost $10 for six months, compared to the $5 for the snack license.

29. "A Southern Delicacy," *Butte (MT) Weekly Miner*, December 7, 1899, 2.

30. Williams-Forson, *Building Houses*, 35. I appreciate Williams-Forson's comments and suggestions on this chapter.

31. For more about Hotchkiss, his work for Stonewall Jackson, and his well-known and important maps of Virginia, see Hearn and Marino, *Civil War Battles*.

32. J. Thomas, "Jedediah Hotchkiss." See also Schulten, *Mapping the Nation*, 189–93. Jed Hotchkiss was the brother of Nelson Hotchkiss, the traveling agent for the Chesapeake and Ohio Railroad and the person who initiated the idea of northern and southern editors visiting each other's regions. Nelson Hotchkiss's idea resulted in *The Pine and the Palm*, as described in this chapter.

33. Hotchkiss, "New Ways," 273.

34. Watkins and Hotchkiss, *Pine and the Palm*, 20. *The Pine and the Palm* was an important book that served to encourage travel to the recently ravaged South. The C&O traveling agent who came up with the suggestion that journalists tour the North and the South was Nelson Hotchkiss, Jedidiah's brother.

35. "The Waiters," *Gordonsville (VA) Gazette*, April 16, 1874.

36. W. W. Scott, a lawyer and the editor of the *Gordonsville (VA) Gazette*, stated that the waiter carriers were described in newspapers in other states, "from Maine to Texas." "The Waiters," *Gordonsville (VA) Gazette*, April 16, 1874. In my research, I have located references to waiter carriers in newspapers from Montana, North Carolina, South Carolina, Tennessee, Washington, DC, and West Virginia.

37. *Richmond (VA) Daily Dispatch*, January 28, 1867.

38. *Presbyterian of the South* (Atlanta), May 31, 1911; *Richmond (VA) Daily Dispatch*, February 4, 1867.

39. *Alexandria (VA) Gazette*, February 21, 1867.

40. *Richmond (VA) Daily State Journal*, August 30, 1871.

41. *Richmond (VA) Daily Dispatch*, August 26, 1867.

42. B. Anderson, *Imagined Communities*.

43. Writers' Program of the WPA, *Virginia*, 500.

44. As Gordonsville historian William H. B. Thomas notes, the account of the town printed in *The Pine and the Palm* "called attention to Gordonsville's position on the main line" of the Chesapeake and Ohio Railroad: "The scene described was one that for the ensuing half century, until after the first World War, would characterize Gordonsville in the minds of travelers and townspeople alike" (*Gordonsville*, 61).

45. Throughout August, September, and October, U.S. newspapers carried reports of the royal visit. There was concern about how the prince would perceive the South and its "peculiar institution," and so Virginia was the farthest south the tour went.

46. Sir Henry Wentworth Acland, accession no. 1986-7-232, National Archives of Canada.

47. At a conference, Williams-Forson suggested that the woman's bare arms may have signified vulgarity (Laboring for Freedom: African American Women Workers in Public Places and Domestic Spaces [panel], Organization of American Historians Conference, Philadelphia, April 5, 2019).

48. Thaggert, *Images of Black Modernism*, 6.

49. *Native Virginian* (Orange County, VA), January 14, 1870.

50. Walter Edward Harris, "Gordonsville and Its Future," *Richmond (VA) Times Dispatch*, June 28, 1905.

51. One concern white residents may have had was the aurality of the food vendors. Jessica B. Harris's research on nineteenth-century food vendors focuses on vendors who worked in urban areas. Charleston, South Carolina, for example, although larger and more populous than Gordonsville, also had food vendors. A letter to the editor of the *Charleston (SC) Post and Courier* offered a "warning" about the sound and "the legalized audacity of the negros who hawk their wares . . . about our streets" (J. Harris, "I'm Talkin' 'bout the Food").

52. As related in a brief history of the journal in 1892, *Southern Workman* was first published in January 1872 as a four-page folio. Its goal was to give "general views of education work for the [Negro and Indian] races and of race questions in various aspects" (*Southern Workman* 21, no. 1 [January 1892], 3). For more information on Dashiell, a white woman whose full name was Landonia Randolph Sparrow Dashiell, see Elizabeth Engelhardt, "Cookbook Story," 70–71.

53. Dashiell, "Aunt Sanna Terry."

54. Ibid., 455.

55. Ibid., 449.

56. Compare the *Scribner's* 1872 drawing to fig. 3.1. In the drawing, the women are under the eaves. The platform appears to be the better place to sell the food.

57. Engelhardt, "Cookbook Story," 70, 82.

58. See Wallace-Sanders, *Mammy*.

59. Schweizer, *On Waiting*, ii, 5.

60. "The loss of stories sharpens the hunger for them. So it is tempting to fill in the gaps and to provide closure where there is none" (Hartman, "Venus in Two Acts," 8).

61. For more on the difficulty of locating African American women in the archive, see D. White, "Mining the Forgotten."

62. Loving, "Fried Chicken." Similar bans against African American food vendors occurred in other southern locations. In Natchez, Mississippi, there were protests against "Negro restauranteurs and fish-women, who set up tables on the sidewalks" (Wharton, *Negro in Mississippi*, 128). In Atlanta, Georgia, African Americans were banned from selling food on Wall Street during the Fourth of July holiday in 1904. The chief of police complained that the vendors' booths were "eye-sores" and the "odor of fried fish and tainted ham" were "quite noticeable" ("Depot Booths are Abolished; Negros Can't Open Lunch Stands on Wall Street," *Atlanta Constitution*, June 29, 1904, 3).

63. In May 1897, Robert Watkins was elected to be the town sergeant; "elected" is the term used in the trustees' minutebook, but it appears that Watkins was the only candidate. Watkins was paid $25 a month for his services until 1898, when his salary was increased to $30 a month. *Minutebook of the Meetings of the Trustees of the Town, Regarding Election of Officers, Establishment of a City Water Works, Other Routine Business, 1889–1902, Gordonsville, VA*, Albert and Shirley Small Special Collections Library.

64. "Mr. R.G. Watkins is running a first-class restaurant at the station in Gordonsville. . . . The food is delicious and the prices moderate" (*Orange [VA] Observer*, February 27, 1925).

65. This is revealed in Watkins's obituary, "R. G. Watkins," *Richmond (VA) Times Dispatch*, November 22, 1925. Just after the ban against the waiter carriers was enacted, Watkins suffered a major heart attack and subsequently died. It is not clear when in 1925 the ban went into effect, but my research suggests that it began in the late summer or early fall, when traveling shows such as circuses would have arrived in town via the railroads. If my inference regarding the September 1925 reference to Watkins and "two waiters" is correct, the ban would have taken place in September.

66. Trouillot, *Silencing the Past*, 25–26.

67. Gordonsville Town Council Records, 1919–31 (Gordonsville).

68. Williams-Forson also credits Gilmore as a source of information (*Building Houses*, 235).

69. Matthew Griffith, "Three Gordonsville 'Waiter Carriers' Recall 'Fried Chicken Center of the World' Days," *Richmond (VA) Times Dispatch*, June 13, 1948, 32.

70. Ibid.

71. "Waiter Carrier Recalls 'Fried Chicken' Days," *Orange (VA) Review*, July 9, 1970, B-9.

72. Griffith, "Three Gordonsville 'Waiter Carriers.'"

73. One final, fictional displacement of the waiter carriers occurs in a tongue-in-cheek *Gordonsville (VA) Gazette* newspaper article, written in 1874 to illustrate what Gordonsville would look like in 1925 if a railroad line between Fredericksburg and Charlottesville were completed, a line that would have negatively impacted railroad traffic in Gordonsville. The editor noted that the colored people who sold "crisp and brown fried chicken and hot coffee or cool lemonade" were gone, "now colonized in Santo Domingo" ("The Deserted Village," *Gordonsville Gazette*, June 18, 1874). Curiously, 1925 was the year the waiter carriers were in fact banned, as noted in the chapter.

74. "Community Events," Town of Gordonsville, www.townofgordonsville.org, accessed June 3, 2018. The attempt to document the lives of the waiter carriers corresponds to the town's growing desire to memorialize aspects of the town's history. The last interview with a waiter carrier, for example, was conducted on the eve of the town's centennial celebration and parade in 1970. A historic Gordonsville organization was formed by the mid-1970s. The organization bought historic buildings in the downtown Gordonsville area and submitted applications to have certain locations designated as National Historic Sites. In 2021, the festival took place in October.

Chapter 4. Handmaidens for Travelers: Archiving the Pullman Company Maid

1. Husband, *Story of the Pullman Car*, 155. See also Buder, *Pullman*, 17. It is difficult to determine George Pullman's racial politics definitively. A series of editorials appeared in the *Atlanta Constitution* and *Atlanta Daily Constitution* of 1875, condemning George Pullman for supporting the Civil Rights Act of 1875, which prohibited segregation in public accommodations. As others have noted, the Pullman Company's and the railroad lines' support of the act was motivated more by economic reasons rather than the desire to acknowledge the rights of African American passengers. ("Pullmanism," *Atlanta Constitution*, June 19, 1875).

2. See Love, *Life and Adventures of Nat Love*, 116–38; Oscar Micheaux's semiautobiographical novel, *The Conquest*; McKay, *Long Way from Home*, 10, 175, 217; Michael Davis and Clark, *Thurgood Marshall*, 41; Allen and Henderson, *Brotherhood of Sleeping Car Porters*; Parks, *Voices in the Mirror*, 64–67; Malcolm X, *Autobiography*, 73–74.

3. Some of these many books include Brazeal and Wolman, *Brotherhood of Sleeping Car Porters*; W. Harris, *Keeping the Faith*; Santino, *Miles of Smiles*; P. McKissack and F. McKissack, *Long Hard Journey*; Arnesen, *Brotherhoods of Color*; Hughes, *Anthology of Respect*; Perata, *Those Pullman Blues*; Tye, *Rising from the Rails*; and Foster, *They Call Me George*. Porters appeared frequently and briefly in early U.S. films from the early twentieth century until the 1950s. Film scholar Jacqueline Stewart points out that the first film by an African American centered on a Pullman porter, William

Foster's silent film *The Railroad Porter* (1913). See Stewart, *Migrating to the Movies*, xvii–xix and 194–96.

4. Distinctions should be made between the service workers who are the focus of this chapter and the manual laborers who physically constructed the railroad across the U.S. landscape in the nineteenth century, the "railroad hands" described by Lorenzo J. Greene and Carter G. Woodson or immortalized by such figures as the legendary John Henry. See Greene and Woodson, *Negro Wage Earner*, 101–2. I am interested in workers who provided service to passengers within the compartment and were responsible for passenger comfort, not those workers who helped to build or manually construct the railroads. My focus is on the dynamics that take place within the train car between the Black female Pullman Company maid and primarily white passengers.

5. The Newberry Library's finding aid for the Pullman Company records describes how the library obtained the documents. In 1948, the library acquired several company scrapbooks. Later company records were donated to the Newberry by George Pullman's granddaughter. "By far the largest portion of the archives was salvaged when the Pullman Company ceased operations in 1969." Two historians were responsible for going through "records stacked ceiling high" in "huge green metal storage containers at an unheated warehouse in Pullman." The historians were "liberal in their selection of personnel records" (Briggs and Peters, *Guide to the Pullman Company Archives*, vii).

6. Yates, *Control through Communication*, 71.

7. The owner, George M. Pullman, also created a town that, as in other sections of U.S. life, excluded African Americans. In 2016, a representative of the Historic Pullman Foundation in Pullman, Illinois, claimed that at least one apparently African American family lived in the town of Pullman in the nineteenth century.

8. See, for example, Simpson and Rutherford, *Bibliography*.

9. Porter Application Register, 06/02/02, vol. 2, Pullman Company Archives.

10. I thank Dr. Earnestine Jenkins for alerting me to this image. For more information about the Hooks Brothers, see Jenkins, "Hooks Brothers of Memphis."

11. Spero and A. Harris, *Black Worker*, 432.

12. Bates, *Pullman Porters*, esp. ch. 3.

13. The quotation is from Bates, *Pullman Porters*, 9. Chateauvert, *Marching Together*, 19: "Female unionists and male union leaders expressed their labor protests in terms of race discrimination and in the language of black manhood rights. This rhetorical emphasis deflected members' awareness of gender inequality, allowing them to focus their attention on gender compatibility."

14. J. A. Rittenhouse was one likely supervisor who came into contact with porters and maids.

15. Other questions concerned how to refer to the maids without breaking the Newberry's own research rules or violating the maids' privacy. Although some of the Pullman Company personnel records are now outside of the embargo period, I have used the initials of the maids to maintain some privacy. For a detailed discussion on

archives and the issues contemporary scholars will need to address, see Helton et al., "Question of Recovery."

16. "Local Matters," Richmond, December 29, 1882, Pullman Company Scrapbooks, 12/00/01, Pullman Company Archives.

17. "Messrs. Pullman and Fields' New Sleeping Car—Excursion to the Summit," *Chicago Tribune*, August 17, 1859, original emphasis.

18. The Pullman Company underwent several name changes. When George Pullman began constructing the sleeping car in 1859 with his friend Benjamin Field, their company was known as Pullman and Field. George Pullman incorporated in 1867 under the name the Pullman Palace Car Company. When the company was charged with operating a monopoly, the company divided into two. See Leyendecker, *Palace Car Prince*, 37.

19. Washington, *Booker T. Washington Papers*, 7:xxiii, 7:312; see also 7:324. In 1903 Governor Frazier of Tennessee wanted a law to prevent African Americans from riding in Pullman sleeping cars. Washington wrote directly to Lincoln in protest. In 1926 A. Philip Randolph commented that although Abraham Lincoln freed the slaves, his son "has bent his influence and name to the notorious exploitation of Negroes as *Pullman slaves*" (quoted in Brazeal, *Brotherhood of Sleeping Car Porters*, 43, original emphasis).

20. Washington, *Booker T. Washington Papers*, 4:180, 3:214.

21. The Pullman Company bought out the Wagner Car Company in 1900.

22. *Railroad Record* (Atlanta), May 29, 1882, Pullman Company Scrapbooks, microfilm 1213, reel 1, Pullman Company Archives.

23. Although porters were a part of the Pullman Company since its beginnings in 1867, tracing the Pullman maid is more difficult. Employee cards indicate the start of a person's employment, and the earliest employment date for a maid I have found, on microfilm in the Newberry Library, is 1901, for a maid working out of the New York division. Microfilm 1433, Pullman Company Archives.

24. "Handmaidens for Travelers," *Pullman News*, January 1923, 291. For more on "in-house magazines" or "shop papers," and their objective of personalizing the workplace, see Yates, *Control through Communication*, 74–77.

25. "Handmaidens for Travelers."

26. *Pullman News*, May, 1924, 2.

27. "Some of the Comforts Found in the New Pullman Single Room Car," *Pullman News*, April 1927, 418–19.

28. 06/02/02, box 9, f.180, Pullman Company Archives.

29. There were some hazards with the curling iron. See, for example, "Girl Burned by Curling Iron; Sues Pullman Co," *Chicago Tribune*, March 26, 1929, 1.

30. See, for example, James H. Hogans, "Things Seen, Heard, and Done Among Pullman Employe[e]s," *New York Age*, December 5, 1925, 10. Maid Mabel Fitts Taylor was profiled several times in this column.

31. 06/01/03, f719, box 31, Pullman Company Archives.

32. Frances Mary Albrier, page 76, interviewed by Malca Chall, OH-31, T-3276, Interviews of the Black Women Oral History Project.

33. Medical Examination of Maids, 06/05/01, f21, box 1, Pullman Company Archives.

34. Albrier interviews, pages 76–77.

35. Ibid., pages 79–81. See also Eget, "Envisioning Progressive Communities." For an example of a Pullman porter memoir, see Robert E. Turner, *Memories of a Pullman Porter*.

36. Husband, *Story of the Pullman Car*, 155.

37. Gitelman, *Paper Knowledge*, 11–12, 30.

38. Ibid., 1.

39. Some porters and maids pledged loyalty to the Pullman Porters Benefit Association of America (PPBAA), "basically an organization to extend [Pullman] company influence," according to Bates (*Pullman Porters*, 51–52).

40. One supervisor, for example, noted a maid's "large breasts" as distinguishing marks. Employee card for Maid E.A.L., 06/02/01, box 309, Pullman Company Archives.

41. Employee card for Maid M.H., 06/02/03, box 112, Pullman Company Archives.

42. Employee card for Maid A.E.W., 06/02/01, box 296, Pullman Company Archives.

43. Yates's definition of "control" is not as exploitative as we may now come to think of it, particularly in light of the Pullman Company's interactions with its African American employees. Rather than its somewhat pejorative interpretation, Yates defines "control" as "the operations of an organization . . . coordinated to achieve desired results" (*Control through Communication*, xvi). And yet, because of what we know of the Pullman Company's problematic employment practices, particularly with its African American employees, a less benign concept of control is not inappropriate when examining the employee cards.

44. Yates, *Control through Communication*, 68.

45. Blair, *Henry James*, 202.

46. Richter, *Home on the Rails*, 119. Richter continues by noting that one can measure the growth of the Pullman Company by the thickening of responsibilities required of conductors and porters.

47. Richter, *Home on the Rails*, 120, 124.

48. F. Taylor, *Principles of Scientific Management*.

49. Smith, *How Race Is Made*, 50.

50. *Instructions for Maids*, 1925, 05/01/06, folder 28, box 2, Pullman Company Archives.

51. Ibid.

52. Hartman, "Venus in Two Acts," 2.

53. Ibid.

54. "Dear Sirs," Application file for Maid N.P., 06/02/02, box 9, Pullman Company Archives.

55. Employee card for Maid N.P., 06/02/03, box 296, Pullman Company Archives.

56. Employee card for Maid E.W., 06/02/03, box 296, Pullman Company Archives.

57. Gitelman, *Paper Knowledge*, 2.

58. See, for example, Batchen, "Vernacular Photographies"; Campt, *Image Matters*.

59. D. Kaplan, "Vernacular Photographies," 230.

60. Maid N.B.C., 06/02/03, box 309. It would be interesting to know if these photographs were taken by the company photographer, Henry R. Koopman, or by someone else. Larry Peterson notes that the Pullman Company's "huge cash reserves allowed it first to employ a regular photographer and then in 1888 to create a photography department, as well as pay for the most advanced reproduction technologies" (90). See Peterson, "Photography and the Pullman Strike."

61. Letter to R. J. Ruddy, Box 3, Brotherhood of Sleeping Car Porters Papers.

62. Ibid. Note that the woman made the claim not against the Pullman conductor but the *train* conductor. Just as Pullman hired its own porters and maids, Pullman hired its own conductors, apart from the railroad line's conductors. For more on the distinction between the railroad conductor and the Pullman conductor, see Perata, *Those Pullman Blues*, xxv–xxvi.

63. There is, for example, no envelope attached to the letter or a stamp indicating the letter was either sent or received.

64. Gitelman writes the following about nominal blanks: "[blank forms are] one small part of the way that bureaucracy assumes an objective character"(*Paper Knowledge*, 31).

65. Maid L.W.J., 06/02/03, box 309, Pullman Company Archives.

66. Employee card of Maid E.S.N., 06/02/03, box 113, Pullman Company Archives.

67. Hine, "Rape and the Inner Lives." Hine's term suggests the performance Black women adopted to protect themselves in a variety of scenarios.

68. Chateauvert notes that the 1930 constitution drops "and Maids." *Marching Together*, 60.

Terminus

1. As a sign of the interest in Murray, the documentary, *My Name is Pauli Murray*, was released in 2021.

2. The female in Murray's first-year class left during the first year, leaving Murray "the only woman in [her] class for the entire three-year course" (Murray, *Song*, 237). Two or three female law school students enrolled after Murray's first year. Subsequent quotations from this work appear parenthetically in the text.

3. Murray and Eastwood, "Jane Crow and the Law." Murray had a long career fighting for social equality and against segregation that space precludes me from recounting here. One important example of a challenge Murray posed to segregation included Murray's refusal to move toward the back of a bus in Virginia, for which Murray and a female partner, Adelene McBean, were arrested in March 1940. See Murray, *Song*, 178–93; Drury, "Experimentation," 226–35; Azaransky, *Dream Is Freedom*, 19–22; Bell-Scott, *Fire-Brand and the First Lady*, 61–64; Rosenberg, *Jane Crow*, 78–96; and Saxby, *Pauli Murray*, 84–93. Glenda E. Gilmore confirms that the account of a couple arrested for segregating a bus in Virginia was an eyewitness account by Harold Garfinkel, originally published in *Opportunity* magazine (Garfinkel, "Color

Trouble"; Gilmore, *Defying Dixie*, 322–25). Notably, Garfinkel assumed Murray was a young man.

4. In addition to the many articles written about Murray, several books about Murray have been published: Azaransky, *Dream Is Freedom*; B. Cooper, *Beyond Respectability*; Bell-Scott, *Firebrand and the First Lady*; Rosenberg, *Jane Crow*; Saxby, *Pauli Murray*. Murray's own writings have been republished; see *Song*; *Dark Testament*; and *Proud Shoes*.

5. B. Cooper, *Beyond Respectability*, 102, 113. See also Hardison, 4.

6. Simmons-Thorne, "Pauli Murray and the Pronominal Problem." For more on this subject, see Rosenberg, "A Note on Pronouns and Other Word Choices," in *Jane Crow*, xvii. The Pauli Murray Foundation uses female pronouns. Biographers Sarah Azaransky (*Dream Is Freedom*), Troy Saxby (*Pauli Murray*), and Rosalind Rosenberg (*Jane Crow*) also use female pronouns, while Simmons-Thorne uses masculine nouns to refer to Murray. The profile page highlighting the Pauli Murray College at Yale University carefully avoids pronouns altogether (https://paulimurray.yalecollege.yale.edu/subpage-2).

7. As noted in the introduction (note 68), I am using definitions from the Human Rights Campaign.

8. In *Song in a Weary Throat*, the mature Murray used female references for herself. See, for example, how she describes herself as "not the only woman on the faculty" at a university in Ghana (434). Having experienced travel as a young girl with Aunt Pauline and as "one of a crowd of teenage girls" at Hunter College (*Song*, 92), Murray would have been familiar with the limitations placed on girls and women who want to travel. This prior experience would have enabled Murray to compare and contrast the experience of train riding while presenting as female and while presenting as male.

9. A. Cooper, "Woman vs. The Indian," in *Voice From the South*, 89.

10. Additionally, although it appears to be in response to a different episode or multiple episodes rather than the one recounted here, Murray, like Terrell, was afraid of a possible assault. Rosenberg writes that Murray was "terrified of rape since at least the age of ten" (*Jane Crow*, 44).

11. This period is also significant because, as Drury points out, Murray's given name changed from "Anna Pauline" to the more gender-ambiguous "Pauli" ("Experimentation," 63). Another significant travel experience includes the period in 1933 when Murray was a field representative for *Opportunity* magazine, one of the leading periodicals of the Harlem Renaissance or the New Negro Movement. Murray enjoyed this job because it enabled "mov[ing] around and meet[ing] people socially" (*Song*, 121). To stay away from Jim Crow travel, Murray bought a used Chevrolet roadster and drove at night to avoid heavy traffic.

12. Murray's road trip in a car inspired Murray's first published poem, "Song of the Highway," published immediately after "Three Thousand Miles on a Dime in Ten Days" in *Negro*.

13. Drury calls "Three Thousand Miles on a Dime in Ten Days" the "richer story of the two versions" because "it suggests [Murray's] passions and emotional complexity" ("Experimentation," 68).

14. Like the "wild girl hoboes" described by Erin Battat, Murray in "Three Thousand Miles" can briefly refuse "wage work and domesticity"(*Ain't Got No Life*, 32, 40.)

15. Nancy Cunard included Murray's "Three Thousand Miles on a Dime in Ten Days" to anthologize in *Negro* (1934); on Cunard and that volume, see Carla Kaplan, *Miss Anne in Harlem*, 279–338, and Rachel Farebrother, "Panorama."

16. Rosenberg, *Jane Crow*, 42.

17. Drury, "Experimentation," 72–73. Other important items published in *Negro* include Langston Hughes's "I, Too" and Zora Neale Hurston's "Characteristics of Negro Expression" and "Spirituals and Neo-Spirituals." As Rachel Farebrother noted in correspondence with me, Murray's decision not to reveal the narrator of Pete's race is, to some extent, undercut by the fact that Cunard included author photos only for Black contributors.

18. Drury, "Experimentation," 68.

19. As Rachel Farebrother pointed out to me, there is an even more striking feeling of freedom in the scrapbook compared to Murray's presence in *Negro* where there was a controlling (white) editor.

20. Murray's hospital notes, quoted in Drury, "Experimentation," 159–60.

21. Drury, "Love, Ambition," 301.

22. "The Life and Times of an American Called Pauli Murray," Pauli Murray Papers.

23. The contents and description of this scrapbook are very helpfully provided by Drury in "Love, Ambition," 299. Drury notes that "The Vagabond" photograph was taken during the March 1931 trip with Dorothy Hayden (Drury, "Experimentation," 73).

24. For more information on Camp TERA, a project supported by Eleanor Roosevelt and the place where Murray saw Mrs. Roosevelt for the first time, see Drury, "Experimentation," 81–100; Murray, *Song*, 122–26; Bell-Scott, *Firebrand and the First Lady*, 3–7, 13–15. Murray got into trouble with the camp director because Murray did not stand up when Mrs. Roosevelt entered a corridor (*Song*, 125). Murray's interest in communism, and, according to Drury, the friendship with Holmes, led to Murray departing the camp early.

25. This discussion of Murray and the relationship with Peggie Holmes is drawn from Drury, "Experimentation," 81–100. Drury's dissertation is one of the best sources examining Murray's gender nonconformity.

26. 1935 diary, Pauli Murray Papers.

27. McKittrick, *Demonic Grounds*, x.

28. Rosenberg describes other clippings that appear near this page (*Jane Crow*, 30).

29. Scrapbook, Pauli Murray Papers. Saxby makes the point about Murray confronting the "bathroom dilemma" that is familiar to people with fluid gender identities (*Pauli Murray*, 47). "Except for the fact that such narratives rarely depict Black characters," as Drury notes ("Experimentation," 65–66).

30. Note here how the concern about assault is acknowledged in a straightforward way, distinctly different from Cooper's and Terrell's discussion of assault through coded, delicate language.

31. Saxby, *Pauli Murray*, xvi. Murray's archive is especially notable considering that most African American (wo)men of that period do not have such expansive archival material of their lives. A Black woman who comes close to having such an extensive archive and who lived during the mid-twentieth century is Mary Church Terrell. Her papers are located in the Library of Congress, Howard University, as well as her alma mater, Oberlin College. In the bibliography of *Unceasing Militant*, Allison Parker notes that Terrell's descendants also have a "private collection" of Terrell material, some of which was donated to Oberlin.

32. Drury, "Love, Ambition," 296.

33. Ibid.

34. The Scottsboro case shows how much "situational riding," the treatment the Black passenger receives depending on who else is in the train compartment, can lead to arrestment of freedom. It is remarkable to consider the degree to which the Scottsboro case resembles the wrongful arrest of five Black and Latino boys on charges of raping a white woman in Central Park in 1989. All were convicted and incarcerated, only to be much later exonerated in 2002 through DNA evidence.

Bibliography

Archival Sources and Libraries

Albert and Shirley Small Special Collections Library. University of Virginia, Charlottesville.

Brotherhood of Sleeping Car Porters Papers. Chicago History Museum, Chicago.

David Rumsey Map Collection. David Rumsey Map Center. Stanford Libraries.

Exchange Hotel Civil War Medical Museum. Gordonsville, VA.

George Pullman Papers. Chicago History Museum, Chicago.

Gordonsville Town Council Records. Gordonsville Town Hall. Gordonsville, VA.

Gordonsville Town Council Records. Library of Virginia. Richmond.

Great Northern Railway Collection. Minnesota Historical Society, St. Paul.

Hooks Brothers Photographers Collection. Department of Art. University of Memphis, Memphis, TN.

Interviews of the Black Women Oral History Project, 1976–1981. Schlesinger Library on the History of Women in America. Schlesinger Library. Radcliffe Institute. Harvard University, Cambridge, MA.

Library and Archives Canada. National Archives of Canada.

Mary Church Terrell Papers. Manuscripts and Archives Division. Library of Congress, Washington, DC.

Pauli Murray Papers, Arthur and Elizabeth Schlesinger Library. Radcliffe Institute for Advanced Study. Harvard University, Cambridge, MA.

Pullman Company Archives. Newberry Library, Chicago.

Theodore Kornweibel Jr. Collection. California State Railroad Museum, Sacramento.

Virginia Museum of History and Culture/Virginia Historical Society, Richmond.

Newspapers

Alexandria (VA) Gazette
Atlanta Constitution

Atlanta Daily Constitution
Bangor (ME) Daily Whig and Courier
Boston Liberator
Boston Transcript
Butte (MT) Weekly Miner
Charlottesville (VA) Daily Progress
Chicago Tribune
Christian Recorder (AME Church, Philadelphia, PA)
Gordonsville (VA) Gazette
Memphis Appeal Avalanche
Minneapolis Tribune
Native Virginian (Orange County, VA)
New York Daily Graphic
New York Times
Orange (VA) Observer
Orange (VA) Review
Presbyterian of the South (Atlanta)
Richmond (VA) Daily Dispatch
Richmond (VA) Daily State Journal
Richmond (VA) Times Dispatch
Semi-Weekly Raleigh (NC) Register
Sonoma (CA) Index-Tribune
St. Louis Globe Democrat
Virginia Free Press (Charlestown, VA [WV])
Weekly Corinthian (Corinth, MS)

Other Works

Aguiar, Marian. *Tracking Modernity: India's Railway and the Culture of Mobility.* Minneapolis: University of Minnesota Press, 2011.
"Alcorn County 1890 Tax List." *Northeast Mississippi Historical and Genealogical Quarterly,* December 1982, 65–69.
Alexander, Elizabeth. "'We Must Be about Our Father's Business': Anna Julia Cooper and the In-Corporation of the Nineteenth-Century African American Woman Intellectual." *Signs* 20, no. 2 (1995): 336–56.
Alexander, Elwin P. *Down at the Depot: American Railroad Stations from 1831 to 1920.* New York: Clarkson N. Potter, 1970.
Allen, Robert L., and Joyce Henderson. *The Brotherhood of Sleeping Car Porters: C. L. Dellums and the Fight for Fair Treatment and Civil Rights, 1925–1978.* Boulder, CO: Paradigm, 2015.
Anderson, Benedict. *Imagined Communities: Reflections on the Origin and Spread of Nationalism.* New York: Verso, 2006.
Arnesen, Eric. *Brotherhoods of Color: Black Railroad Workers and the Struggle for Equality.* Cambridge, MA: Harvard University Press, 2001.

"Assessment of Personal Property and Polls." *Northeast Mississippi Historical and Genealogical Quarterly*, September 1982, 29–33.

Augé, Marc. *Non-Places: An Introduction to Supermodernity*. New York: Verso, 2008.

Ayers, Edward. 1992. *Promise of a New South: Life after Reconstruction: 15th Anniversary Edition*. New York: Oxford University Press, 2007.

Azaransky, Sarah. *The Dream Is Freedom: Pauli Murray and American Democratic Faith*. New York: Oxford University Press, 2011.

Baker, Henry. "The Negro in the Field of Invention." In *Twentieth-Century Negro Literature*, edited by D. W. Culp, 399–413. New York: Arno Press, 1969.

Baker, Houston A., Jr. *Blues, Ideology, and Afro-American Literature: A Vernacular Theory*. Chicago: University of Chicago Press, 1984.

Balducci, Temma. *Gender, Space, and the Gaze in Post-Haussmann Visual Culture: Beyond the Flâneur*. New York: Routledge, 2017.

Barrow, Robin. "Rape on the Railway: Women, Safety, and Moral Panic in Victorian Newspapers." *Journal of Victorian Culture* 20, no. 3 (2015): 341–56.

Batchen, Geoffrey. "Vernacular Photographies." *History of Photography* 24, no. 3 (2000): 262–71.

Bates, Beth Thomkins. *Pullman Porters and the Rise of Protest Politics in Black America, 1925–1945*. Chapel Hill: University of North Carolina Press, 2001.

Battat, Erin. *Ain't Got No Life: America's Great Migrations and the Making of an Interracial Left*. Chapel Hill: University of North Carolina Press, 2014.

Bay, Mia. "From the 'Ladies' Car' to the 'Colored Car': Black Female Travelers in the Segregated South." In *The Folly of Jim Crow: Rethinking the Segregated South*, edited by Stephanie Cole and Natalie J. Ring, 150–75. Arlington: University of Texas Press, 2012.

———. *To Tell the Truth Freely: The Life of Ida B. Wells*. New York: Hill and Wang, 2009.

———. *Traveling Black: A Story of Race and Resistance*. Cambridge, MA: Harvard University Press, 2021.

Beaumont, Matthew. "Railway Mania: The Train Compartment as the Scene of a Crime." In *The Railway and Modernity: Time, Space, and the Machine Ensemble*, edited by Matthew Beaumont and Michael Freeman, 125–53. Oxford: Peter Lang, 2007.

Bell-Scott, Patricia. *The Firebrand and the First Lady: Portrait of a Friendship. Pauli Murray, Eleanor Roosevelt, and the Struggle for Social Justice*. New York: Vintage Books, 2016.

Berg, Walter G. *Buildings and Structures of American Railroads: A Reference Book for Railroad Managers, Superintendents, Master Mechanics, Engineers, Architects, and Students*. New York: J. Wiley & Sons, 1893.

Best, Stephen. *The Fugitive's Properties: Law and the Poetics of Possession*. Chicago: University of Chicago Press, 2004.

Blair, Sara. *Henry James and the Writing of Race and Nation*. New York: Cambridge University Press, 1996.

Bliss, James. "Black Feminism Out of Place." *Signs: Journal of Women in Culture and Society* 41, no. 4 (2016): 728.

Bolster, W. Jeffrey. *Black Jacks: African American Seamen in the Age of Sail.* Cambridge, MA: Harvard University Press, 1997.

Bradford, Sarah H. *Harriet Tubman: The Moses of Her People.* 1886. New York: Corinth Books, 1961.

Brazeal, Brailsford R. *The Brotherhood of Sleeping Car Porters: Its Origin and Development.* New York: Harper, 1946.

Briggs, Martha T., and Cynthia H. Peters. *Guide to the Pullman Company Archives.* Chicago: Newberry Library, 1995.

Brown, Charlotte Hawkins. *The Correct Thing to Do, to Say, to Wear.* Sedalia, NC: Charlotte Hawkins Brown, 1941.

Bruce, John Edward. *The Black Sleuth.* Edited and introduced by John Cullen Gruesser. Boston: Northeastern University Press, 2002.

Bryant, J. L. "A Usable Pastoralism: Leo Marx's Method in *The Machine in the Garden.*" *American Studies* 16.1 (1975): 63–72.

Buchanan, Thomas. *Black Life on the Mississippi: Slaves, Free Blacks, and the Western Steamboat World.* Chapel Hill: University of North Carolina Press, 2004.

Buckmeister, Henrietta. *Let My People Go: The Story of the Underground Railroad and the Growth of the Abolition Movement.* New York: Harper and Bros., 1941.

Buder, Stanley. *Pullman: An Experiment in Industrial Order and Community Planning, 1880–1930.* New York: Oxford University Press, 1967.

Bynum, Victoria E. "Negotiating Boundaries of Race and Gender in Jim Crow Mississippi: The Women of the Knight Family." In *Mississippi Women: Their Histories, Their Lives,* edited by Martha H. Swain, Elizabeth Anne Payne, and Marjorie Julian Spruill, 2:174–91. Athens: University of Georgia Press, 2010.

Camp, Stephanie. *Closer to Freedom: Enslaved Women and Everyday Resistance in the Plantation South.* Chapel Hill: University of North Carolina Press, 2004.

Campt, Tina. *Image Matters: Archive, Photography, and the African Diaspora in Europe.* Durham, NC: Duke University Press, 2012.

Carby, Hazel V. "It Jus Be's Dat Way Sometime: The Sexual Politics of Women's Blues." In *Gender and Discourse: The Power of Talk,* edited by Alexandra Dundas Todd and Sue Fisher, 227–42. Norwood, NJ: Ablex, 1988.

———. "Policing the Black Woman's Body in an Urban Context." In *Identities,* edited by Kwame Anthony Appiah and Henry Louis Gates Jr., 115–32. Chicago: University of Chicago Press, 1995.

———. *Race Men.* Cambridge, MA: Harvard University Press, 1998.

Certeau, Michel de. "Railway Navigation and Incarceration." In *The Practice of Everyday Life,* 111–14. Translated by Steven Randall. Berkeley: University of California Press, 1984.

Chafe, William H., Raymond Gavins, and Robert Korstad, eds. *Remembering Jim Crow: African Americans Tell about Life in the Segregated South.* New York: New Press, 2001.

Chateauvert, Melinda. *Marching Together: Women of the Brotherhood of Sleeping Car Porters*. Urbana: University of Illinois Press, 1998.

Chatelain, Marcia. *South Side Girls: Growing Up in the Great Migration*. Durham, NC: Duke University Press, 2015.

Chesnutt, Charles. *The Marrow of Tradition*. 1901. Edited by Werner Sollors. Reprint, New York: W. W. Norton, 2012.

———. "A Matter of Principle." 1899. In *Stories, Novels, and Essays*, 149–68. Edited by Werner Sollors. New York: Library of America, 2002.

Conningham, Frederic A., and Mary Barton Conningham. *An Alphabetical List of 5735 Titles of N. Currier and Currier & Ives Prints: With Dates of Publication, Sizes and Recent Auction Prices*. New York City: Priv. print by F. A. and M. B. Conningham, 1930.

Cooper, Anna Julia. *A Voice From the South by a Black Woman of the South*. Xenia, OH: Aldine Printing House, 1892.

Cooper, Brittney C. *Beyond Respectability: The Intellectual Thought of Race Women*. Urbana: University of Illinois Press, 2017.

Cope, R. Douglas. *The Limits of Racial Domination: Plebian Society in Colonial Mexico City, 1660–1720*. Madison: University of Wisconsin Press, 1994.

Craft, William, and Ellen Craft. *Running a Thousand Miles for Freedom*. 1860. Reprint, Athens: University of Georgia Press, 1999.

Crenshaw, Lewis D. *A History of the Quinquennial Reunion of the Class of 1908, University of Virginia, June 14 to 18, 1913*. Roanoke, VA: Stone Printing and Manufacturing Co., 1913.

Currier and Ives [Nathaniel Currier and James Merritt Ives]. "A Kiss in the Dark: Mischievous Conductor,—"Dark Tunnel, through in half an hour!" Scene,—When the Train struck the light in just 3 minutes. 1881." New York: Currier & Ives. Lithograph. Library of Congress Prints and Photographs Division, Washington, DC. www.loc.gov/item/2002707713/.

Currier and Ives [Nathaniel Currier and James Merritt Ives], and Thomas Worth. "A Limited Express: Five seconds for Refreshments!" Photograph by Thomas Worth. New York: Currier & Ives, ca. 1884. Lithograph. Library of Congress Prints and Photographs Division, Washington, DC. www.loc.gov/item/97507578/.

Daly, Nicholas. "Railway Novels: Sensation Fiction and the Modernization of the Senses." *ELH* 66, no. 2 (1999): 461–87.

The Damage Suit Disease: A Compilation of Editorials, Letters and Addresses Upon Personal Injury Litigation Against Railroads in Mississippi. Chicago: Chicago Legal News Press, 1913.

Dashiell, Landon. "Aunt Sanna Terry." *Southern Workman* 47, no. 9 (1918): 449–55.

Davis, Angela Y. *Blues Legacies and Black Feminism: Gertrude "Ma" Rainey, Bessie Smith, and Billie Holiday*. New York: Pantheon Books, 1998.

Davis, Michael D., and Hunter R. Clark. *Thurgood Marshall: Warrior at the Bar, Rebel on the Bench*. New York: Carol, 1992.

Dinerstein, Joel. *Swinging the Machine: Modernity, Technology, and African American Culture between the World Wars.* Amherst: University of Massachusetts Press, 2003.

Douglass, Frederick. "Civil Rights and Judge Harlan." *American Reformer*, November 1883, 388.

Drury, Doreen M. "'Experimentation on the Male Side': Race, Class, Gender, and Sexuality in Pauli Murray's Quest for Love and Identity." PhD diss., Boston College, 2000.

———. "Love, Ambition, and 'Invisible Footnotes' in the Life and Writing of Pauli Murray." *Souls* 11, no. 3 (2009): 295–309.

Du Bois, W. E. B., and Henry Louis Gates Jr., ed. *The Souls of Black Folk: The Oxford W. E. B. Du Bois.* New York: Oxford University Press, 2007.

Duffy, Edna. *The Speed Handbook: Velocity, Pleasure, Modernism.* Durham, NC: Duke University Press, 2009.

Edge, John T. *Fried Chicken: An American Story.* New York: G. P. Putnam's Sons, 2004.

Eget, Patricia L. H. "Envisioning Progressive Communities: Race, Gender, and the Politics of Liberalism, Berkeley, California and Montclair, New Jersey, 1920–1970." PhD diss., Rutgers University–New Brunswick, NJ, 2011.

Ellison, Ralph. "Boy on a Train." In *Flying Home and Other Stories*, edited by John Callahan, 12–21. New York: Random House, 1996.

———. "The Little Man at Chehaw Station: The American Artist and His Audience." In *The Collected Essays of Ralph Ellison*, edited by John F. Callahan, 493–523. New York: Modern Library, 1995.

Engelhardt, Elizabeth S. D. "The Cookbook Story: Transitional Narratives in Southern Foodways." In *Writing in the Kitchen: Essays on Southern Literature and Foodways*, edited by David A. Davis and Tara Powell, 69–85. Jackson: University Press of Mississippi, 2014.

English, Daylanne. *Each Hour Redeem: Time and Justice in African American Literature.* Minneapolis: University of Minnesota Press, 2013.

Erbacher, Eric C., Nicole Maruo-Schröder, and Florian Sedlmeier, eds. *Rereading the Machine in the Garden: Nature and Technology in American Culture.* New York: Campus Verlag, 2014.

Ernest, John. "Representing Chaos: William Craft's *Running a Thousand Miles for Freedom*." *PMLA* 121, no.2 (2006): 469–83.

Fairman, Charles. "The Civil Rights Cases." In *Do Great Cases Make Bad Laws?*, edited by Lackland H. Bloom, 137–49. New York: Oxford University Press, 2014.

Farebrother, Rachel. "A 'Panorama' of Black Internationalism: Resistance and Antagonism in Nancy Cunard's *Negro* Anthology (1934)." *Slavery and Abolition: A Journal of Slave and Post-Slave Studies* 41, no. 1 (March 2020): 93–109.

Foster, Cecil. *They Call Me George: The Untold Story of Black Train Porters and the Birth of Modern Canada.* Windsor, Ontario: Biblioasis, 2019.

Foucault, Michel. "Of Other Spaces." *Diacritics* 16, no.1 (1986): 22–27.

Freud, Sigmund. "The Uncanny." In *The Standard Edition of the Complete Psychological Works of Sigmund Freud*, vol. 17, *An Infantile Neurosis and Other Works.* London: Hogarth Press, 1917–19.

Fuentes, Marisa. *Dispossessed Lives: Enslaved Women, Violence, and the Archive.* Philadelphia: University of Pennsylvania Press, 2016.

Gaines, Jane. *Fire and Desire: Mixed Race Movies in the Silent Era.* Chicago: Univ. of Chicago Press, 2001.

Gardner and Gaines' City Directory of Corinth, for 1875–76. Jackson, TN: D. M. Wisdom and Co. Printers, 1875.

Garfinkel, Harold. "Color Trouble." Reprinted in *Best Short Stories of 1941*, edited by Edward J. O'Brien, 97—119. New York: Houghton Mifflin, 1941.

Giddings, Paula. *A Sword among Lions: Ida B. Wells and the Campaign against Lynching.* New York: Amistad, 2008.

Gikandi, Simon. "Rethinking the Archive of Enslavement." *Early American Literature* 50, no. 1 (2015): 81–102.

Gilmore, Glenda Elizabeth. *Defying Dixie: The Radical Roots of Civil Rights, 1919–1950.* New York: W. W. Norton, 2008.

———. *Gender and Jim Crow: Women and the Politics of White Supremacy in North Carolina, 1896–1920.* Chapel Hill: University of North Carolina Press, 1996.

Gilroy, Paul. *The Black Atlantic: Modernity and Double Consciousness.* Cambridge, MA: Harvard University Press, 1993.

Gitelman, Lisa. *Paper Knowledge: Toward a Media History of Documents.* Durham, NC: Duke University Press, 2014.

———. *Scripts, Grooves, and Writing Machines: Representing Technology in the Edison Era.* Stanford, CA: Stanford University Press, 1999.

Gobel, Mark. *Beautiful Circuits: Modernism and the Mediated Life.* New York: Columbia University Press, 2010.

Goldsby, Jacqueline. *A Spectacular Secret: Lynching in American Life and Literature.* Chicago: University of Chicago Press, 2006.

Grant, H. Roger, and Charles W. Bohi. *The Country Railroad Station in America.* Boulder, CO: Pruett, 1978.

Gray's New Map of Gordonsville, Orange County, Virginia. Drawn from Special Surveys, 1878. Philadelphia: O. W. Gray & Son.

Greene, Lorenzo J., and Carter G. Woodson. *The Negro Wage Earner.* 1930. Reprint New York: Russell and Russell, 1969.

Gross, Ariela. *What Blood Won't Tell: A History of Race on Trial in America.* Cambridge, MA: Harvard University Press, 2008.

Gross, Kali. *Colored Amazons: Crime, Violence, and Black Women in the City of Brotherly Love, 1880–1910.* Durham, NC: Duke University Press, 2006.

Grow, Lawrence. *Waiting for the 5:05: Terminal, Station, and Depot in America.* New York: Main Street/Universe Books, 1977.

Hale, Grace Elizabeth. *Making Whiteness: The Culture of Segregation in the South, 1890–1940.* New York: Pantheon Books, 1998.

Hall, Annie E. "What Can the Colored Woman Do to Improve the Street Railroad Dep[o]rtment." In *The United Negro: His Problems and His Progress, Containing the Addresses and Proceedings, the Negro Young People's Christian and Educational*

Congress, Held August 6–11, 1902, edited by I. Garland Penn and J. W. E. Bowen, 454–56. Atlanta: D. E. Luther Publishing, 1902.

Hardison, Ayesha. *Writing through Jane Crow: Race and Gender Politics in African American Literature.* Charlottesville: University of Virginia Press, 2014.

Harris, Jennifer. "Barbara Pope." *Legacy,* 32, no. 2 (2015): 281–297.

Harris, Jessica B. "'I'm Talkin' 'bout the Food I's Sells': African American Street Vendors and the Sound of Food from Noise to Nostalgia." In *The Larder: Food Studies Methods from the American South,* edited by John T. Edge, Elizabeth S. D. Engelhardt, and Ted Ownby, 333–41. Athens: University of Georgia Press, 2013.

Harris, William Hamilton. *Keeping the Faith: A. Philip Randolph, Milton P. Webster, and the Brotherhood of Sleeping Car Porters, 1925–37.* Urbana: University of Illinois Press, 1977.

Hartman, Saidiya. *Scenes of Subjection: Terror, Slavery, and Self-Making in Nineteenth-Century America.* New York: Oxford University Press, 1997.

———. "Venus in Two Acts." *Small Axe,* no. 26 (June 2008): 1–14.

Hearn, Chester, and Mike Marino. *Civil War Battles: The Maps of Jedidiah Hotchkiss.* San Diego: Thunder Bay Press, 2008.

Helton, Laura, Justin Leroy, Max A. Mishler, Samantha Seely, and Shauna Sweeney, eds. "The Question of Recovery: An Introduction." *Social Text* 33, no. 4 (2015): 1–18.

Hicks, Cheryl D. "'Bright and Good Looking Colored Girl': Black Women's Sexuality and 'Harmful Intimacy' in Early-Twentieth-Century New York." *Journal of the History of Sexuality* 18, no. 3 (2009): 418–56.

Higginbotham, Evelyn Brooks. "African American Women's History and the Meta-language of Race." *Signs* 71, no. 2 (1992): 251–74.

Higginbotham, Leon. "The Supreme Court's Sanction of Racial Hatred: The 1883 Civil Rights Cases." In *Shades of Freedom: Racial Politics and Presumption,* 94–107. New York: Oxford University Press, 1996.

Hine, Darlene Clark. "Rape and the Inner Lives of Black Women in the Middle West: Preliminary Thoughts on the Culture of Dissemblance." *Signs* 14, no. 4 (1989): 912–20.

Hirsch, Susan E. "Rethinking the Sexual Division of Labor: Pullman Repair Shops, 1900–69." *Radical History Review* 35 (1986): 26–48.

Hoffer, Willamjames Hull. *Plessy v. Ferguson: Race and Inequality in Jim Crow America.* Lawrence: University Press of Kansas, 2012.

Hotchkiss, Jedediah. "New Ways in the Old Dominion: The Chesapeake and Ohio Railroad." *Scribner's,* December 1872, 137–59, 273.

Hughes, Lyn. *An Anthology of Respect: The Pullman Porters National Historic Registry of African American Railroad Employees.* Chicago: Hughes Peterson, 2007.

Human Rights Campaign. "Sexual Orientation and Gender Identity Definitions." Resources, Human Rights Campaign. https://www.hrc.org/resources/sexual -orientation-and-gender-identity-terminology-and-definitions. Accessed October 20, 2021.

Hunter, Louis C. *Steamboats on the Western Rivers: An Economic and Technological History*. Cambridge, MA: Harvard University Press, 1949.

Hurston, Zora Neale. *Dust Tracks on a Road*. Edited by Robert Hemenway. Urbana: University of Illinois Press, 1984.

Husband, Joseph. *The Story of the Pullman Car*. Chicago: AC McClurg, 1917.

Jacobs, Harriet A. *Incidents in the Life of a Slave Girl Written by Herself*. Edited by L. Maria Child. Boston: Published for the Author, 1861.

Jefferson, Thomas. *Notes on the State of Virginia, Illustrated with a Map, including the States of Virginia, Maryland, Delaware and Pennsylvania*. London: Printed for John Stockdale, opposite Burlington-house, Piccadilly, 1787.

Jenkins, Earnestine. "The Hooks Brothers of Memphis: Artist-Photographers of the 'New Negro' Movement in the Urban South." In *Memphis: 200 Years Together*, edited by Karen B. Golightly and Jonathan Judaken, 84–99. Memphis and New Orleans: Susan Schadt Press, 2019.

Johnson, James Weldon. *Along This Way: The Autobiography of James Weldon Johnson*. In *James Weldon Johnson: Writings*. 1933. Reprint New York: Library of America, 2004.

Jones, Virgil Carrington. Foreword to *Gordonsville, Virginia: Historic Crossroads Town*, by William H. B. Thomas, vii–ix. Verona, VA: McClure, 1971.

Kaplan, Carla. *Miss Anne in Harlem: White Women of the Black Renaissance*. New York: Harper, 2013.

Kaplan, Daile. "Vernacular Photographies: Responses to a Questionnaire." *History of Photography* 24, no. 3 (2000): 229–31.

Karuka, Manu. *Empire's Tracks: Indigenous Nations, Chinese Workers, and the Transcontinental Railroad*. Oakland: University of California Press, 2019.

Kawash, Samira. *Dislocating the Color Line: Identity, Hybridity, and Singularity in African-American Literature*. Stanford, CA: Stanford University Press, 1997.

Kelley, Blair L. M. *Right to Ride: Streetcar Boycotts and African American Citizenship in the Era of Plessy v. Ferguson*. Chapel Hill: University of North Carolina Press, 2010.

King, Edward. "The Great South: A Ramble in Virginia: From Bristol to the Sea." *Scribner's*, April 1874, 645–74.

———. *The Great South: A Record of Journeys in Louisiana, Texas, the Indian Territory, Missouri, Arkansas, Mississippi, Alabama, Georgia, Florida, South Carolina, North Carolina, Kentucky, Tennessee, Virginia, West Virginia, and Maryland*. Hartford, CT: American Publishing Co., 1875. http://docsouth.unc.edu/nc/king/king.html#p110.

Kirby, Lynne. *Parallel Tracks: The Railroad and Silent Cinema*. Durham, NC: Duke University Press, 1997.

Kornweibel, Theodore. *Railroads and the African American Experience: A Photographic Journey*. Baltimore: Johns Hopkins University Press, 2010.

Lee, Julia H. "Estrangement on a Train: Race and Narratives of American Identity." *ELH* 75, no. 2 (2008): 345–65.

Leslie, Kent Anderson. *Woman of Color, Daughter of Privilege: Amanda America Dickson, 1849–1893*. Athens: University of Georgia Press, 1995.

Leyendecker, Liston Edgington. *Palace Car Prince: A Biography of George Mortimer Pullman*. Nitwot: University Press of Colorado, 1992.

Lofgren, Charles A. *The Plessy Case: A Legal-Historical Interpretation*. New York: Oxford University Press, 1987.

Love, Nat. *Life and Adventures of Nat Love, Better Known in the Cattle Country as "Deadwood Dick," by Himself*. Chapel Hill: University of North Carolina Press, 2017.

Luxenberg, Steve. *Separate: The Story of* Plessy v. Ferguson*, and America's Journey from Slavery to Segregation*. New York: W. W. Norton, 2019.

Mack, Kenneth W. "Law, Society, Identity, and the Making of the Jim Crow South: Travel and Segregation on Tennessee Railroads, 1875–1905." *Law and Social Inquiry* 24 (1999): 377–409.

Malcolm X, with Alex Haley. *The Autobiography of Malcolm X*. New York: Ballantine Books, 1992.

Maltz, Earl M. "'Separate but Equal' and the Law of Common Carriers in the Era of the 14th Amendment." *Rutgers Law Journal*, 17, nos. 3–4 (Spring–Summer 1986): 553–68.

Mann, Thomas. "A Railway Accident." In *Stories of Three Decades*, 320–27. Translated by H. T. Lowe-Porter. New York: Knopf, 1936.

Marcus, Sharon. "Psychoanalytic Training: Freud and Railways." In *The Railway, Modernity, Time, Space, and the Machine Ensemble*, edited by Matthew Beaumont and Michael Freeman, 155–76. New York: Peter Lang, 2007.

Marx, Leo. *The Machine in the Garden: Technology and the Pastoral Ideal in America*. 1964. Reprint New York: Oxford University Press, 2000.

Masur, Kate. *An Example for All the Land: Emancipation and the Struggle over Equality in Washington, D.C.* Chapel Hill: University of North Carolina Press, 2010.

———. "'A Rare Phenomenon of Philological Vegetation': The Word 'Contraband' and the Meanings of Emancipation in the United States." *Journal of American History* 93, no. 4 (2007): 1050–84.

Matlock, Jann. "Vacancies: Hotels, Reception Desks, and Identity in American Cinema, 1929–1964." In *Moving Pictures/Stopping Places: Hotels and Motels on Film*, edited by David B. Clarke, Valerie Crawford Pfannhauser, and Marcus A. Doel, 73–142. New York: Lexington Books, 2009.

May, Vivian M. *Anna Julia Cooper, Visionary Black Feminist: A Critical Introduction*. New York: Routledge, 2012.

———. "'By a Black Woman of the South': Race, Place, and Gender in the Work of Anna Julia Cooper." *Southern Quarterly* 45, no. 3 (Spring 2008): 127–52.

McCaskill, Barbara. "'Yours Very Truly': Ellen Craft—The Fugitive as Text and Artifact." *African American Review* 28, no. 4 (1994): 509–29.

McHenry, Elizabeth. "Toward a History of Access: The Case of Mary Church Terrell." *American Literary History* 19, no. 2 (2007): 381–401.

———. *To Make Negro Literature: Writing, Literary Practice, and African American Authorship*. Durham: Duke University Press, 2021.

McKay, Claude. *A Long Way from Home*. New Brunswick, NJ: Rutgers University Press, 2007.

McKissack, Pat, and Fredrick McKissack. *A Long Hard Journey: The Story of the Pullman Porter.* New York: Walker, 1995.

McKittrick, Katherine. *Demonic Grounds: Black Women and the Cartographies of Struggle.* Minneapolis: University of Minnesota Press, 2006.

McPherson, James Alan, and Miller Williams. *Railroad: Trains and Train People in American Culture.* New York: Random House, 1976.

Meeks, Carroll L.V. *The Railroad Station: An Architectural History.* New Haven, CT: Yale University Press, 1956.

Meikle, Jeffrey L. "Leo Marx's *The Machine in the Garden.*" *Technology and Culture* 44, no. 1 (2003): 147–59.

"The Memphis and Charleston Railroad: Profit and Loss Account." *Merchants' Magazine and Commercial Review,* November 1, 1866, 361.

Mencken, August. *The Railroad Passenger Car: An Illustrated History of the First 100 Years, with accounts by Contemporary Passengers.* Baltimore: Johns Hopkins University Press, 1957.

Micheaux, Oscar. *The Conquest: The Story of a Negro Pioneer.* 1913. Reprint Lincoln: University of Nebraska Press, 1994.

Minter, Patricia Hagler. "The Failure of Freedom: Class, Gender, and the Evolution of Segregated Transit Law in the Nineteenth-Century South." *Kent Law Review* 70, no. 3 (1995): 993–1009.

Mitchell, Michelle. *Righteous Propagation: African Americans and the Politics of Racial Destiny after Reconstruction.* Chapel Hill: University of North Carolina Press, 2004.

Morrison, Toni. *Sula.* 1973. New York: Vintage, 2004.

Murray, Pauli. *Dark Testament: And Other Poems.* 1970. New York: Liveright, 2018.

———. "The Liberation of Black Women." In *Words of Fire: An Anthology of African American Feminist Thought,* edited by Beverly Guy Sheftall, 186–97. 1970. Reprint New York: New Press, 1995.

———. *Proud Shoes: The Story of an American Family.* Boston: Beacon, 1999.

———. *Song in a Weary Throat: Memoir of an American Pilgrimage.* 1987. New York: Liveright, 2018.

———. "Three Thousands Miles on a Dime in Ten Days." In *Negro: An Anthology,* edited by Nancy Cunard, 67–70. New York: Frederick Ungar, 1934.

Murray, Pauli, and Mary Eastwood. "Jane Crow and the Law: Sex Discrimination and Title VII." *George Washington Law Review* 34, no. 2 (1965): 232–56.

Nelson, Alice Dunbar. *Give Us Each Day: The Diary of Alice Dunbar-Nelson,* edited by Gloria T. Hull. New York: Norton, 1984.

Painter, Nell Irvin, ed. *Narrative of Sojourner Truth.* New York: Penguin, 1998.

———. *Sojourner Truth: A Life, a Symbol.* New York: W. W. Norton, 1996.

Parker, Alison. *Unceasing Militant: The Life of Mary Church Terrell.* Chapel Hill: University of North Carolina Press, 2021.

Parks, Gordon. *Voices in the Mirror: An Autobiography.* New York: Doubleday, 1990.

Perata, David. *Those Pullman Blues: An Oral History of the African American Railroad Attendant.* Lanham, MD: Madison Books, 1999.

Peterson, Larry Dean. "Photography and the Pullman Strike: Remolding Perceptions of Labor Conflict by New Visual Communication." In *The Pullman Strike and the Crisis of the 1890s: Essays on Labor and Politics*, edited by Richard Schneirov, Shelton Stromquist, and Nick Salvatore, 87–129. Urbana: University of Illinois Press, 1999.

Pike, Gustavus D. *The Jubilee Singers and Their Campaign for Twenty Thousand Dollars*. Boston: Lee and Shepard, 1873.

Porter, Edwin S., prod. *"What Happened in the Tunnel."* New York: Edison Manufacturing Co., 1903. Video, 1:23 min. Paper Print Collection, Library of Congress. www.loc.gov/item/00694331/.

Porterfield, James D. *Dining by Rail: The History and Recipes of America's Golden Age of Railroad Cuisine*. New York: St. Martin's, 1998.

Presner, Todd Samuel. *Mobile Modernity: Germans, Jews, Trains*. New York: Columbia University Press, 2007.

Pryor, Elizabeth Stordeur. *Colored Travelers: Mobility and the Fight for Citizenship before the Civil War*. Chapel Hill: University of North Carolina Press, 2016.

Quinzio, Jeri. *Food on the Rails: The Golden Era of Railroad Dining*. Lanham, MD: Rowman and Littlefield, 2014.

T.F.R. "The Pleasures of the Dining Car." *Railway Magazine* 7 (July–December 1900): 520–21.

Revill, George. "Perception, Reception, and Representation: Wolfgang Schivelbusch and the Cultural History of Travel and Transport." In *Mobility in History: Reviews and Reflections*, edited by Peter Norton, et al., 31–48. Neuchâtel, Switz.: Editions Alphil, 2002.

———. *Railway*. London: Reaktion Books, 2012.

Richards, E. M. "Our Western Correspondence." *Scientific American* 3, no. 11 (September 8, 1860): 163.

Richards, Jeffrey, and John M. Mackenzie. *The Railway Station: A Social History*. New York: Oxford University Press, 1986.

Richter, Amy. *Home on the Rails: Women, the Railroad, and the Rise of Public Domesticity*. Chapel Hill: University of North Carolina Press, 2005.

Robinson, Amy. "It Takes One to Know One: Passing and Communities of Common Interest." *Critical Inquiry* 20, no. 4 (1994): 715–36.

Robinson, Stephen. "African American Citizenship, the 1883 *Civil Rights Cases* and the Creation of the Jim Crow South." *History: The Journal of the Historical Association* 102, no. 350 (April 2017): 225–41.

Rosenberg, Rosalind. *Jane Crow: The Life of Pauli Murray*. New York: Oxford University Press, 2017.

Ross, Alexander Milton. *Recollections and Experiences of an Abolitionist*. Toronto, 1876.

Ruchames, Louis. "Jim Crow Railroads in Massachusetts," *American Quarterly* 8, no. 1 (Spring 1956): 61–75.

Rusch, Frederik L., ed. *A Jean Toomer Reader: Selected Unpublished Writings*. New York: Oxford University Press, 1993.

Sanborn, Geoffrey. "The Plagiarist's Craft: Fugitivity and Theatricality in Running a Thousand Miles for Freedom." *PMLA* 128, no. 4 (2013): 907–22.

Sandoval-Strausz, A. K. "Travelers, Strangers, and Jim Crow: Law, Public Accommodations, and Civil Rights in America." *Law and History Review* 23, no. 1 (Spring 2005): 53–94.

Santino, Jack. *Miles of Smiles, Years of Struggle: Stories of Black Pullman Porters.* Urbana: University of Illinois Press, 1989.

Saxby, Troy. *Pauli Murray: A Personal and Political Life.* Chapel Hill: University of North Carolina Press, 2020.

Schivelbusch, Wolfgang. *The Railway Journey: The Industrialization of Time and Space in the Nineteenth Century.* Berkeley: University of California Press, 1986.

Schulten, Susan. *Mapping the Nation: History and Cartography in Nineteenth-Century America.* Chicago: University of Chicago Press, 2012.

Schweizer, Harold. *On Waiting (Thinking in Action).* New York: Routledge, 2008.

Scruggs, Lawson A. *Women of Distinction: Remarkable in Works and Invincible in Character.* Raleigh, NC: L. A. Scruggs, 1893.

Shrady, Theodore, and Atlantic Coast Line and Seaboard Air Line Railroads Historical Society. *The Sleeping Car: A General Guide.* Bay Pines, FL: Atlantic Coast Line and Seaboard Air Line Railroads Historical Society, 2004.

Simmons-Thorne, Naomi. "Pauli Murray and the Pronominal Problem: A De-essentialist Trans Historiography." *Activist History Review*, May 30, 2019. https://activisthistory.com/2019/05/30/pauli-murray-and-the-pronominal-problem-a-de-essentialist-trans-historiography/.

Simpson, Jack, and Matt Rutherford. *A Bibliography of African American Family History at the Newberry Library.* Chicago: Newberry Library, 2005.

Simpson, Mark. *Trafficking Subjects: The Politics of Mobility in Nineteenth-Century America.* Minneapolis: University of Minnesota, 2005.

Smith, Mark M. *How Race Is Made: Slavery, Segregation, and the Senses.* Chapel Hill: University of North Carolina Press, 2006.

Solnit, Rebecca. "Walking after Midnight: Women, Sex, and Public Space." In *Wanderlust: A History of Walking*, 232–46. New York: Penguin Books, 2000.

Spero, Sterling D., and Abram L. Harris. *The Black Worker: The Negro and the Labor Movement.* 1931. Reprint, New York: Atheneum, 1974.

Stepto, Robert B. *From Behind the Veil: A Study of Afro-American Narrative.* Urbana: University of Illinois Press, 1979.

Sterling, Dorothy. *Making of an Afro-American: Martin Robinson Delany, 1812–1885.* New York: Doubleday, 1971.

Stewart, Jacqueline. *Migrating to the Movies: Cinema and Black Urban Modernity.* Berkeley: University of California Press, 2005.

———. "What Happened in the Transition?: Reading Race, Gender, and Labor between the Shots." In *American Cinema's Transitional Era: Audiences, Institutions, Practices*, edited by Charlie Keil and Shelley Stamp, 103–30. Berkeley: University of California Press, 2004.

Still, William Grant. *A Brief Narrative of the Struggle for the Rights of the Colored People of Philadelphia in the City Railway Cars; and a Defence of William Still, Relating to His Agency Touching the Passage of the Late Bill & Read before a large public meeting, held in Liberty Hall, Lombard St. below Eighth, Apr. 8th, 1867.* 1867. Reprint Wilmington, DE: Scholarly Resources, 1970.

Strother, Horatio T. *The Underground Railroad in Connecticut.* Middletown, CT: Wesleyan University Press, 2011.

Sumler-Edmond, Janice. "The Quest for Justice: African American Women Litigants, 1867–1890." In *African American Women and the Vote, 1837–1965,* edited by Ann D. Gordon with Bettye Collier-Thomas, 100–119. Amherst: University of Massachusetts Press, 1997.

Sundquist, Eric J. *To Wake the Nations: Race in the Making of American Literature.* Cambridge, MA: Belknap Press of Harvard University Press, 1993.

Tarpley, Joan R. "Blackwomen, Sexual Myth, and Jurisprudence." *Temple Law Review* 69 (1996): 1343–88.

Taylor, Frederick Winslow. *The Principles of Scientific Management.* 1911. Reprint New York: Norton, 1947.

Taylor, Susie King. *Reminiscences of My Life in Camp with the 33D United States Colored Troops Late 1st S.C. Volunteers.* Boston: N.p., 1902.

Terrell, Mary Church. *A Colored Woman in a White World.* Washington, DC: Ransdell, 1940.

Thaggert, Miriam. *Images of Black Modernism: Verbal and Visual Strategies of the Harlem Renaissance.* Amherst: University of Massachusetts Press, 2010.

Thomas, Jerry B. "Jedediah Hotchkiss, Gilded-Age Propagandist of Industrialism." *Virginia Magazine of History and Biography* 84, no. 2 (1976): 189–202.

Thomas, William G. *The Iron Way: Railroads, the Civil War, and the Making of Modern America.* New Haven, CT: Yale University Press, 2011.

Thomas, William H. B. *Gordonsville, Virginia: Historic Crossroads Town.* Verona, VA: McClure, 1971.

Totten, Gary. *African American Travel Narratives from Abroad: Mobility and Cultural Work in the Age of Jim Crow.* Amherst: University of Massachusetts Press, 2015.

——. "Embodying Segregation: Ida B. Wells and the Cultural Work of Travel." In *Representing Segregation: Toward an Aesthetics of Living Jim Crow, and Other Forms of Racial Division,* edited by Brian Normal and Piper Kendrix Williams, 167–84. Albany: State University of New York Press, 2010.

Traser, Donald R. *Virginia Railway Depots.* Richmond, VA: Old Dominion Chapter, National Railway Historical Society, 1998.

Trouillot, Michel-Rolph. *Silencing the Past: Power and the Production of History.* Boston: Beacon, 2015.

Turner, Robert E. *Memories of a Pullman Porter.* New York: Exposition, 1954.

Tushnet, Mark. "'To Enable the Black Race to Take the Rank of Mere Citizen': The Civil Rights Cases, 1883." In *I Dissent: Great Opposing Opinions in Landmark Supreme Court Cases,* 45–67. Boston: Beacon, 2008.

Twelbeck, Kirsten. "Eden Refounded: Post Civil War Literary Gardening." In *Rereading the Machine in the Garden: Nature and Technology in American Culture*, edited by Eric C. Erbacher, Nicole Maruo-Schröder, and Florian Sedlmeier, 58–76. New York: Campus Verlag, 2014.

Twinam, Ann. *Purchasing Whiteness: Pardos, Mulattos, and the Quest for Social Mobility*. Stanford, CA: Stanford University Press, 2015.

Tye, Larry. *Rising from the Rails: Pullman Porters and the Making of the Black Middle Class*. New York: Henry Holt, 2004.

Wallace-Sanders, Kimberly. *Mammy: A Century of Race, Gender, and Southern Memory*. Chapel Hill: University of North Carolina Press, 2008.

Washington, Booker T. *The Booker T. Washington Papers*. Edited by Louis Harlan and Raymond W. Smock. 14 vols. Urbana: University of Illinois Press, 1972–89.

———. *Up From Slavery*. 1901. In *Three Negro Classics*, edited by John Hope Franklin, 23–205. New York: Avon, 1999.

Watkins, N. J., and Nelson H. Hotchkiss. *The Pine and the Palm Greeting: or, The Trip of the Northern Editors to the South in 1871, and the Return Visit of the Southern Editors in 1872, Under the Leadership of Maj. N.H. Hotchkiss*. Baltimore: J. D. Ehlers, 1873.

Welke, Barbara. *Recasting American Liberty: Gender, Race, Law and the Railroad Revolution, 1865–1920*. New York: Cambridge University Press, 2001.

———. "When All the Women Were White and All the Blacks Were Men: Gender, Class, Race and the Road to Plessy, 1855–1914." *Law and History Review*, Fall 1995, 261–316.

Wells-Barnett, Ida B. *Crusade for Justice: The Autobiography of Ida B. Wells*. Edited by Alfreda M. Duster. Chicago: University of Chicago Press, 1970.

———. *The Memphis Diary of Ida B. Wells*, edited by Miriam DeCosta-Willis. Boston: Beacon, 1995.

Wharton, Vernon Lane. *The Negro in Mississippi, 1865–1890*. Chapel Hill: University of North Carolina Press, 1947.

White, Deborah Gray. *Ar'n't I a Woman: Female Slaves in the Plantation South*. New York: W. W. Norton, 1985.

———. "Mining the Forgotten: Manuscripts Sources for Black Women's History." *Journal of American History* 74, no. 1 (1987): 237–42.

———. *Too Heavy a Load: Black Women in Defense of Themselves, 1894–1994*. New York: W. W. Norton, 1999.

White, Eric B. *Reading Machines in the Modernist Transatlantic: Avant-Gardes, Technology and the Everyday*. Edinburgh: Edinburgh University Press, 2020.

Wilkerson, Isabel. *The Warmth of Other Suns: The Epic Story of America's Great Migration*. New York: Vintage, 2010.

Williams, Linda. "Of Kisses and Ellipses: The Long Adolescence of American Movies." *Critical Inquiry* 32, no. 2 (2006): 288–340.

Williams-Forson, Psyche A. *Building Houses out of Chicken Legs: Black Women, Food, and Power*. Chapel Hill: University of North Carolina Press, 2006.

Winschel, Terrence J. "John Marshall Stone." In *American National Biography*, 858–59. New York: Oxford University Press, 1999.

Woodward, C. Vann. *Reunion and Reaction: The Compromise of 1877 and the End of Reconstruction.* New York: Oxford University Press, 1966.

———. *The Strange Career of Jim Crow.* 1966. Reprint New York: Oxford University Press, 2002.

Writers' Program of the WPA. *Virginia: A Guide to the Old Dominion.* New York: Oxford University Press, 1940.

Yates, JoAnne. *Control through Communication: The Rise of System on American Management.* Baltimore: Johns Hopkins University Press, 1989.

Index

Page numbers in *italics* refer to illustrations.

MIRIAM THAGGERT is an associate professor of English at SUNY-Buffalo and the author of *Images of Black Modernism: Verbal and Visual Strategies of the Harlem Renaissance.*

Women, Gender, and Sexuality in American History

The Women's Joint Congressional Committee and the Politics
of Maternalism, 1920–1930   *Jan Doolittle Wilson*

"Swing the Sickle for the Harvest Is Ripe": Gender and Slavery
in Antebellum Georgia   *Daina Ramey Berry*

Christian Sisterhood, Race Relations, and the YWCA, 1906–46
Nancy Marie Robertson

Reading, Writing, and Segregation: A Century of Black Women
Teachers in Nashville   *Sonya Ramsey*

Radical Sisters: Second-Wave Feminism and Black Liberation
in Washington, D.C.   *Anne M. Valk*

Feminist Coalitions: Historical Perspectives on Second-Wave Feminism
in the United States   *Edited by Stephanie Gilmore*

Breadwinners: Working Women and Economic Independence, 1865–1920
Lara Vapnek

Beauty Shop Politics: African American Women's Activism
in the Beauty Industry   *Tiffany M. Gill*

Demanding Child Care: Women's Activism and the Politics
of Welfare, 1940–1971   *Natalie M. Fousekis*

Rape in Chicago: Race, Myth, and the Courts   *Dawn Rae Flood*

Black Women and Politics in New York City   *Julie A. Gallagher*

Cold War Progressives: Women's Interracial Organizing for Peace and Freedom
Jacqueline Castledine

No Votes for Women: The New York State Anti-Suffrage Movement
Susan Goodier

Anna Howard Shaw: The Work of Woman Suffrage   *Trisha Franzen*

Nursing Civil Rights: Gender and Race in the Army Nurse Corps
Charissa J. Threat

Reverend Addie Wyatt: Faith and the Fight for Labor, Gender, and Racial Equality
Marcia Walker-McWilliams

Lucretia Mott Speaks: The Essential Speeches   *Edited by Christopher Densmore,
Carol Faulkner, Nancy Hewitt, and Beverly Wilson Palmer*

Lost in the USA: American Identity from the Promise Keepers
to the Million Mom March   *Deborah Gray White*

Women against Abortion: Inside the Largest Moral Reform Movement
of the Twentieth Century   *Karissa Haugeberg*

Colored No More: Reinventing Black Womanhood in Washington, D.C.
Treva B. Lindsey

Beyond Respectability: The Intellectual Thought of Race Women
Brittney C. Cooper

Leaders of Their Race: Educating Black and White Women in the New South
Sarah H. Case

Glory in Their Spirit: How Four Black Women Took On the Army
during World War II   *Sandra M. Bolzenius*

The University of Illinois Press
is a founding member of the
Association of University Presses.

Composed in 10.5/13 Minion Pro
by Kirsten Dennison
at the University of Illinois Press
Manufactured by Sheridan Books, Inc.

University of Illinois Press
1325 South Oak Street
Champaign, IL 61820-6903
www.press.uillinois.edu